PRIMATOLOGY, ETHICS AND TRAUMA

Primatology, Ethics and Trauma offers an analytical re-examination of the research conducted into the linguistic abilities of the Oklahoma chimpanzees and uncovers the historical reality of this research without fabrication. It has been 50 years since the first language experiments on chimpanzees. Robert Ingersoll was one of the researchers from 1975 to 1983. He is well known for being one of the main carers and best friend of the chimpanzee, Nim Chimpsky, but there were other chimpanzees in the University of Oklahoma's Institute for Primate Studies, including Washoe, Moja, Kelly, Booee and Onan, who were taught sign language in the quest to discover whether language is learned or innate in humans. Antonina Anna Scarnà's expertise in language acquisition and neuroscience offers a vehicle for critical evaluation of those studies.

Ingersoll and Scarnà investigate how this research failed to address the emotional needs of the animals. Research into trauma has made scientific advances since those studies. It is time to consider the research from a different perspective, examining the neglect and cruelty that was inflicted on those animals in the name of psychological science. This book re-examines those cases, addressing directly the suffering and traumatic experiences endured by the captive chimpanzees, in particular the female chimpanzee, Washoe, and her resultant inability to be a competent mother.

This book discusses the unethical nature of the studies in the context of recent research on trauma and offers a specific and direct psychological message, proposing to finally close the door on the language side of these chimpanzee studies. This book is a novel and groundbreaking account. It will be of interest to lay readers and academics alike. Those working as research, experimental and clinical psychologists will find this book of interest, as will psychotherapists, linguists, anthropologists, historians of science and primatologists, as well as those involved in primate sanctuary and conservation.

Robert Ingersoll (BSc, MS) has been a tireless champion of captive chimpanzees since the 1970s. He entered the world of primates as an undergraduate student at the University of Oklahoma's Institute for Primate Studies, where the research focus was on cognition, language, and interspecies communication between chimpanzees and humans, using American Sign Language. He quickly came to see the chimpanzees as friends rather than as research subjects. After several productive years, funding for the program was cut by the university, and the chimpanzee colony was sold to a medical research laboratory for invasive research. This led Ingersoll on a crusade to free his chimpanzee friends that has lasted decades.

Antonina Anna Scarnà (BSc Hons, DPhil, PGCTHE, PGCert, CPsychol) is a psychologist and neuroscientist with expertise in language, personality and psychological disorders. Her doctorate was on the composition of the monolingual and bilingual lexicon, and she explored the factors that affect object naming and reading. She has conducted award-winning research into non-drug treatments for dopamine in bipolar disorder and schizophrenia at Oxford University, United Kingdom, where she runs courses in brain and behaviour/neuroscience, personality and psychological disorders, covering topics including personality traits, addiction and social behaviours. She teaches various international tutorial courses and has been running the popular Oxford University online Introduction to Psychology course.

PRIMATOLOGY, ETHICS AND TRAUMA

The Oklahoma Chimpanzee Studies

Robert Ingersoll and Antonina Anna Scarnà

Routledge
Taylor & Francis Group

LONDON AND NEW YORK

Designed cover image: Author

First published 2023
by Routledge
4 Park Square, Milton Park, Abingdon, Oxon OX14 4RN

and by Routledge
605 Third Avenue, New York, NY 10158

Routledge is an imprint of the Taylor & Francis Group, an informa business

British Library Cataloguing-in-Publication Data
A catalogue record for this book is available from the British Library

ISBN: 978-1-032-41347-1 (hbk)
ISBN: 978-1-032-41348-8 (pbk)
ISBN: 978-1-003-35765-0 (ebk)

DOI: 10.4324/9781003357650

Typeset in Bembo
by Apex CoVantage, LLC

CONTENTS

ACKNOWLEDGEMENTS

Robert Ingersoll

It would be impossible to acknowledge all the friends and acquaintances who played a role in the development of this book. Thanks to all the folks who have supported me privately and publicly over the course of this journey. Many of you won't be mentioned who should be, and I hope you understand.

First, I'd like to say that without Belle Ball, my beautiful wife, this book would not have gotten off the ground, and I would not even be here to write it. Her encouragement and support over these last 35 or so years made this a reality. Her help along the way has been immeasurable in my work, and in my life.

I would like to acknowledge Dr. Rafael Merriman and his liver team at the California Pacific Medical Center, who saved me with a lifesaving liver transplant.

Thank you to Patti Ragan for allowing me to visit and work with the staff and apes at Center for Great Apes, to Priscilla Feral at Primarily Primates, and to Raina Smith at Chimp Haven, for allowing me to visit their sanctuaries. I would also like to thank Elizabeth Hess, and Simon Chinn and James Marsh for bringing Nim's story to life on screen in the film, *Project Nim*.

I would also like to acknowledge all my Jungle Jim's employees over the years, especially Jennifer Gilbert, who was particularly important to Jungle Jim's efforts, and my long-time friend, Shaun O'Brian, for 35 years of contributions to non-human primate welfare.

A few people are no longer with us, but their contributions are important. I thank Dr. Shirley McGreal, Chris Byrne, Wally Swett, Dwight Russell, and Dr. Bill Lemmon for allowing me access to the Institute for Primate Studies. In particular, I would like to remember Dr. Jim Mahoney. I can't express how important Dr. Mahoney was to my development as a human being.

I would like to thank Mr. Billy Strings and his amazing band for providing us with an escape when we needed a break from writing this book.

Last but not least, without Antonina Anna Scarnà there would be no book. Her knowledge of all the topics in this book, and her determination to tell the story of these chimps and the trauma they experienced in a truthful and scientific way cannot be over-emphasised.

I would like to dedicate this book to all the chimpanzees I have been honored to know and love over my journey. To Nim, Washoe, Onan, Denyse, Kelly, Booee, Bruno, Sheba, Toddy, Knuckles, Kitty, Loulis, Midge, Abigail and Sequoyah. And to all the chimps who are still stuck in the cages.

Antonina Anna Scarnà

Thanks to everyone who shared their thoughts with me about language, trauma and chimpanzees: Joyce Butler, Noam Chomsky, Roger Fouts, Ron Helterbrand, Elizabeth Hess, Mary Lee Jensvold, Marie-Paule Mahoney, James Marsh, Tom Martin, Desmond Morris and Esteban Rivas.

Remembering James Mahoney and Shirley McGreal, who dedicated their lives to helping primates to find safety, and Tiny, who features in so many stories about keeping them safe. Remembering my best friend, Gordon Claridge, who sadly died just before this work started but whose emails and books guided me through it. I am hugely grateful to Gary Browning, Peter Collett, Miguel Farias and George Stuart, and to Bob's wife, Belle Ball, for her patience, help and understanding. Special thanks to my wonderful friends and family.

The chimpanzee stories are combined with the human ones. I am honoured to work with, and get to know, the spirit of Washoe. I would like a special space to remember her infant, Sequoyah. Thanks also to the memory of Loulis, and the others: Abendigo, Abigail, Booee, Carolyn, Dar, Denyse, Jacob, Kelly, Kitty, Lily, Midge, Moja, Onan, PB, Pablo, Sally, Sheba, Sherry, Tatu and the others, and everything they taught us.

Lastly, if it hadn't been for the film, *Project Nim*, this work would never have happened. I am hugely grateful to two of the most magnificent sentient beings whose existence has rocked this world and changed my life. Those are, of course, Nim Chimpsky and his wonderful friend, Bob Ingersoll.

CHIMPANZEE FAMILY TREES

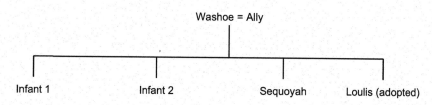

FIGURE FM.1 Washoe's family tree.

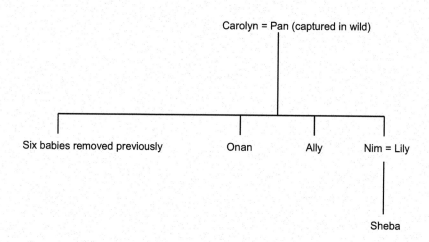

FIGURE FM.2 Nim's family tree.

INTRODUCTION

It has been 50 years since the first language experiments on chimpanzees. Robert Ingersoll was one of the carers from 1975 to 1983 for the chimpanzees Washoe, Moja, Tatu, Kelly, Sherry, Booee, Onan, Nim, Denyse, Abigail and numerous others. It is time to consider those research studies from a different perspective, taking responsibility for the neglect and cruelty that was inflicted on those animals in the quest of psychological study. By definition, these studies failed to address the emotional needs of the animals. We re-examine those cases, addressing directly the suffering and traumatic experiences endured by the chimpanzees.

Various studies have already attempted to tell their stories. The case of Nim Chimpsky is well documented and accurately told in the book *Nim Chimpsky: The Chimp Who Would Be Human* by Elizabeth Hess, and in the James Marsh and Simon Chinn documentary, *Project Nim*. However, other books present the chimpanzee histories with omission, exaggeration and confusion regarding the true events. This book will uncover the historical reality without fabrication. Nim and some of the other Oklahoma chimpanzees will feature here, but the focus is on Washoe, whose story has been inauthentically and incompletely told.

It has taken around 50 years to reveal the facts about what happened in the lives of those chimpanzees. One of the strengths of the passage of time is that information can be presented without the biases that existed for the researchers in the 1970s and 1980s. Robert is in possession of a detailed log book that was kept about Washoe, where details were recorded about her daily care and wellbeing including her births. We have also spoken to others who were present during those times. Now that biological science can speak confidently and accurately about trauma, we present those cases in a different light and with emphasis upon the hallmarks of its psychological scars.

Those chimpanzees taught the researchers as much as the researchers taught them. While the primary aims of those studies were to examine language processes,

DOI: 10.4324/9781003357650-1

the non-verbal and prelinguistic behaviours were more relevant. By definition, any language learning that happened was representative of learning by chimpanzees that were being held captive. No matter how scientifically rigorous those studies seemed, they lacked ecological validity and did not represent what truly happens when primates communicate. The researchers were responsible for producing studies that mimicked science and that were not planned or controlled properly, and so remained pseudoscientific. Some of the studies may have *felt* scientific in nature, but even within a broad dimension of "language study", they remain invalid.

Normal language processing is non-verbal, semantic and emotional. It is carried in the dynamic between the being and the other, and in how that individual interacts with others and with the environment. Whether a chimpanzee is able to "do" human language is beyond a binary question. The fact that these chimpanzees were held in captivity following traumatic beginnings and without their emotional or physical needs being met fully reflects the uselessness of the language information to the scientific quest. At best, the studies remain examples of cross-species relationships. It is time to stop considering them valid studies of language learning and to recognise the cruelty inflicted on the animals during the course of the work.

We discuss the unethical nature of the studies in the context of recent research on trauma. We would never take an infant from its mother, rear that infant in an unnatural environment with a succession of carers keeping it captive, and expect it to learn a foreign language while neglecting its needs. Most of the time, we rear our young with care and nurturance and in consideration of development and progression in growth. When that goes awry, those youngsters grow up unable to raise their own young in a manner free of maladaptive behaviours. Much of the damaged behaviours demonstrated by the chimpanzees were because of being traumatically captured in the wild, subjected to unhealthy and unnatural environments, and starved of modelling of healthy group behaviours. The extent of the trauma that Washoe and the other chimpanzees endured is particularly clear if we replace the figure of the primate with that of a human: if we swap chimp for child.

Washoe has been dead since 2007. We reflect upon the experiences she endured through her lifetime: her birth in the wild in West Africa, the abandonment and loss through being removed from her mother, who was shot, the introduction of new parents with the expectation of integration and adaptation to human routines and interventions. Washoe was raised in a trailer, which would have provided the very opposite space compared with that needed from her natural habitat in the wild, and with the continued imposition of learning sign language. The introduction of language to a primate species creates significant problems pertaining to attachment and self-identity, which have rarely been discussed. The longer-term implications of that work were not considered and have not been discussed openly since. The world did not know much about chimpanzees, let alone about psychological well-being in those times. It is tragic that hardly any of those original researchers have taken responsibility regarding the trauma in those primates. Washoe gave birth twice. Both times resulted in babies who died, the first of congenital deformities and the second, Sequoyah, reportedly due to pneumonia. There are conflicting accounts about the death of this baby. We are able to present the facts about this death and other events with accuracy and confidence. Robert and I would like to be voices for Washoe and those other chimpanzees, in order to reconsider their experiences with the dignity they deserve.

The chimpanzees taught us all; not just the researchers who worked directly but also those who have read the books, watched the films and taught the materials over the years. They taught us that existence goes beyond language and words. Nim Chimpsky is known and respected long past his death in 2000, demonstrating his legacy that lives on in every person touched by these stories. There is a bigger context for those findings: they reflect human attitudes towards ownership of animals and other aspects of nature on our planet. We need to address our attitudes towards nature and environmental issues and to change some of our existing arrogance towards our roles as curators of it. It is important that we begin to honour Washoe and the other beings in the way we should have done years ago, to consider the work from the perspective of the trauma endured by the chimpanzees as well as their caregivers, and to finally close the door on the language aspect of these studies.

1

FIFTY YEARS LATER

It started with a comment on Instagram. Robert (Bob) Ingersoll, carer and best friend of the chimpanzee, Nim Chimpsky, posted a photograph of a paintbox from his home in Oklahoma, in July 2021. Across the seas in Scotland where I was staying with my then partner, I replied to his post. I teach Introduction to Psychology online for Oxford University, and usually live in Oxford. I told Bob how his appearance in the film *Project Nim* influenced my students. We were studying his work that week. I discuss the findings from the 1970s primate studies. In recent years, this has been with reference to the film and the special bond that Nim and Robert forged. I must have seen the film at least a hundred times. When it came out in 2011, I watched out of curiosity, as those studies I first learned about in my undergraduate days were projected onto the screen. The work looked different via the home footage and interviews. I had many questions about the studies. Not about the language aspect – I felt passionately that these were useless as studies of language acquisition, captive chimps can only tell us what captive chimps can learn – but about the traumatic events endured by the chimps, and the history, experiences and emotions that each of the researchers and carers brought to those studies. I was surprised these important points had not been addressed. I was honoured and astonished, then, when following my Instagram comments Bob kindly offered to give my students a question-and-answer session. His generosity of time and spirit was great that afternoon. Current and previous students, friends and family members who had heard me raving about Nim over the years listened as Bob generously and thoughtfully gave one of the best sessions I have ever heard. He was only supposed to speak for 45 minutes, but there were many questions, and the session went on for 2 hours. My students were moved. His experiences with Nim brought together and touched an audience from across the globe.

DOI: 10.4324/9781003357650-2

Bob tells our meeting like this:

> About 9 months ago, I was scrolling through Instagram and my eye caught a familiar image that I'd seen hundreds of times before. The image was the cover of the DVD of *Project Nim*, a film in which I appear and am very familiar with. I read the post under the picture. Antonina Anna Scarnà, an Oxford professor, was screening *Project Nim* for her Intro to Psych class. When I am made aware of an academic institution screening the film, I offer to do a Q&A session for the professor or teacher taking the class. I contacted Anna on Instagram and offered to guest in her class. She responded promptly and expressed her gratitude for my offer. We nailed down the details, and after a few days, I attended the class, along with my wife, Belle, who had filmed several of the segments of historical footage that appear in *Project Nim*. We agreed to a 30–45 minute time frame, and would go longer if the class gave us indication of wanting to do so. Over 2 hours later, we had to wrap it up, but I'm sure we could have gone on longer. It was one of, if not *the*, best Q&A sessions I've ever done in support of *Project Nim*.
>
> In the first 10 minutes of the post-film discussion, I realised that Anna might be the person that I had been seeking, for many years, to collaborate on a book about my experiences with the Oklahoma IPS [Institute for Primate Studies] chimps, especially the birth and death of Washoe's infant son, Sequoyah, about whom I had a diary of care from those days. After the class I spoke with Belle, and she was supportive of the idea, so the next day, I contacted Anna and proposed a possible collaboration. That's how it started. I knew, based on her background, extensive knowledge of language acquisition, and the factors that were being discussed during the chimp ASL days, that she might be willing to dig into the subject more thoroughly.
>
> In no time, we were deep in discussion and research in primate books and other relevant literature, both current and past. All of that became this book. A great stroke of luck to accidentally run into Anna, who had apparently been screening *Project Nim* to her Oxford students for several years. It is fortunate for me and for the language study chimps to have Anna as an ally.

There are many reasons why Bob's relationship with Nim represented something existential and not just a man studying a chimpanzee. Two major life events happened to Bob to make him rethink his priorities. The first was a motorbike accident when he was 18 years old and in the US Air Force. Bob was run over by a drunk driver and almost lost his life. He was in hospital for 9 months and given last rites. The second was extreme illness followed by a liver transplant 2 years prior to our meeting. Facing his own death not once, but twice, brought a sense of clarity and purpose. After the first near-death experience, he vowed to make something of himself, and enrolled in a Psychology degree course at Oklahoma University. After the second, he vowed to collate the chimpanzee materials and experiences and to be the voice for the chimpanzees, to make accurate the inaccuracies, and to share his stories and experiences.

Being a survivor is being in a place of isolation. Bob devoted his life to the sanctuary of primates. There is more to the chimpanzees' experiences than shown in the books and the film. After years of thinking about the issues in our respective cocoons of survival, we were both asking, independently: Why do human beings do these things? What do we now do with the experiences? What is still wrong with our world? Together, Bob and I have been asking: What can we learn from the chimpanzee studies? How can we pass on the knowledge? How do we give those chimpanzees the dignity and respect that they deserve? We present the results of those discussions here.

There were many reasons why I, Anna, could empathise with little Nim. Finding himself in a number of alien environments, Nim was made to take on the foreign language of signing and seemed pleased every time he was understood. Although I am fluent in English, it is not my first language. I grew up in an Italian community in England in the 1970s and was raised with no English. This was not so unusual for Bedford, UK, at that time. The market town just outside London is home to a large number of immigrants from the 1950s onwards: Irish, Jamaican, Nigerian, Iranian, Indian, Pakistani, Polish and Italian families lived alongside native English inhabitants. Before the internet, it was possible to stick within one's native bubble and not speak any English. Regular trips back to Italy as part of a large and extended family facilitated this, and it was easy to have no sense of English identity. The identity inside the home was incongruent with that of the external environment, and of the nation. I was familiar with the havoc that an unclear and changing identity can bring and had Nim-like experiences of my own.

Just like Nim's carers, my parents were young and impressionable. I am almost the same age as Nim, and my parents would have been the same age as Bob. As an only and solitary child for the first years of life, I struggled with English and started school with a split identity and hotchpotch of languages, clumsily navigating my way around a foreign social code. Somehow I made the grade and studied Experimental Psychology at university. In my second term, we covered Behavioural Psychology. There, I learned about Nim, Washoe and other primates who had been raised within their own version of incongruence. I conducted undergraduate research on why dyslexia went undiagnosed in Italian children. Italian has a transparent orthography, so it is easy to read it, even if you are dyslexic. The cluster "gh" is always "guh" regardless of whether it is in the beginning (ghiaccio = ice), middle (Lamborghini) or end of a word (funghi = mushrooms). Try that in English. It can be ghost, straight or cough. It can be understood through tough, thorough thought, though. All those things that had stumbled me up as a child were suddenly useful tools for investigation of language learning.

I was offered and took up a doctoral place to study the composition of the lexicon (mental dictionary), comparing monolingual English speakers with bilingual Italian-English speakers. By this time, some of the older Italians in Bedford were suffering strokes or other brain problems, and it was beneficial to study their language breakdown over time. Would they revert to Language 1, the Italian they had learned in their native environments, or would they prefer Language 2, the English picked up over decades settling in England? To look at language attrition in bilinguals, it was first necessary to consider its acquisition. In the 1990s there were not many neuropsychological studies on this – especially not from England, where the norm is to speak English most of the time. Together with my supervisor, Professor Andrew Ellis, I measured language acquisition, object naming and word reading in one and in two languages.

Over my doctorate years, we found more clues about language production. The age at which words are acquired affects the efficiency with which they are produced later in life. I often thought about contacting Nim's researchers to discuss learning by the chimps. I wondered, what if there had been a chimp equivalent? I saw the question differently. Were those chimps actually becoming bilingual, by being taught American Sign Language (ASL)? What if those sign-language-fluent chimps had strokes, too? Would they forget their sign language and revert to "chimp language"? Or would they always hold both languages in their brains? Of course, I hadn't accounted for *how* the chimps themselves came to *be*, and how formative that would be to the whole language-learning study in primates.

When *Project Nim* was released in 2011, I was several years post-doctorate and moved from studying bilingual people to those with bipolar disorder, in the Department of Psychiatry at the University of Oxford. With questions about the link between language and emotion at the back of my mind, my working life focussed on teaching courses, conducting research and writing papers. The Nim studies aided my teaching from a theoretical perspective for years. The film demonstrated to students how languages and cultures are learned. My mind went back to those problems caused by an unclear and changing identity. It was noteworthy with Nim that the human carers were bringing their "stuff" into their interactions. Some seemed more emotionally literate than others, and stood in for absent chimp parents, siblings, grandparents, for poor Nim, who would have been part of a big social group in the wild. Fortunately, one or two other caregivers kept him within healthy boundaries, such as Joyce Butler, whose special touch seemed to keep him emotionally safe. And of course, Robert, who was loyal to Nim to the end. Now here I was, in front of my computer, fielding questions for Nim's best friend, all the way from Oklahoma to near Oban, via Oxford. Without the film and without Nim, there would have been no such discussion, and this book would not have been.

That initial discussion led to hours of talking, thinking and analysing with Bob and interviews with some of the caregivers of those other chimpanzees, of Washoe, Carolyn, Onan, Ally, Lucy and others. I did not remember which animal was studied by whom, or the exact details of what had occurred and when. I learned that each chimpanzee had a complicated life story. The information needed collating, like a big ancestry study. Who did what, to whom? I spent the best part of 6 months doing the equivalent of a doctorate in Chimpanzee Studies.

It became clear that many of the accounts that are given about some of the chimpanzees that were studied are inaccurate. Some of the information was incomplete or sparse. Other aspects were inconsistent. I found out through discussions with Robert that there is so much more than what can be presented within a 93-minute documentary about one chimp. Each chimpanzee had an identity, a birth story, a history and an ending. Just like humans. When you meet someone for the first time, you think about what they are presenting to you. What's your name, where are you from, what do you do, where did you grow up, are you married, do you have children? With those chimpanzee case studies, some aspects were reported, but we are left wanting to know more. Why was this about Nim? What about those other chimps? How did they come to be? How did they live afterwards? How did they die? Did they have chimp offspring? Are they still alive? Where do they live? How?

The truth of these chimps' lives needs to be told, and this book will correct some of those inaccuracies. The history will be presented without speculation. We do not wish to heroise or to castigate anyone who was or is involved in this work. We simply wish to communicate the truth. It is clear that some individuals have dedicated, and continue to dedicate, their lives to providing sanctuary to those chimpanzees and their offspring as well as to other animals that were captured, exploited, sold, kept as pets or abandoned. Some of those individuals have died since the studies were conducted; indeed, a few of them died while we were writing this book. We would like to honour their memory, and their work is discussed here. It is hugely important to document and make available in print the truth about those studies. We hope to make scientists, policymakers, psychologists, historians and other readers aware of what went on, and what goes on. Here we are, as I write this, 6 months later, the product of those talks.

Robert (Bob) Ingersoll features in the film as one of Nim's carers. Bob had a particular relationship with Nim, with a very different interaction to the others. While many students were able to look after and train Nim, some were more empathetic than others and had different roles. Bob's relationship was remarkable for being affectionate yet boundaried. The wonderfully warm bond and understanding that developed between the two of them is prominent, especially towards the end of the documentary. We see from the home video clips that Nim had an air of confidence and, most importantly, trust, around Bob, which was not always apparent with his other carers. In fact, the documentary presents various incidents where Nim ignored, or worse, attacked his carers, especially when he felt resentful about his care. I realised over my repeated viewings of *Project Nim*, that the factor that united Bob and Nim was a mutual understanding of each other's trauma.

Bob and Nim's unspoken understanding was based on a bidirectional and mutual acceptance of troubled personal history. Bob's trust was held by Nim. It is particularly apparent in the last part of the film, once Nim is rescued from the Laboratory for Experimental Medicine and Surgery in Primates (LEMSIP) and taken to the Black Beauty Ranch. Nim was exceptionally insightful of human emotion. Stephanie LaFarge says, "He knew every dynamic that was in the room, instantly". Jenny Lee explains how, as a 14-year-old, Nim knew when she was upset: "He would come over and he would just come and sit with you, and hug you, and then just kiss the tears away . . . and it was amazing . . . just . . . unconditional" (*Project Nim*).

In the group session that Bob kindly gave to my class, it became apparent that while my focus had been on Nim, he was not a lone chimpanzee. The film could just have easily been Project Midge, or Project Moja, or Project Onan. The story of Project Washoe had already been told in the literature, but the inconsistencies, obfuscation and lack of detail about some of the most important parts of the story made the truth difficult to access. One book, *Next of Kin*, by Roger Fouts (Fouts & Mills, 1998), who was Washoe's principal investigator, told the story in a fairy-tale-like fashion, while *Silent Partners* by investigative journalist Eugene Linden (1986) seemed a solid piece of analytical narrative but did not present all the facts. These authors could only work with the tools and information that were made available to them at the time. The story of Washoe herself had never been told explicitly and with detail, accuracy and clarity, from multiple points of view, and so we hope to put forward the facts about her existence here.

As my discussions with Bob continued, it became apparent that what had started off as experiments about what humans could teach chimpanzees about language had become more about what the chimpanzees taught the humans. There were many twists and turns to the experiences of the chimpanzees in captivity. Even if *Project Nim* covered some of the work that went on behind the scenes to rescue the animals from invasive medical research, it was nothing close to the amount of energy and activity that went on. Robert, alongside James Mahoney, the chief veterinarian at the LEMSIP in New York, and others, fought for many chimpanzees, using deftness and insider knowledge to move the animals to safety. There were undercover projects, phone calls, letters, all in the backdrop of rescuing Nim, but with other chimps and monkeys also ultimately being rescued. Throughout this period, researchers were producing books about their experiences with the chimpanzees and still arguing as to whether what the chimps were learning was language or not. The continued debate whether chimpanzees are capable of grammar, syntax and words missed a huge and glaring point, which had been clear on my TV screen back in the UK. These were not studies about language. They were studies about survival.

The chimpanzees endured days in dingy enclosures, behind bars or in laboratories. They were incarcerated by and among humans when they should have been socialising with other primates. Over the course of the next few months, Robert and I discussed the main issues about the "science" of the studies. That context forced us to consider wider moral and ethical issues, in particular the issue of what makes us human. Consideration about what makes us different from other beings required us to concentrate on how we came to exist on this planet, why we humans think that we rule it, and how we can treat our planet with respect, and what on earth (literally) can be done going forwards. The work made me consider how to preserve life on this planet, starting with my own.

I came back to Oxford from Scotland and re-organised my life. I left my relationship, gave up alcohol and decided not to eat sentient beings while I was writing about them. I began to take better care of myself, and to give attention to my everyday life decisions, such as what I ate and where I went. How can you respect the animals that you are studying if you do not respect yourself? Bob had already had these insights through his chimpanzee experiences over his lifetime. The full story about life after Nim was still unknown to me, and I had a lot to learn. Our Oklahoma-Oxford link was established.

After Nim was sold to LEMSIP, Bob opened a shop named Jungle Jim's, just outside the campus of the University of Oklahoma (OU) in Norman, Oklahoma. Figure 1.1 shows one of the posters displayed inside Jungle Jim's.

With Nim gone, Bob was bereft. He used his voice to alert people about the sale of the famous OU chimps to medical research, using the slogan "Save the OU Chimps". In those pre-internet days, Jungle Jim's functioned as a sort of social media platform. It was a vehicle for raising the chimp issues, and Bob used it to amplify his voice for his activism. A long-time Grateful Dead enthusiast, he recalls how "One of the fun parts was having the opportunity to not only sponsor the 'Grateful Dead Hour' on the local FM rock station, but we also had the chance to educate the public and to poke the University in terms of its responsibilities towards the former OU chimps". An introduction to the Dead Hour broadcast on 11 January 1998, has the DJ David Kelso (who sadly died in September 2021) inviting listeners to Jungle Jim's for their Grateful Dead paraphernalia and to get information on "helping out some friends". Kelso tells the listeners about the sign-ing chimps of the 1970s and about the research being done at the University of Oklahoma, how Robert was involved, and how he didn't want "the genius animals

FIGURE 1.1   One of the posters displayed inside Jungle Jim's store.

being shipped off to medical labs". He explains Robert's crusade to get some of the animals out of these ugly situations and encourages listeners to find out how to help "our friends, our closest relatives on the ecological scale" by visiting Jungle Jim's on Campus Corner.

While the University of Oklahoma had lauded the chimps during the language studies, it tried to erase its connection to the animals from university documents thereafter, and it did not admit responsibility in helping them. Jungle Jim's placed adverts in the OU student newspaper, raising awareness of the plight of Nim's and others' experiences among the OU students, and making it clear that these studies were conducted in Oklahoma just 2.5 miles from campus and were not being discussed. "University officials didn't want to talk about this because they really made a big mistake", says Robert, "They sold those chimps down the river".

Jungle Jim's does not exist any longer, but its memory lives on. Former students who worked there frequently share memories on Robert's social media pages. Alongside Jungle Jim's, Robert engaged in work with numerous rescue organisations around the world, and that work continues. In getting to know him further, it is apparent that almost all of his life decisions are based around the care of those and other primates. It is fair to say that Bob has dedicated his life to the welfare of captive primates. He is recognised as a pioneer in animal rights activism, pushing enormous efforts into ending all animal testing. He is an advisor for the sanctuary Center for Great Apes, and for Save the Chimps, and continues to make known the issues around primate captivity. Even during the writing of this book, he was often busy building homes and being heavily involved in the Oklahoma Primate Sanctuary (OPS), a sanctuary for rescued primates on his doorstep in central Oklahoma, which he has been involved in since its inception in 1993. The rescuing of primates by him has continued, 50 years on.

I grew up in the 1980s in England. These were years of fear. We grew up under a disappearing ozone layer and against the backdrop of a threat of nuclear war. There was a constant worry of the pressing of the button, and talks between Thatcher and Reagan. There was the Falklands War. There were problems with the Romanian dictator Ceauşescu, who outlawed abortion and contraception and decreed that women should bear at least five children, resulting in more than 150,000 infants being abandoned in orphanages. There was a one-child policy in China with its government decreeing women to have intrauterine devices for birth control after their first child, subjecting them to forced sterilisation, and fining families for having more than one child, leading to sex-selective abortion of girls and the abandonment of many children, usually girls, in overcrowded orphanages. There were famines in Africa. These were dark clouds. The narrative I heard was that the earth was not a safe place for females, and that it is a place ruled by males who cause harm towards, and control, women and ordinary people. At school, there was always a school disco or a charity event to raise money for these plights. Indeed, in 1991, I was so shocked by a news report showing rocking, isolated babies in the Romanian orphanages cast aside in their cots, that I organised a school charity event to raise money for this plight and arranged for a journalist to report it in the local Bedford & Kempston Citizen newspaper. As an 8-year-old I was asked by my Italian teacher to write about something I was scared about. I wrote an essay on how I, a child, would live without my dead parents, adapting and surviving after the nuclear war I kept hearing about. After adolescence came young adulthood, in more terror. The millennium bug loomed, then 11 September 2001 happened, and the bombing of Afghanistan continues with current worries of a world with COVID, and now the Ukrainian crisis, which unfolds as I type. It is fair to say that my generation is one that grew up in terror. We knew panic and chaos and prepared for a doomsday, and felt despair for the harm we were, and are, inflicting on our planet.

I attended a Voluntary Aided, Catholic school in Bedford, and class debates were often about nature, social issues and population management. Conversations centred on the threat of nuclear war, the plight of Greenham Common and the Newbury bypass. There were reports of cruelty against animals in the name of beauty. I chose to be vegetarian for several years, and as a child spent weekends writing to companies about their testing of products on animals. In those days, toiletries and cosmetics were routinely tested on beagles and rabbits. My letters were to the British Union for the Abolition of Vivisection, now Cruelty Free International, which campaigns against animals being used in laboratories around the world. I had read the books by the English author Enid Blyton and learned about her work representing the People's Dispensary for Sick Animals (PDSA), a veterinary charity in the United Kingdom, which was founded in 1917 by Maria Dickin to provide care for sick and injured animals of the poor. There were constant threats about species becoming endangered, discussions about the Campaign for Nuclear Disarmament, the Women's Liberation Movement and their publication, *Spare Rib*. There were many wrongs to put right on this planet. We were economically comfortable but psychologically terrorised. I say this to demonstrate that when I met Bob, it was not the first time that I had given these social and political issues attention, but over the more recent years I had been thrown off track by work and life commitments. We have to produce and flourish, in order to survive. Some of the economic decisions such as where to live, which clothes to wear, which food to eat and which pets to have are now mine to make, and my social responsibility as the adult in this house. What have I noticed in these years? That we are constantly dipping into nature and exploiting its bounty, hand-in-hand with the conditioned belief that we, as humans, are the most important creatures on planet earth, with rule over animals. Recent news stories have resurfaced many of these issues during COVID: climate change, deforestation, fossil fuels, fracking, forest fires, vegetarianism, self-objectification, Botox. People of my generation who are now in the throes of raising families, running households and holding down jobs are responsible for consumer decisions, and we use our chauvinistic ideas about our exclusivity and entitlement to make daily economic decisions, often to the detriment of our animal neighbours. Something has to change.

The work presented in this book forced me to reconsider these world issues. Analysing the interactions between humans and animals made me think about my own attitudes towards group behaviour, and this form of human elitism. I was back to considering how to right wrongs: climate change, capitalism, sexism, humanism, zoos. How can we take action? What did Nim teach us? In those months, after stopping consumption of alcohol and meat, I became more aware of interpersonal relationships and human interaction with the planet. Despite the fact that a global pandemic caused isolation and disabling of activities such as travel, I reached a peak of personal development. I am a scientist at core, and we do not like to use abstract and non-verifiable terms such as "spirit" or "soul", but it is correct to say that I have been touched by a peculiar form of energy and action, and that its cause is Nim.

It has been 50 years since the original language experiments on chimpanzees. Nim Chimpsky was born in Oklahoma in 1973. The story of Nim and of the other experimental chimpanzees has been told in various books: *Nim Chimpsky: The Chimp Who Would Be Human* by Elizabeth Hess (2008), *Silent Partners* by Eugene Linden (1986), *Next of Kin* by Roger Fouts with Stephen Mills (Fouts & Mills, 1998), and in the touching testimony by the late James Mahoney, *From Elephants to Mice: Animals Who Have Touched My Soul* (Mahoney, 2010). The stories have not always been told with accuracy or in complete form. We present the true renditions of the events here. Although this book undoubtedly discusses Nim and the other chimpanzees, the writings focus on Washoe. We also describe the involvement of several chimp carers. Some of the individuals who looked after these primates were overlooked from the original explanations or their roles were underemphasised or ignored, which we hope to rectify.

The past cannot be changed. Mistakes were made, and those studies remain ethically questionable. It is important now to consider what we have learned from the experiences and to retell the stories with the *correct* details in order to do justice to the animals and to act with integrity and dignity towards other beings. A huge number of scientific and philosophical implications were unearthed throughout the studies. The most basic, yet perhaps the biggest philosophical concern, was that these chimpanzees did not have their needs met in an adequate way. What happens if we swap the figure of the chimpanzee with that of a child? A tremendous amount of trauma is uncovered. We would never take an infant from its mother, rear it in an unnatural environment, keep it captive, expect it to learn a foreign (cross-species) language, and neglect its needs as it grows. We rear our young with care, tending to their needs, and in consideration of their development and progression in growth. Many of the maladaptive behaviours demonstrated by the chimpanzees were due to their having been torn from their mothers as infants. Over the years, various tales of how these chimpanzees were raised "as humans" have emerged. We would like this book to be the vehicle for setting those stories straight and the process by which we should reflect upon and rationalise the experiences of those chimpanzees to prevent any harm occurring again.

Why Chimpanzees?

In her study on consciousness and octopi, Sy Montgomery says that, "Humans are not unique in possessing the neurological substrates that generate consciousness . . . nonhuman animals, including all birds and mammals, and many other creatures, including octopi, also possess these neurological substrates" (Montgomery, 2015). The primate studies focussed so much on the cognitive aspects of language that they neglected to consider the neurological makeup of the animals. In our human arrogance, we tried to use those studies to consider what makes us human, at the expense of considering what it means to be chimpanzee.

Washoe's story has been neglected from the aspect of trauma, which the chapters in this book revisit. There also follows discussion of the other Oklahoma chimpanzees, but we would very much like Washoe to be considered the "star of the show" in these pages, as she was in life.

Washoe was born in the wild and reared in captivity. Although language was studied in other primates, Washoe was the first chimpanzee to successfully demonstrate two-way communication with another animal using ASL. The details about how she came to academia are sketchy, but she was first studied by a husband-and-wife team of scientists, Allen and Beatrix Gardner. Allen was a psychologist interested in verbal learning, and Beatrix was interested in ethology, which is the biology of behaviour. Over the years, they conducted research into sign language on many chimpanzees. They had studied film of a failed attempt by psychologists Keith and Catherine Hayes at the Yerkes National Primate Research Center, with the involvement of Yale and Harvard universities, to teach spoken language to the female chimpanzee, Viki, about 15 years before Washoe. The chimpanzee was intelligible, moving her lips into the proper shape but not able to generate the appropriate sounds. Viki was able to "speak" the words *cup, mama, papa, up*, in "a hoarse stage whisper" (Fouts & Mills, 1998, p. 24), although it was reported that each word had taken 6 months to master. The Gardners considered whether the problem might have been more of a physical than a mental one in the chimpanzees, since chimps lack the vocal apparatus to create the same articulations as humans. They believed that chimpanzees could learn sign language, specifically ASL, and "Project Washoe" was started.

Washoe was born in Africa and given the name Kathy. According to Roger Fouts, Washoe had been abducted from the jungle in Africa to become part of the American Space Program. It is not made clear what the exact steps were between her mother in Africa and the Gardners in Reno, which is in the northwest section of the US state of Nevada and is the county seat and the largest city of Washoe County, after which Washoe was renamed.

The Gardners acquired Washoe through the Space Program people who provided chimpanzee babies for the Air Force. Roger Fouts was employed by the Gardners as Washoe's main caregiver and became the principal investigator of the language studies on her. In *Next of Kin*, Washoe's origins are described as "a rather romantic mystery" to him. He knew that she had been "wild-collected" in Africa

(p. 38), and that the Gardners had acquired her at 10 months from the Holloman Aeromedical Laboratory in New Mexico, and she was a part of the American Space Program. "Wild-collected" is one of several sanitised terms used by research teams. It means stalking a mother chimpanzee, shooting her and stealing her baby. This sanitised name presents the behaviours as permissible and accepted.

In the 1950s and 1960s, the American military procured chimpanzees from hunters in Africa who stalked any mother chimpanzees carrying babies. Usually, the mother was shot out of her hiding place in a tree. If she fell on her stomach with her infant clinging to her chest, both mother and baby would die. However, when the mother chimpanzee shielded the infant by falling on her back, the baby would be easy to seize. Fouts explains how "The screaming infant would then be bound hand and foot to a carrying pole and transported to the coast, a harrowing journey usually lasting several days" (Fouts & Mills, 1998, p. 41).

Washoe's beginnings will have been strongly trauma-ridden. It is likely that she was abducted from her mother after having witnessed her being shot, would have been bound to a carrying pole and transported, screaming, to the coast for a journey lasting several days. Not all infant primates would survive this trip. The chimpanzees would then be sold to a European animal dealer for $4 or $5. The dealer would keep them in a small box until the American buyer would arrive a few days later, in this case the Air Force. Fouts explains the continuation of the ordeal: "Those still alive when the buyer came were crated up and sent to the United States, a journey that mirrored the slave trade of the earlier centuries" (p. 42). It is believed that for every one chimpanzee that survived from the crates to arrive in the US, around 10 chimpanzees would have died. When the US stopped using the chimpanzees for space projects in the 1960s, another dreadful fate befell the chimpanzees, and they would be used, instead, in medical experiments and toxicity studies.

There is not much more clarity than Wahoe being "wild-collected", but it is thought that individuals from the Primate Foundation of Arizona, and Jo and Paul Fritz, were involved with the acquisition of Washoe from the Air Force. The Fritzes were friends with William (Bill) Lemmon, the prominent psychologist at the University of Oklahoma who founded the research facility named the IPS, which had been formed in the early 1960s. Washoe was moved there on 1 October 1970, under the care of Fouts, and Robert joined in 1975. Lemmon also probably played a role in acquiring Washoe. He had played an advisory role to the Gardners before Roger Fouts was even a student of theirs. It is unclear why Fouts does not mention this in his book, but it is known that Lemmon must have been involved early on with Washoe.

In Fouts's book, Lemmon is painted as an evil villain who had not helped on any level with Washoe. Robert knew both men and believes this is an inaccurate exaggeration. Lemmon was a difficult man, but he was not evil. Fouts describes Lemmon as "calculating", as "a natural politician who knew how to charm journalists with quotable wisdom" (p. 119), as having "a bizarre plan for studying the maternal behavior of chimpanzees" (p. 107). An interesting and dramatic allusion is made by

Fouts of Lemmon resembling Dr. Moreau of the H.G. Wells novel, *The Island of Dr. Moreau*, which is about "a brilliant but megalomaniacal scientist who holes up on a Pacific island so he can carry out controversial experiments on animals" (p. 120). Fouts explains how, like Dr. Moreau, Lemmon had been cast out of academia by his colleagues and "took up residence on the scientific fringe" (p. 120). The allusion goes on for several pages in Fouts's book. Mysteriously, he also says that "The Gardners seemed to know more about Lemmon than they said" (p. 125) but does not elaborate. The reader is left wondering how much of the description is fact, and how much has been woven into a would-be tale. It is certainly clear that Roger Fouts experienced feelings of inferiority towards Bill Lemmon.

The difficult dynamic between Fouts and Lemmon is highlighted further by Eugene Linden, who describes Lemmon as having power over his colleagues and an ability to dominate chimpanzees. Lemmon's power was "underscored at various times when chimpanzees broke out of the main cage complex" (Linden, Silent Partners, 1986, p. 40). A situation is described where Lemmon called a local dog-catcher to round up a group of chimpanzees. When the dogcatcher declined, Lemmon went after the chimpanzees himself, bullying the males back into the cages, "something that nobody else at the institute – including Roger Fouts – would have been able to pull off" (p. 41). Linden explains further how "In fact, when an adult female named Candy broke out, Roger backed off toward water (chimpanzees cannot swim) and let Lemmon get her back into her cage" (p. 41). It appears that Fouts was rather jealous of Lemmon's ability to control the chimpanzees. The two men dealt with the chimpanzees in different ways. Lemmon was more authoritative and unliked by Fouts, but "In other ways, however, Roger Fouts was a serious threat to Dr. Lemmon" since the younger Roger had arrived in Oklahoma with a highly achieving Washoe, who had the potential to win grants. Linden explains how there was obviously tension between the two men which would surface in both trivial and serious ways and says how "One former graduate student described their relationship as 'like two alpha [dominant] male chimpanzees butting heads' . . ." (p. 41). In her account, *Nim Chimpsky: The Chimpanzee Who Would be Human*, Elizabeth Hess explains how "Lemmon expected Fouts to follow his orders while continuing to take care of the chimpanzees and generate more outside funding for them. In return, Lemmon was prepared to take the young psychologist under his wing and into his inner circle of believers . . .", and how Fouts "had an intense dislike of Lemmon and found Lemmon's attitude toward his chimpanzees to be reprehensible. There was so much tension between him and Lemmon that Fouts could barely stand to be at IPS some days". It is described how "[Lemmon] played with Fouts and watched him squirm" (Hess, 2008). If this were a human family, it would have been difficult for a child. Being raised in the midst of such squabbling figures in such constant conflict would have caused confusion and tension. How would it have been for Washoe to live in the shadows of these dynamics? Or for the other students in Fouts's and Lemmon's laboratories?

It is useful to consider the relationship between these two men when considering the treatment of Washoe. What were these researchers bringing to the studies? If this were a human fostering or adoption placement, extensive consideration would be given to the background and dynamics within the fostering family. Here, no attention was ever paid to such dynamics, or to the personal trauma that each researcher was bringing to their individual and respective relationships with Washoe. Who was now the father figure for Washoe? Was it Fouts, or was it Lemmon? Was a father figure necessary? She had grown up with the Gardners. Other human relationships also featured in the chimpanzees' identities, various graduate students and researchers of different ages and with varied trauma histories themselves. What were those individuals to her? If Washoe were a human being under retrospective analysis, we would go through her family very carefully to consider the familial linkage with each of her family members and the trauma bonds passed on over generations. The social positionings in Washoe's life were constantly unclear.

Much later, once Washoe was fully grown, the Gardners, Fouts and Lemmon, and others, considered returning her to the Gambia where a prior IPS chimpanzee named Lucy, owned and raised by Maurice (Maury) Temerlin, was returned by Janis Carter. Robert lobbied heavily for Washoe to be returned to the Gambia at the time, but on reflection, he has realised that this would not have been in Washoe's best interests. The difficulties that Janis faced with Lucy were only recently reported in the film, *Lucy, the Human Chimp* (Alex Parkinson, 2021). Had Bob known then how complicated the transition to Africa had been, he would not have argued for it. Back in the 1970s, nobody had considered what to do with an *adult* chimpanzee, as they were not kept for psychological experiments much beyond around age 4 or 5 years, although Lemmon did keep adult chimpanzees which he kept on breeding, as per his plan.

There is a moral duty to use as much of the data collected as possible from those controversial studies. We need to present an accurate and authentic picture. The image commonly portrayed in the media is of older naturalists kissing chimpanzees that are being returned to the wild after time spent in sanctuary. This is damaging in itself and does not convey the reality. Chimpanzees are not cute, fluffy creatures that offer hugs and kisses in gratitude for human sanctuary. They are larger than humans and they bite. Not only is it damaging to present a saccharine and fake version to the public, but it also reflects a type of human arrogance and animal exploitation. Chimpanzees, especially as adults, are extremely strong and dangerous creatures. To give the image on social media that there are compassionate cuddles, even kisses, from chimpanzees is harmful. Sadly, social media audiences will look on in their millions, liking posts, perhaps even shedding tears at such heartwarming images of compassion from the creatures, when in fact they are watching without critical awareness. Peddling chimpanzees for these images is tacky and objectifies them. Any such return to the wild or to sanctuary is a private moment and should be kept so in order to retain the dignity to the animals.

There is relatively little time to rescue chimpanzees and other primates from extinction. One of the most important conclusions of Fouts's book is that if we do not take action, "we will wake up one day soon only to discover that we've destroyed the living link to our own evolutionary past" (Fouts & Mills, 1998, p. 370). If we do not get on with preserving these beings, they will be gone from the wild in very few years. Our children will not see them. This is why there is a sense of urgency within which we convey this message. We should be concerned about our wiping out a species of creatures with whom we share around 98% of our DNA. If we can do this to our closest DNA neighbours, what else are we capable of doing? Where will our level of destruction end?

It is this sense of urgency that we wish to convey through this book. We hope that readers will forgive any omissions, but this book was written within just months of our initial speaking (we have not even met in person yet), and we are desperate to pass on the information from these studies. The message of this book is to consider how best we can proceed from the information that was acquired. How do we ensure those studies are never repeated? What do we pass on to future generations of scientists, researchers, anthropologists, therapists and our children? How can we treat chimpanzees and other animals with respect? What can we do now, which is in the best interests of these chimpanzees?

2
NARRATIVES FOR FLOURISHING

Whoever teaches us language bears a responsibility for ensuring that we develop narratives that lead to our flourishing. It has taken the field of psychology decades to understand the role of language in wellbeing. How was that same science at a point where it was deemed acceptable to steal a newborn chimpanzee from its mother and to raise it within a human family, in a quest to learn about language? In *Project Nim*, Herb Terrace says, "Wouldn't it be interesting to find out what a chimpanzee would be feeling? The breakthroughs would be if a chimpanzee could put together sentences in structure" (*Project Nim*, 2011). According to Roger Fouts, "Since 98.7 percent of the DNA in humans and chimps is identical, some scientists (but not Noam Chomsky) believed that a chimp raised in a human family, and using ASL (American Sign Language), would shed light on the way language is acquired and used by humans" (Fouts & Mills, 1998). Terrace was a behavioural psychologist and conceived *the Nim study* as a challenge to Chomsky's hypothesis that only humans have language.

The researchers and carers were not prepared for "the wild animal within" (Stephanie LaFarge, *Project Nim*, 2011). The study was conducted in a state of non-preparation. "There was utter chaos" (Laura-Ann Petitto, *Project Nim*, 2011). Terrace neglected the needs of Nim in growing from a child to an adult chimpanzee, "two, three times the human's size" (Laura-Ann Petitto). In *Silent Partners*, Eugene Linden explains the muddled thinking behind the language experiments; the "quagmire" posed by the language researchers. He explains how "there is more to be learned from looking at the quagmire from a distance than by entering it and attempting to determine its shape by peering through the murk" (Linden, 1986, p. 60). Along with other cognitive scientists of the time, Terrace assumed that the language debate could be settled by basing his suppositions on his view, in which he was settling the language debate; "Terrace's facts are not everybody's facts" (Linden, 1986, p. 61). The debate was oversimplified: "It's as though a sixteenth-century

DOI: 10.4324/9781003357650-3

astronomical society decided that when, under Vatican pressure, Galileo recanted his belief in a heliocentric solar system, the matter was then settled, and they could get back to business as usual" (Linden, 1986, pp. 61–62).

Terrace has given an excessive amount of attention to Chomsky's theory even in recent years. Nobody has ever pointed out that Chomsky's ideas were representative of a psychology of the 1960s and are relics of a previous psychology. They came from Chomsky's position as a philosopher and theorist. He was not an experimental psychologist. Chomsky may be one of our best-known intellectuals, but he speaks from his standing as an anarcho-syndicalist and libertarian socialist. His ideas about the language acquisition device (LAD) and Universal Grammar are hypothetical. Nobody has ever opened up a brain and pointed to the LAD. Chomsky's ideas represent a hypothetical organisation of language planning and articulation. Research into language processing has made huge advances since Chomsky's proposals. Those initial ideas were novel in the 1960s, and while they influenced the field, it was only later that the tools became available to analyse and challenge them in a scientifically rigorous manner. For Terrace to still be discussing Chomsky in the 2000s is an anachronism.

To put this into perspective, when I started my doctoral work in 1996, there were only four functional magnetic resonance imaging (fMRI) brain scanners in the UK. As I type this, I can count four in Oxford alone. A magnetoencephalography (MEG) centre was also built in 2008 as a part of the Oxford Centre for Human Brain Activity (OHBA) in the Department of Psychiatry in the University of Oxford. MEG measures the magnetic fields generated by electric currents in the brain. When brain cells fire, they create magnetic fields. These are picked up by electrodes which were traditionally placed on the scalp, and which are fitted inside a device that sits on the head like a helmet, so the process of measurement is non-invasive. The technique only picks up firing from the cortex, so it cannot measure brain activity within the limbic regions in the centre of the brain, but that is not necessary in order to measure language function. MEG has already been used to map cortical function for a number of different languages, including English, Spanish and Chinese (Valaki et al., 2004; Zhang et al., 2010).

The OHBA Centre in Oxford now houses a multi-modality imaging centre which has state-of-the-art techniques for measuring and stimulating activity in the living human brain. This includes an integrated 128-channel electroencephalography (EEG) system which can measure scalp potentials during the MEG experiment, so that the EEG signals are recorded in the same dataset as the MEG channels. This means that one can employ three different techniques to measure brain activity directly, in the space of just 1 hour. Other universities in the UK, the US and worldwide have similar facilities. For neuroscientific advancement to explode in this way was unforeseen when Chomsky described his version of the linguistic brain. Yet so-called behavioural psychologists and cognitive scientists are still discussing language in the context of the hypotheses of the 1960s and relying on evidence from animal data unrepresentative of typical human brain activity.

Noam Chomsky on Nim Chimpsky

How does it feel to have a famous chimpanzee named after you? It is surprising that Noam Chomsky does not comment more on this. There is one YouTube interview: 'Noam Chomsky on Nim Chimpsky and the Emergence of Language' and one email interview with Matt Aames Cucchiaro in 2007/2008, 'The Myth of Ape Language', both before the release of the film, *Project Nim*, so it is possible that his opinions have changed since these interviews, but it is clear that Chomsky does not hold the studies in great regard. Both commentaries are disappointingly shallow and, lacking in any evidence, highly speculative.

One has to remember that the radical claims about language by Chomsky were made in the 1950s and 1960s, before it was clear that he is a theorist rather than a scientist. Chomsky first wrote his famous papers in response to B.F. Skinner's theories, when the world was divided into the nature-*or*-nurture discourse. With recent studies employing more sophisticated techniques, we are now in a position of demonstrating nature *via* nurture. In his 2007/2008 interview, Chomsky's comments were that these animal learning studies were "totally meaningless" and gave the impression that the primate researchers were delusional in their beliefs that they were teaching chimps to sign. To claim that "It's all totally meaningless, so I don't participate in the debate", is not a particularly intellectual way to consider the decades of ape research, and to reduce it to an argument that "it is considered significant that apes (or birds, which tend to do much better) can be trained to mimic some superficial aspects of human language" is hypothetical, and just as reductionist as the early theories that he was reviewing.

It is clear that he does not hold the chimpanzees, or some of the caregivers, in any positive regard. He says about Nim:

> If he wanted a banana, he'd produce a sequence of irrelevant signs and throw in the sign for banana randomly, figuring that he'd brainwashed the experimenters sufficiently so that they'd think he was saying "give me a banana."

This comment was made before the film, which includes several clips where Nim makes the sign for wanting a banana, demonstrating clearly that the sign was meaningful, in context, and not produced at random, and in no way indicative of any "brainwashing".

Chomsky continues:

> And he was able to pick out subtle motions by which the experimenters indicated what they'd hope he'd do. Final result? Exactly what any sane biologist would have assumed: zero.

It appears that Chomsky has been studying a different animal. The experimenters teaching Nim language were far from subtle, and the caregivers giving him bananas did not have to indicate any motions to have him signing back. Again, it is demonstrated on a number of occasions in the film that the quality of communication between chimp and human is more sophisticated than this, and the further clips from Robert's personal collection reflect deeper and more insightful processing of concepts in the chimpanzees.

Perhaps most telling of Chomsky's undermining of the studies and of the chimpanzees as sentient beings, is in this remark:

> Then comes the sad part. Chimps can get pretty violent as they get older, so they were going to send him to chimp heaven. But the experimenters had fallen in love with him, and tried hard to save him. He was finally sent off to some sort of chimp farm, where he presumably died peacefully – signing the Lord's Prayer in his last moments.

One wonders if Chomsky was aware of the book about Nim by Elizabeth Hess, where it was made clear that there was no fantasy about "chimp heaven", the Lord's Prayer or religiosity about Nim in the caregivers. Facetious statements are beyond deep intellectual discussion. It is clear that Chomsky – like most of the external observers and critics of the primate studies – has not considered the chimps in the context of contemporary neuroscientific or psychodynamic research.

The YouTube clip of Chomsky also has inaccuracies and contradictions, but he makes the important point about the *order* in which the words were acquired. It is known that the age at which words are acquired is important in human language. It is a key factor in object naming. Disappointingly, the clip suggests that Chomsky is behind the times in his discussion of the research: "Brain science" has already configured time signatures for language production in the hemispheres and cortical areas (Cornelissen et al., 2009). Research work using MEG and brain scanning on dyslexic individuals compared with healthy control participants has already revealed the nature and time signature of object naming and word production (Cornelissen et al., 2009), and other studies using fMRI were able to identify the cortical areas employed by both monolingual and bilingual speakers, in naming words in their first and second languages (Kim et al., 1997). It was found that native and second languages have a spatial relationship in the human cortex, within the frontal lobe, language-sensitive regions (Broca's area). Second languages acquired in adulthood ("late" bilinguals) are spatially separated from native languages. However, when acquired during the early language acquisition stage of development ("early" bilinguals), native and second languages tend to be represented in common frontal cortical areas. In both late and early bilingual speakers, the temporal-lobe language-sensitive regions (Wernicke's area) show little or no separation of activity based on the age of language acquisition. These findings demonstrated the existence of language-specific regions in Broca's area which underpin multiple language functions.

Organisation of language processing is also widely affected by language-specific characteristics in bilinguals, across languages. Two languages can be similar depending on some linguistic features, and not others. For example, Italian and Spanish are the same across semantic as well as phonemic features, and it was found that similar areas of the cortex were activated during their production, whereas those which were different across two languages (Italian and Japanese) showed a physical linguistic distance. Also, while for an English-Italian speaker the difference in the phonological inventory of the two languages is larger than that in the semantic system, the opposite is true for Japanese-Italian bilinguals, as Japanese and Italian have overlapping phonemic ranges (Kavanagh, 2007) but are very different socio-culturally. Other research (indeed, Chomsky himself mentions) has noted that speakers who are using sign language activate left hemisphere regions which are common to spoken word production in the brain. As Linden pointed out, "Irre-spective of the merits of an idea, a passionate advocate can promote a theory long after it has ceased to have any utility" (p. 59). He mentions "Noam Chomsky, who has managed to keep the foundering ship of deep structure afloat for two decades principally through his intimidating brilliance and his willingness to debate anyone anywhere who challenges his ideas".

I emailed Chomsky directly, to ask his opinions about these issues. I pointed out that in *Next of Kin*, Fouts says that:

> It is important to point out that human language, whether signed or spoken, is not in any sense "better" than the communication system of wild chimpan-zees. Evolution is not a ladder of "improvement" culminating in the human species; it is an ongoing process of adaptation for millions of related species, each on its own evolutionary pathway.
>
> *(Fouts & Mills, 1998, p. 191)*

Chomsky's reply was:

> I barely wrote about the NIM project but followed it closely throughout. The lead investigator with NIM (Laura-Ann Petitto) and one of the chief designers of the project (Tom Bever) are close friends (Tom's a former stu-dent, now colleague). Both they and others working directly on the project are outstanding scientists.
>
> I was quite skeptical from the start, in part for reasons that you quote from Fouts, though I'd put it differently. The desert ants in my back yard (in Tuc-son) have cognitive capacities that humans can't possibly match. No doubt one could train grad students to more or less mimic the waggle dance of some bee species, but it would be of no scientific interest. I never understood what would be the importance of training a chimp to mimic some aspects of human language, if that could be attained.
>
> Human language is not just a "more intricate" communication system. In its fundamental properties, it has no analogue in the animal world. While of course used for communication, it seems fundamentally to be a system for generating thought – pretty much the traditional view, pre-20th century, and I think on the right track. All of this has become much clearer in more recent

years with advances in studies of language acquisition and on core principles of language. Including the few relevant discoveries in the neuroscience of language (an extremely difficult area, in part because of ethical barriers to direct experimentation, in part because of lack of any animal models apart from very superficial properties). The conclusions about radical divergence are supported further by what has come to light about language evolution.

In response to your question, I wasn't the one who felt that the researchers were deluded by the apparent successes. That was their conclusion after they analyzed the protocols carefully. I was frankly surprised at how little NIM achieved after intensive training, revealing, I think, the radical divergence of human language from animal communication, becoming ever more clear.

I don't know of any evidence that apes can acquire even the most elementary rudiments of sign language, even anything like human words, as Petitto and Seidenberg discussed years ago.

As for other studies, hard to say, especially for those who refuse to release protocols. I know of none that have been subjected to the careful scrutiny of the NIM study.

When I challenged these points, he replied:

I've looked over the evidence and discussed the matter extensively with Nim's major trainers. I agree with the conclusion of those who ran the project, after studying the frame-by-frame videos carefully, that NIM never mastered even the basic rudiments of sign, and that they had been deluded to think so. No doubt that data are susceptible to various interpretations. I never had any contact with Terrace, who I don't think was close to the research.

It is certainly unusual that Chomsky's theory continues to be held up as a reason for why these chimpanzees could or could not sign. Chomsky is still aligned with being a theorist rather than a scientist, and there has been no experimental research by Chomsky, yet his theory continues to be cited with frequency. Indeed, one of the main researchers of Nim, chief investigator and organiser, Terrace, still cites Chomsky as a way of explaining the Nim results. In his book, *Why Chimpanzees Can't Learn Language and Only Humans Can* (2019), he explains how "Nim Chimpsky's failure to produce sentences in American Sign Language . . . confirmed Chomsky's view that language was uniquely human". It is perhaps worth noting that this book was produced from a set of university seminars (the Leonard Hastings Schoff Memorial Lectures), rather than Terrace having written this argument out of main consideration of the language debate alone. The University Seminars at Columbia University sponsor an annual series of lectures, and a member of the Columbia faculty is invited to deliver three lectures before a general audience, which are then published. This approach is different to writing a book out of integrity and full consideration of the topic and may have influenced Terrace's reporting of the supposed lack of Nim's language learning.

He claims that "it obscured the fact that the real reason for the failure was Nim's inability to learn words" (p. 167). This does not match what we see from Nim's behaviours. Footage of Nim's signs shows that he was able to sign a number of utterances confidently, as Terrace himself noted from his own study on the cumulative record of signs that Nim learned to produce in New York (Terrace, Figure 2.2, p. 41). Terrace says that "By his third birthday, Nim had learned to produce 125 signs". Which is it? Did Nim produce accumulating signs, or was it "a failure"? Terrace explains that "they were an artifact of imitation" (p. 40), but there is no scientific way of demonstrating this. Even in humans, how would anyone dis/prove that language is due, at least in part, to imitation?

From my own doctoral research in language acquisition, I note that what we call "language" is the attaching of a linguistic tag to a concept. It is clear that the chimpanzees had clear concepts, symbols and ideas about objects in nature, such as flowers, trees, fruit, body parts and babies, and had also acquired semantic knowledge also about artefacts that were not "natural" to them: pens, paper, tools, cameras, soda pop, cigarettes and marijuana. They were able to conceptualise these and to attach forms of linguistic tags to them. It simply happened that those linguistic tags had to be in the form of signs using hands, rather than articulations using the larynx and tongue and mouth, although some recent studies indicate that some primates do use those, too.

Both Terrace and Chomsky appear to express confusion in their scientific understanding. It is not surprising given that the evidence is from such fluid and outdated ideas. Even to this day their positions on whether chimpanzees can learn language or not are unclear. James Mahoney says in *Project Nim*: "We realised that Prof. Terrace says that they can sign single words but that they cannot 'do' grammar . . . but this is not the case. Certain of the Oklahoma chimps could use sign language, and were trying to sign with us . . . . We wrote down on sheets of paper which we posted all over the place, on doors on walls and everywhere we could find, certain signs and we would hope that as time went by, everyone would pick up at least a certain amount of sign language."

There are two important points to note here. First, single-word imperatives such as LOOK, EAT, GIVE convey a different grammatical tense from GOOD and RIGHT. The single word HELP! conveys a different meaning to PEACE. There is a suggestion that that chimpanzees *cannot* use these conversationally, but the multitude of home movies, many of which were part of *Project Nim*, demonstrate the opposite. The second important point to note is that at the Laboratory for Experimental Medicine and Surgery in Primates (LEMSIP), the humans had to be taught the chimp signs so that they could use the signs with chimps to comfort them: SHOES, HUG, PLAY, OUT.

One definition of language is that it is a structured system of communication that can be used in reception *and also* in transmission. It is ironic that Mahoney and other humans had to teach themselves the signs that the chimps were using, which were taught to them by humans. It is possible that Terrace's confusion stems from this. A chimpanzee may not be wired to learn human language, but if taught, will learn something akin to language, and will be able to produce it in order to communicate with humans.

Terrace's confusion is further demonstrated in his publications. In 1987 Terrace published his book: *Nim: A Chimpanzee Who Learned Sign Language*, but the 2019 book was *Why Chimpanzees Can't Learn Language and Only Humans Can*. This book gives little discussion about neuroscientific research or of the brain regions involved in language processing. Terrace gives the impression that the failure is of the chimpanzees rather than of his experiments. Yet as this chapter demonstrates, there exists an abundance of published evidence from both MEG and fMRI brain scanning which determine the loci (a hint at where Chomsky's LAD might be located) and which identify specific cortical areas involved in language processing. There is even evidence from canines. Research demonstrates how dogs use the same brain mechanisms as humans to process words, as well as intonation. Dogs are able to understand vocabulary and tone of voice to decipher complex meanings. In an investigation of lexical processing in canines, Andics et al. (2016) studied the brain responses of 13 dogs using fMRI when their owners' voices were played. The dogs were presented with praise or neutral words spoken using praising intonation compared with neutral intonations. There was a bias for left hemisphere processing of interpretation of word meaning regardless of intonation, and this allowed the dogs to discriminate between praise and neutral words. There was also increased activity in primary reward regions when both lexical and intonation information were consistent with praise. The right middle ectosylvian gyrus responded to intonation only, rather than word meaning. This is the same process demonstrated in humans, where listeners separately analyse lexical and intonational cues to arrive at a unified representation of communicative content. This demonstrates that canines have the capacity for language processing, even in the absence of its production.

Instead, Terrace explains that while his paper was asserting confidently that Nim knew several signs, his confidence was gone by 1979 as he realised his videos were showing Nim responding to reward signals. He makes much of these as "negative results". Let us remember that these results would have determined research funding issues at the time. One wonders if this sudden volte-face of Terrace was in part his washing of hands from the project. By suggesting negative findings, he would no longer receive research funding, and the problem of Nim's expensive upkeep would be passed on. This would serve as justification of ending Project Nim and sending Nim to Oklahoma. Robert believes that Terrace never planned to keep him past the age of 5 years.

Terrace uses the Clever Hans example as explaining Nim's learning. This is a paper by Pfungst from 1911. Things have moved on in psychology since then, but to explain: Clever Hans was a German horse whose trainer claimed could solve arithmetic problems. When the trainer wrote "3 × 2 = ?" Hans tapped his foot six times. A group of scientists explained that Hans was solving the problem by hearing the breathing of the trainer, who would hold his breath after posing the problem and inhale on every tap, exhaling once Hans had reached the requisite number of taps (Pfungst, 1911). To use this tale to explain Nim's learning reflects the facetiousness with which Terrace regards Nim's communication, which not only undermines but demonstrates how little Terrace understood Nim. There are many examples from *Project Nim* and from home movie clips where Nim is signing spontaneously and of his own accord. For instance, Bob talks about the walks he and Nim went on for hours and hours:

> We signed about what we saw. We would encounter a gate and he would jump off my back and run up to the gate and sign OPEN OPEN, which is two hands palm-to-palm, and then opening like a book, so OPEN OPEN and then HURRY YOU ME RIDE THERE.

In the clips made available to me, it is clear that Nim will have the gate opened for him, regardless of whether he will sign or not. He will be allowed up on Bob's back, regardless of any signing. Yet he still chooses to sign UP, UP, HURRY, HURRY.

Terrace identifies the prelinguistic stage we have as infants. He describes the nature of the emotional and social engagement between infant and mother/care-taker as vital. Yet he makes no link of this in the very chimpanzee he studied. One has to question the scientific rigour of the scientist who (a) does not look out for such basic factors in his hypotheses ahead of his practical work and (b) who keeps publishing alternative accounts of the science. By definition, scientific results that have to have their interpretations changed every few years are not scientific. This is not hypothesis-driven, theory-making, experimental work.

In my experimental work on lexical composition in humans for my doctorate, I described the various stages required in processing language. Terrace makes no reference to these stages. He identifies a pre-lexical *state* in development but surprisingly does not refer to any model of lexical processing. Here is a simple explanation of how we do words: Think of the brain as having a sort of dictionary of words. Lexicalisation (this is the scientific name for simple object naming) is the set of processes which affect the retrieval of lexical items (object names, or words) from the mental lexicon (the dictionary). These lexical items can be divided into two parts. The lemma contains semantic and grammatical details about a word. Meaning and syntax are available here. The *lemma* would tell us, for instance, whether it is a command word (imperative) like PLAY; a describing word (adjective) like RIGHT; or a noun, like SHOE. It would also tell you whether it means RIGHT as in correct or RIGHT as in the opposite to LEFT. At the second stage called the *lexeme*, there is morphological and phonological information (Levelt & Schriefers, 1987). The meaning part of the lemma is matched with semantic information from the pre-verbal message to activate lexical items, which then activates information about syntax and grammar, resulting in a surface structure processed by a sort of phonological planning. At the final stage, this phonetic plan is converted to overt speech. The speech production process is incredibly fast and highly automatic in humans (Levelt, 1989). It takes around 500 to 1,500 milliseconds to name single objects. In that short space of time, if you are speaking a language that contains grammatical genders, you will also be retrieving information about whether that object is, say, masculine or feminine, and information to help us make the adjective agree, or to help with inconsistencies, like knowing that SHEEP can be singular or plural.

It is likely that chimpanzees reached both stages in anticipation of producing a sign. In the signing of SHOE, for example, Nim was able to demonstrate that a shoe went on his foot, which demonstrates successful access of the semantics and the lemma. In the processing of the word SHOE itself, he showed lexeme access – albeit as the act of putting the hands together to form the appropriate sign rather than as a construction of phonemes. If Nim was asked "Where does this go?" about the shoe, he was able to show that the shoe went on the foot, again demonstrating successful lexical access for the word SHOE. Object naming in humans requires phonological access after this semantic stage is processed, with the articulatory process of moving the mouth and jaw to produce the words. Since chimpanzees do not have the articulatory processes to be able to utter those words in the same way as humans, at this stage the output for them was in the actual signing of language.

It seems that Terrace is saying that chimpanzees are able to access the lemma but not lexeme stage, which contradicts his statement that "There's no evidence that a nonhuman animal can engage in conversation" (Terrace, 2019, p. 5). Terrace's most recent interpretations also miss a number of other significant points. First, he makes the assumption that humans *always* access both stages in normal speech. This is not the case. Humans often find themselves in a "tip-of-the-tongue" state, or finish each other's words, or don't bother finishing them, or simply do not name the objects at all. We do not name every item we have a name for. When you enter a room, do you name the floor, the ceiling, the walls, the table, the chair? And you would not make the assumption that you do not know those object names simply because you do not produce their names. The second mistake Terrace makes is in assuming that humans always name items correctly. We frequently make visual or semantic, or name agreement errors. Third, Terrace makes these assumptions without considering that online and offline learning in humans is different. We found performance to differ significantly when participants were asked to name objects in a speeded naming task under laboratory conditions, versus being able to name those same objects in normal conversation (Scarnà & Ellis, 2002). Terrace makes assumptions that the chimpanzees did not know language, yet on page 41 of *Why Chimpanzees Can't Learn Language and Only Humans Can* demonstrates a cumulative record of the signs Nim learned. Would we divide up the signs that humans had learned through those which were prompted by others, and those which were not? We would consider it unnatural to think of language learning in this way, yet Terrace argues that Nim was prompted to sign. He fails to mention that humans prompt each other all the time. It is a natural part of the turn-taking that occurs in speech.

Terrace makes an assumption reflecting an arrogance of the language topic as a whole: "[T]he social development . . . (of those) who are autistic is limited". He fails to acknowledge that autism is a spectrum condition with varying levels of language deficiency. It is easy to mistakenly assume that individuals with autism have language deficiency, when in fact they suffer the "absence of communicative intent" due to social deficits disguising themselves as expressive language impairment (Happé & Frith, 1996). It is easy to mistake a reduced social drive to talk as delayed or impaired language development (Mody & Belliveau, 2018). To suggest that these children "are poignant reminders of the importance of a 'stimulating loving environment' for the development of language" (p. 134) is incorrect and, indeed, insulting to families of autistic children. Plenty of autistic children are from stimulating, loving and enriched environments. There are cases in humans where language is present but where the decision is made not to use it. In selective mutism, for instance, individuals (usually children, although it can persist into adulthood) speak fluently in some situations but choose to remain silent in others, due to overwhelming anxiety. One would not say that the selectively mute individual does not possess language. Indeed, both Terrace and Chomsky make the mistake of assuming that because it is not using conventional human language, a chimpanzee does not *have* language. ASL differs from conventional spoken human language; it does not have the same syntactical structure, and words are represented differently. It is not a good output for judging if a being can process syntax. It appears that Terrace is changing the definition of language to suit the results. I emailed Terrace about these points, inviting him to give his opinions, but he did not reply. Lastly, let us not forget that these were traumatised animals. It is likely that they knew more language than they showed, due to overwhelming fear, anxiety, upset and disappointment. It is likely that they were not demonstrating it to their true ability, just as anxious children do not perform to capacity.

Using chimpanzees was an unusual way to study language. It is surprising that Terrace was even allowed to proceed, given his previous attempts to keep another chimpanzee, Bruno, and given the previous attempts to teach Washoe and others. I say this from my position as a scientist also interested in the construction of language. I, too, have considered how words, sentences and structure come together to give this uniquely human and creative capability, yet I was able to investigate without use of animals. My thesis used human participants only, who were invited to the laboratory to answer questions about how old they were when they learned object names, to judge how frequently they used those words/read their names, and how imageable, familiar and nameable those items were. Participants named pictures or read aloud these object names as fast as possible; one group of bilinguals in their first language, another in their second language. They read aloud words which were very similar across English and Italian (carrot-carota) and those which were very different across the two languages (pencil-matita). I measured object naming and word reading performance in healthy volunteers and then in both monolingual and bilingual patients with brain damage and aphasia (language loss) after strokes or brain injuries. The idea was that understanding how language comes apart might help us to understand how it comes together. At no point were any non-human animals required. A computerised model was also constructed, and that validated the human findings.

It is time to put a close to these questions about chimpanzee language learning. These debates about whether apes could learn language and whether it was the "correct" word, or syntax, or due to reward or motivation distracted the researchers from some of the more important aspects of the studies, which were the physical and emotional needs of the animals. Whether a primate learns through moulding or not is irrelevant if that animal's needs are not being met. How the animals would be accommodated as they grew was not considered. The researchers failed to address the biggest scientific flaw in their studies: that any language produced by these chimpanzees would only represent language learning by a chimpanzee in captivity and would therefore be irrelevant to models of normal human language processing.

In *Project Nim*, Mahoney says that "there's no way you can carry out research on animals, and for it to be humane. It can't be humane, because you've already put them in a cage". Although I did not use animal participants, I conducted my research work in a university alongside a thriving animal laboratory. My best friends were animal researchers. Just as in Bob's day, people who worked with animals tended to party together, finding not only an intellectual focus but a social one, too, going to the college bar or local pub after work. We drank alcohol, smoked, and spent hours together, talking about animal behaviours and science. I suppose one way in which they differed was that my UK animal scientist friends did not discuss any one animal in isolation but referred to their groups of rats, pigeons or snails. One friend worked on intelligence in snails, and we would laugh at his adverts encouraging people to take snails from their gardens and bring the creatures to work in plastic margarine tubs. Another counted pecking behaviours in pigeons, and another friend separated baby rats from their mothers and counted tail flicks to measure stress before and after various brain lesions. I was a conscientious student but also a desperate one who wanted to please her supervisor, so I would arrive before him, and leave the office after him, and I kept antisocial hours in the quest to demonstrate my conscientiousness at analysing data and writing my thesis. The animal lab students and researchers were great as a social distraction because they were always around. Rats had to be fed, pigeons watered, behaviours measured, and those researchers were highly productive. "Publish or perish", we were all told. Nobody much considered that to publish meant, quite literally, for these animals to perish.

The case was similar in Oklahoma. Ron Helterbrand, who was a student in Oklahoma at that time, describes a similar pressure:

> It has been over forty years. I've gone back and forth about some of the decisions that were made. I have been angry, but as I've gotten older, I can also see that Roger was under the pressure to "publish or perish". He was dealing with Bill Lemmon. I worked for Bill one summer as a handler and could see how there would be conflict between the two. It was his facility and Roger was a guest. Roger wanted more control and he wouldn't be able to have it at the farm. I visited Roger in Ellensburg (Washington) about a year or so

after they left. Roger was definitely more relaxed and in control there, than he had been in Oklahoma.

Roger was trying his best at this. He was the lead investigator. It came down to his trying to keep his research going forwards. I felt that the data we were getting weren't great. The unintentional fudging data to prove findings, and if they didn't prove the hypothesis, they were deemed a failure. This wasn't necessarily Roger's fault. Most of the work we were doing involved having students sit and watch to see if Washoe was teaching Sequoyah and later, Loulis, signs. There were really no rules around which behaviour or signs were to be noted, meaning that it was all subjective to the opinion of the student recording the data. Most of the students we had recruited to observe were rookies who really didn't understand very much about chimp behaviour. Some of those students were also trying to make their mark inside the programme and unfortunately would record things that really weren't sign but were normal chimp to chimp communication. In my opinion, the mechanics of the recorded data, deep down, were flawed.

Roger did show humanity. Booee, one of the chimps, had had his brain split because it was assumed he had epilepsy. He had exhibited seizures [severing the corpus callosum between the two brain hemispheres is sometimes performed in humans to stop epileptic seizures]. Roger hated all that medical experimentation. It was a really rough time [referring to after later events involving the chimpanzees]. Things were falling apart. When you're in college doing research, you want everything to be perfect.

Ron has mixed feelings about the research, and he describes the student dynamic in the laboratory: "David (Autry, an undergraduate student), Bob and I were competitive. A few nights ago I was watching the Beatles Documentary, 'Get Back'. It reminded me a little bit about how the three of us used to work together but we were like brothers who went through a lot together. We would get into fights, not physical fights, but verbal spats. We were all housemates together at various time during the chimp years." Ron is also able to describe the dynamics of the time, both between Fouts and Lemmon, and between the students, researchers and carers. The academic group functions like a family, and it is likely that these dynamics would have been felt by the chimpanzees.

It was a lot of fun for me to spend time with the "animal people" in my university in the UK. They became like family to me. Working in the engineering side of human behaviours gives a strong understanding and acceptance that we are creatures of mechanics. Having such exposure to the nuts-and-bolts of what makes us human reduces life to a series of wake, eat, think, drink, work, shit, fuck, patterns. Reducing life to this was an efficient mechanism for surviving university life and for dealing with life's adversities. In the time between the graduation from my undergraduate degree, and starting my doctorate, my mother became ill with non-Hodgkin's lymphoma and died after just 5 months. She was 42 years old, like Washoe was when she died, and so being in the company of people who condensed life to its sum of the parts helped with grief. This way of living came with an understanding that death is just another stage for breathing beings to reach. Better be happy, then. Pass that cigarette, and make mine a double. I can see now how this approach excuses and encourages hedonism, but it is also an effective mechanism for dealing with trauma, because the ability to ignore meaning and avoid "overthinking" forces the individual to live in the here-and-now. We were all being mindful through this method of acting mindlessly.

While it was fun, hanging out with animal psychologists posed philosophical and moral difficulty. My marine biologist housemate described dinners of fluorescent crayfish, experimental participants brought home and cooked after a long day in the lab. I would be drinking beer with someone who had spent their working day decapitating their experimental animals. I was reassured by strict adherences to the UK Home Office regulations for humane methods in experimentation, but I am still asking myself what is humane about decapitating rats. That animal laboratory has closed down since I got my doctorate in 2000. The question remains: how did someone in the same line of work as me reach the idea that raising a chimpanzee under human conditions would be permissible? "It was the '70s" says Jenny Lee in *Project Nim*. A social and historical context can describe but cannot explain what psychologists were doing at that time. It does not excuse it. This is unsatisfactory as an answer. Why was this a study of language, and not a study of, say, trauma, or of emotional needs? In order to understand the curiosity around the linguistic angle, we should consider the rationale and history around the work.

The word "chimpanzee" derives from an African language called Tshiluba, the language of the Democratic Republic of the Congo. It means "mock man" and first appeared in Western vocabulary in 1738. In 1735, the Swedish naturalist Carolus Linnaeus had sorted species by physical similarity and placed humans beside chimpanzees and other apes, naming the order "Anthropomorpha", meaning "resembling man". He further specified human beings as "Homo Sapiens" – "wise me". Thomas Huxley was the first in 1863 to argue that we anatomically resemble apes, presenting anatomical evidence of our relationship to apes via a common ancestor. As chimpanzees have highly sensitive immune systems and are vulnerable to disease, as well as being hard to keep alive, it took some time for them to arrive out of Africa and into Europe.

The London Zoological Gardens first made available a collection of "exotic species" for scientific observation in 1847. Indeed, the chimpanzees' tea party, a type of public entertainment starring chimpanzees dressed in human clothes at a table of food and drink, started at the London Zoo in 1926, and occurred daily during the summer months. British readers may remember these chimpanzees as starring in the television advertisements from 1956, for PG Tips tea. They were discontinued in 1972.

Charles Darwin was able to take notes on the gorilla in the zoo for *The Origin of Species* (1859). The study of the connection between primate and human soon continued in the US. Robert Mearns Yerkes, a psychologist from Pennsylvania, studied animal behaviour and comparative psychology at Harvard, received a doctorate, and joined the faculty in 1902. He observed chimpanzees in Cuba in a colony just outside Havana run by a Cuban woman named Madame Rosalia Abreu, who was enamoured by chimpanzees and had taken over her family's summer estate. In 1915, she announced the birth of the first chimpanzee born into captivity. Yerkes realised that chimpanzees are close enough to humans to be employed as models of human behaviour in research laboratories. They were seen as blank slates with no language or emotion, and certainly no culture. Yerkes returned from the trip determined to raise and observe his own chimpanzees, and bought two chimpanzees, Chim and Panzee, from a zoo. In 1917, Yerkes became president of the American Psychological Society, and he encouraged the society to devise and implement intelligence tests for army recruits during the First World War. This led him to develop the famous Yerkes-Dodson law, matching arousal to performance. During this time and up to the 1920s, he promoted the eugenic movement, unfortunately proliferating ideas of scientific racism which, of course, modern scientific consensus rejects. Yerkes established the Anthropoid Experiment Station to continue primate research in Orange Park, Florida, where the weather was milder for his chimpanzees. This was funded by the Rockefeller Foundation, one of the main funders of the eugenic movement in universities.

After Yerkes's death in 1956, the Station moved to Emory University in Atlanta, Georgia, where it continues to exist today as the Yerkes National Primate Research Center, the oldest scientific institute dedicated to non-human primate research. Yerkes's belief that chimpanzees could be in science led to huge scientific advancement and theories to benefit human behaviour. Yerkes was a pioneer of primate studies, and without his work there would have been no further primate research.

That explains why chimpanzees were studied. Now let us consider why we should study language. There is no unifying theory of language. Instead, language can be best explained through a combination of different theories. Both nature and nature are implicated. Current thinking suggests it is nature via nurture. One of the earliest scientific theories by Skinner (1957), the "father of behaviourism", explained that behaviours including language occur through influence of the environment. Children learn language through behaviourist reinforcement: conditioning, reinforcing and imitating, associating words with meanings. Any correct utterances become rewarded through parental praise or by the child realising that their utterance has communicative value and through incorrect utterances being ignored or corrected. These beliefs only partially explain language development. Terrace was a doctoral student of Skinner and highly influenced by these theories. Contemporary psychologists acknowledge the role of behaviourist theories in language learning but also understand that it is not a black-and-white, on/off process. Many factors affect language learning.

Chomsky criticised Skinner's theory in 1959. He argued that children could never acquire language through input alone and proposed the existence of Universal Grammar, the idea that the human brain has evolved neural circuits containing linguistic information prenatally. He believed children have natural predisposition to language learning by hearing speech and through pre-existing neural structures contained within the LAD. However, to this day, no scientist has sliced a brain open to reveal the exact locus of the LAD. It is a *hypothetical* explanation that became hardwired into scientists' thinking. Chomsky is not a neuroscientist; he is a theorist. There is no section of the brain with "LAD" stamped on it, and no magical switch turning language on and off. It is likely that by describing the LAD, Chomsky was defining those multiple brain regions described previously, that have evolved to make us exceptional at language learning and understanding. If psychologists had kept in mind that the LAD is a theoretical concept, perhaps the chimpanzee studies would have never taken place.

Chomsky noted that "the fact that all normal children acquire essentially comparable grammars of great complexity within remarkable rapidity suggests that human beings are somehow specially designed to do this" (Chomsky, 1959). A key idea was that all children, irrespective of culture and native language, go through the same stages of language development despite huge cultural and experiential differences in the way they are exposed to language. For instance, at age 1 year, a child will verbalise a few, individual words. At age 2 years, the child begins to speak in short sentences containing two to three words. At age 3 years, the child begins speaking in more grammatically sound sentences. By age 4 years, the child's speech is similar to that of an adult. Chomsky focussed on grammar as the most distinctive feature of human language, explaining that "universal grammar" allows humans to generate sentences in languages spoken around the world, and that children instinctively know how to combine a noun (e.g. a boy) and a verb (to eat) into a meaningful, correct phrase (A boy eats). He believed that universal grammar allows the creation of an infinite large number of meanings from a limited number of words. These ideas were hugely influential in the field of linguistics and in cognitive psychology, but they say a lot about grammar and very little about the word level. Without words, it would be impossible to have grammar.

Chomsky's hypotheses about language were limited to explaining language in beings who do know words. Retrospectively, why would we care to know about language in those beings who do not know words? It helps to place these theories in a historical context. This was psychology at a time before reliable brain scanning techniques, so Chomsky's ideas were an attempt to take a metaphorical look inside the brain. His ideas have not held up well since researchers started using the brain scanning techniques of fMRI and MEG in their experiments, although this has never been discussed in the literature.

Language is special precisely because humans do it, and it differs from animal communication. What are the characteristics of language as a human function? It has been reported that one difference is that humans use language even from birth. However, chimpanzees also use a type of language and calling, from their birth, and in a similar way. Second, language is thought to be specific to humans, since they have in their core being the ability to engage in complex creative processing including the use of language in music. It is a form of human arrogance to assume that the ability to combine vocal sounds to produce a sound perceived as pleasingly harmonious and expressing emotion is a human-specific skill. The third reason given for language being specific to humans is that we use language to create new meanings by combining and recombining words. However, there are various examples of the Oklahoma chimpanzees doing this. When rowing their boat past a swan, Roger Fouts signed to Washoe "What's that?" and she replied WATER BIRD, despite never having learned any signs for differentiating birds. Washoe also spontaneously asked Bob what his name was, and together they came up with a sign for BOB. Fouts explains how during their last outing with the chimps, Tatu and Washoe "conversed with each other about FLOWERS, CARS, GRASS, TREES and DOGS" (Fouts & Mills, 1998, p. 321). In other cases, it is reported that Washoe used language "the way human children do: for example, she would sign QUIET to herself when she sneaked into a forbidden room. . . . Or she would sit on her bed and talk to her dolls spread out around her. The way Washoe ran on with her hands like a gregarious deaf child" (Fouts & Mills, 1998, pp. 68–69).

To say that animals cannot use language in a creative manner is another example of human arrogance. In defining "creativity" in animals, we are imposing human judgements about what being creative means. In her research on the African grey parrot Alex, Irene Pepperberg noted that aside from his ability to learn names of individual objects and to identify the objects and their colours regardless of their shape, when in front of a mirror, Alex spontaneously asked the existential question, "What colour?", referring to himself. He was able to learn that his colour was grey after being told six times. This is an example of an animal using language creatively in order to pose a question about itself. Is this any more or less creative than how a child might ask about colour? The Oklahoma primates enjoyed painting and were able to tell their carers what they had painted afterwards. Figure 2.1 shows the painting of a bird by Nim. Not only is it clear that this figure depicts a bird, but when Bob asked Nim what he had painted, Nim's reply was: BIRD.

Terrace intended *Project Nim* to be a direct challenge to Chomsky's premise that language is inherent to humans. Terrace's intention was to teach Nim Chimpsky to use language in the same way as humans do, in order to disprove Chomsky's idea. Terrace intended to blur the language line between humans and non-humans, and to analyse interspecies communication. The nature-versus-nurture question was a part of the debate at the time. How much of language is due to how we are born, and how much of it is as a consequence of how we are raised? Nowadays, we neuroscientists understand that it is nature *via* nurture, and consequently, nurture via nature. Who we are is partly hardwired from birth and partly due to our character-building experiences that occur in our environment. I say this as somebody who initially learned English as a second language, but whose first language it now is. In between, I have learned several other languages and cultures, as is necessary in the human experience. Humans have the capacity to use two languages at the same time. It is a relatively simple and automatic process for "balanced bilinguals" and suggests that while language is not a natural process for animals such as the chimpanzee to learn, humans are engineered to do so – even from being in utero.

The language focus missed a crucial point in the chimpanzee work. These were sentient beings with thoughts, ideas and personality traits of their own, just as

FIGURE 2.1 Nim's painting of a bird. When Bob asked him what he had painted, Nim's reply was: BIRD.

humans are. James Marsh, the director of *Project Nim*, observed in an interview: "[I]f you have children, you soon understand that there's an embryonic personality from birth. You mess with that at your peril. You need to understand what your children are like, rather than try to impose your desires upon them. There's a fine line between letting them be what they are and making them responsible in the world, and that's definitely a theme that I brought to Nim, or some personal experience" (James Marsh to Gemma Kappala-Ramsamy in *The Guardian*, 2011).

There are other theories of language development, and these identify other factors which are crucial to the learning experience. Theories about learning and play were neglected in explaining language acquisition. Psycholinguists continue to question the existence of Universal Grammar, demonstrating that categories like noun and verb are biologically, evolutionarily and psychologically implausible. Pinker (1994) suggested that human language is a specialised "mental module", "a complex, specialised skill, which develops in the child spontaneously, without conscious effort or formal instruction" MacWhinney (1998). Other researchers believe that the neural circuitry required for language acquisition develops over time in response to experience and stimuli, and that mere exposure to language will not lead to acquisition of it unless there is also a supportive environment.

It appears that few, if any, other theories of development were considered in the primate studies. Other developmental theories consider the different stages of cognition (Piaget), observation (Bandura) or social interaction in cognition (Vygotsky, 1978). Vygotsky's sociocultural theory considered the central role that community plays in the process of "making meaning." It viewed human development as a socially mediated process in which children acquire cultural values, beliefs and problem-solving strategies through collaborative dialogues with more knowledgeable members of society. This was not considered in the chimpanzees. With whom were they mixing? Who were the adults in charge? From whom would these chimpanzees, in particular the ones living within human families, obtain their cultural beliefs? Vygotsky's theory considered culture-specific tools, private speech and the zone of proximal development (ZPD) and more knowledgeable other (MKO). The ZPD is the difference between what a learner can do without help and what a learner can achieve with guidance and encouragement from a skilled partner so that the term "proximal" refers to those skills that the learner is close to mastering. The MKO refers to a person, animal or thing, with a better understanding or a higher ability level than the learner in a particular task, process or concept. The MKO might be a teacher or an older adult, but it can also be a peer or even a computer or a pet, with more knowledge or experience. The chimpanzee studies suffered from lack of consideration of these.

The child's sophisticated microlinguistic ability to connect sign and meaning for communication marks the development of new higher mental functions that distinguish the human child from animals. This development goes through several stages. The initial phase includes the fact that another person (an adult) controls the child's behaviour, directing the implementation of any involuntary function. At the second stage, the child becomes a subject, and using this psychological tool, directs the behaviour of another. The child begins to apply those methods of controlling behaviour that others have applied to him/her, and the child to others. These nuances were not considered in the chimpanzees. The expectation on Washoe as with Nim, was to produce grammar and full sentences. On a philosophical level, was it moral to place this expectation on any animal from the outset? Steven Pinker puts it clearly: why would we even expect an animal to learn language? We could turn to the belief that language is part of our genetic inheritance. Instead of considering it a cultural creation, Pinker describes it as a part of an evolutionary adaptation within human DNA designed to carry out important functions. He discusses how the human brain is constructed for language to take place (Pinker, 1994). It is a part of the innate human instinct to communicate, using the special biological apparatus that we are all born with.

These are basic psychological theories about language in humans. We take them very seriously when it comes to our own children. How were the needs for language learning addressed in the chimpanzees? Not one of the original principal investigators has explained this. If anything, the opposite was presented by Fouts, as he describes how "By the early 1990s, it had been an awfully long time since Washoe or the other chimps had been OUT" (p. 320). If something as simple as walks were prohibited in the chimpanzees, what chance did they have for any of their other needs to be met for adequate learning?

How Humans Use Language

A number of factors affect how fast we name objects, with robust experimental evidence for each. It is important to note that in everyday life, we do not name under speeded time conditions; we tend to take our time. Speeded naming was taken as a measure in laboratories because psychologists measured behaviours in reaction times in milliseconds. This helped us identify the time it took to access each of the stages in naming. In everyday life, we tend to take our time and to name things within the context of our usual spoken speech timing. Factors that affect how fast we access the names for objects, are visual complexity, familiarity, name agreement, length, frequency and age of acquisition.

Visual complexity includes the visual characteristics of an object. Naming requires recognition followed by a match to a stored prototype in memory, and name retrieval. This takes longer if recognition involves more complex objects. Visual complexity is also the extent to which an object shares visual features with other objects: a pencil is similar to a pen. Humphreys et al. (1988) demonstrated that structural similarity affects access to a structural description which interacts with other factors affecting the later stages of object recognition, such as picture name frequency.

The next variable to affect naming is familiarity. The more familiar an object, the easier it is to name. For instance, we are more familiar with apples than with armadillos, and so the former is named faster than the latter. Of course, apple is also easier to articulate. Some of the variables work together to ease the process of naming. Familiarity affects both objects being *named*, and object names being *read*. In reading, interactions with certain clusters of letters will be familiar to us. One example in English is the cluster "ch": chocolate, Manchester, much. Seeing the cluster so frequently, we find it easy to identify. Less frequent clusters like "nk" are less familiar and cause us to think harder about what we are reading: unknowing, embankment, think. Written words and reading are less relevant to us here, since the chimpanzee studies were about learning sign rather than written language.

For familiarity, there is *experiential* frequency, and *perceived* familiarity. I might believe that I see a lot of armadillos in my life, but if my life were tracked from my birth to my death, it would be apparent that I do not see as many as I think across my life span. I might see them in books and documentaries, but it is likely that I have over-rated how often I see them. This is a problem for scientists studying name acquisition. One way in which we can account for this is by taking a rated (subjective) measure of how familiar adults think they were with each object, and then going into nurseries and schools and asking children directly to name the same objects, in an objective measure (Morrison et al., 1997). Object familiarity can be distinguished from its frequency. We can see objects every day but do not necessarily produce their name: floor, ceiling, walls – we do not name everything. Familiarity is about how connected we are with that object. Frequency is about how often we use its name, either in spoken or in written form. Names that are familiar to us tend to be those which are concrete rather than abstract, which we find easier to pronounce, encounter more frequently and which have names that are earlier acquired in life.

Humans are sensitive to familiarity. We seek comfort in the familiar even when we have outgrown our old patterns. The unknown adds to our sense of fear, so we prefer to stick with what is predictable to us. This is not limited to naming or choosing objects, but to emotional patterns and life choices. Each chimpanzee in those studies was taken out of its natural comfort zone. Some were taken out of their immediate environment full of familiar things rich in meaning for them: trees, leaves, berries, chimpanzee siblings and parents, to be transported to a different continent altogether before arriving in a laboratory. Others, like Nim, were bred for the purpose of being studied and started life with a highly familiar chimpanzee mother who was taken away and replaced with the unfamiliar. The items that the chimps were being made to become familiar with did not always feature in their innate worlds.

The next variable of interest is name agreement. This is the extent to which we agree on a name for any given object. Objects with low name agreement take longer to name than those with high name agreement; a "sofa" can also be called a "settee" or a "couch", so it is harder to name than "apple" which has a high name agreement and is usually not misnamed as anything else. The more names an item has, the more work our brains have to do to access that name. Lexical access is easy for items with one clear name, "elephant", but trickier for those with multiple names: "mobile phone", "plant", "photo". Our brains have to work harder to decide which tag to select and articulate for those.

A few important points here about ASL. The sign language taught to the chimpanzees is problematic. In terms of sentence structure and grammar, ASL does not follow the rules of English. ASL is not grammatically correct as far as English is concerned. This does not mean it is *not* language, rather, that it is better considered a demonstration of language which runs parallel to English, but which does not copy its sentence structure. The studies criticised the chimpanzees for not knowing syntax, yet there *is* no equivalent syntax in ASL. The wrong instrument was used to ascertain whether these chimpanzees could demonstrate language learning or not. This is a little like using a set of bathroom scales to take one's temperature and assuming that the person using the set of scales is incapable of using them properly.

In ASL there are aspects about the reality principle, spatial agreement and the signer's perspective, which refer to signing about places and other physical objects as they are in real life. If describing where a tree is, one points in its direction; this is the reality principle. The "signing space", or the area in front of the body, is used to show where objects are in relation to each other so that the addressee can understand the location from the visual description. In spoken English, this might be the equivalent of saying "here" versus "there" distinguished from, say, as in older English, "there yonder". Other languages have more overt signifiers. For instance, Japanese has the distinction of "kore" (this), to "sore" (that), to "are" (over there). Eye gaze and head tilt are also used in addition to pointing in ASL. For example, in demonstrating a right turn, there would be a tilt of the head to the left as though looking around the corner to the right. Spatial agreement can also show how far away something is. The hand is used with motions of the index finger to demonstrate whether something is near or far and can also indicate reference to time. If an event will happen in the far distant future, the same modification in signing used to point at faraway objects is used to indicate chronological distance. In the spoken language equivalent, this would be the equivalent of combining "there" and "then". Signer's perspective means that spatial relationships are always signed from the perspective of the signer and *not* adjusted for the perspective of the addressee. For example, if you are describing a room, you would sign it from your perspective as if you were entering the door of the room with the room on the other side of the door from you. You would *not* try to rotate the room in the signing space in front of you to move the door in front of the addressee. Imagine addressing these points when teaching a young chimpanzee (or child) to sign. The chimpanzee does not yet have a solid understanding of object permanence and from a Piagetian perspective is stuck in an egocentric stage. Young children when being egocentric will describe a room from their perspective even when asked to describe it from another observer's perspective. The nature of the English language, paired with underdeveloped representation of the chimpanzee, would have not made ASL the ideal parallel to learning language. Furthermore, none of the researchers were fluent in ASL, which was like instructing an English person to teach a child French, in the absence of their knowing any French themselves.

Name (or word) length has an effect on how easily objects are named. "Dog" is named faster than "elephant". This is the same for reading. *Neighbourhoods* vary both phonologically and orthographically (in writing). This refers to how similar the name is to other words. "Mat" is very similar to "cat", "hat" and "pat". We will have heard and read the cluster <u>at</u> very often, as a consequence, which facilitates our production of that word.

These variables affected the speed and reliability of every one of those signs made by the chimpanzees. Sometimes they would have affected single object names in isolation, and sometimes they would have affected the speed of the chimpanzees' signing string, such as when they were performing an action with other chimpanzees, or with emotion. Washoe signing OUT IT OUT WITH TO GET OUT would have been fast and repetitive.

A very commonly discussed variable in object naming is frequency. As early as 1944, naming studies examined speech and sound effects of word frequency and found a reaction time difference as big as 313 milliseconds between naming high- and low-frequency words (Thorndike & Lorge, 1944). The average item in the English language takes around 700 milliseconds to name. Frequency is measured by taking rated estimates of how often people see the object's name in print, or hear it in speech, or by taking a number of existing materials and simply counting the incidence of a particular word. It is useful for explaining how quickly the object names are produced in speech and in print. For the chimpanzee work, however, word frequency was irrelevant, since they were not reading, and speed was also of less relevance. This explains why Terrace may have overlooked the difference in chimps' performance in controlled conditions with their performance under free conditions and jumped to the conclusion that they were less able than they really were in their language production. The language performance one sees within a laboratory or classroom setting is significantly different to performance observed when the participant is free, comfortable and free from pressure.

The variable of utmost importance to naming is the age at which the object's name was acquired (age of acquisition [AoA]). Carroll and White (1973) first reported the effects of AoA in object naming, although it was often confounded with frequency after that. This is because early acquired items tend to be higher in frequency. The earlier one learns an object's name, the more chances there are in life that that object can be named, especially if that object is concrete and familiar, with a name that appears frequently, like "apple". Other, late acquired names are less imageable and more abstract, less familiar, and appear less frequently in language. Some good examples are "mortgage", "bachelor", "certificate", "divorce". In studies of naming, age of acquisition was overlooked for many years, but it is significant because it is relevant to non-linguistic aspects of life, too. If I see olives from a very young age, the chances are that I am presented with opportunities to eat them more often, and becoming familiar to me, I am more likely to enjoy them. This means that the experiences that one has as an infant are particularly important. They will provide the canvas for later life. Being able to name words and objects early on is particularly important for later life. Specifically in emotional wellbeing, knowing the vocabulary for emotional behaviours is crucial, since it allows us the ability to describe those feelings and experiences as we grow up. Indeed, it is safe to say that our early life experiences provide an important framework for how we write our narratives for trauma later on in life.

Age of acquisition is similar to *order* of acquisition, which has been less well studied. The points about narratives for trauma would be the same in this case. In the human lexicon, quality of vocabulary is dictated by the order in which words are learned which correlates with developmental age. Those short words for imageable nouns are learned first and approximately in this order: Mummy, Daddy, milk, dog, cat, table, chair. They tend to be the words of survival. Longer and more abstract nouns come later: test, exam, degree, mortgage, marriage. Some early acquired but frequently used words are soon put to the back of the mind: dummy, nappy, fairy, witch, wizard. Other later-acquired nouns become very frequent: bills, lawn, work, office. This *order* of acquisition has been explored in studies of second-language acquisition versus bilingualism (Izura & Ellis, 2002) and also in computer simulations of language (Dijkstra & van Heuven, 1998). The original language-learning studies in the chimpanzees could be explored in terms of the order of the learning of the signs by each animal. However, the point remains that by definition these chimpanzees were not representative of typically developing primates. Indeed, as some such as Booee had endured brain surgery for split brain investigation, it is important to realise that their brains would not necessarily have been typically developing or fully functioning. The language work in chimpanzees is pseudoscience. It offers little in the way of validating any aspect of language function.

Introducing primates to human language through signing was incredibly harmful. The very act of giving them a coding system for which they were not biologically adapted, so that they might express themselves *sometimes*, will have been traumatising in itself. The researchers did not know what it would look like to give language to a species that is not geared to have an innate system for language. It is incredibly arrogant of humans to assume that teaching a chimpanzee to sign would have been helpful to both human and animal. The exact opposite is true. The original researchers, such as Terrace, and to some extent, Fouts, have not acknowledged this point. Equipping primates with signs for emotions and a life incongruent to their evolutionary underpinnings which they are not programmed was traumatic, by definition. The animals were given a script for experiences, in the absence of the right people with whom to express them. The chimpanzees were considered experimental participants when it suited the researchers, but too many people were involved in their care: Fouts, Lemmon, owners and keepers of grounds and of other animals, research students, graduate students, undergraduates. Each human carer came with their own set of thoughts, beliefs and crises. Many of them were young and still figuring themselves out. This is the key factor. As is typical of a university setting, there were drugs and alcohol and complex romantic relationships. How many of the researchers were suffering, themselves, from traumatic experiences? It will have been difficult for the researchers who did not to recognise the chimpanzees' behaviours as trauma responses.

Language aside, sentient beings need to attach. It is likely that every animal ever studied under laboratory conditions has been traumatised, by definition of being experimented upon in an environment unnatural to it. Of course, it is easy to criticise in retrospect, and we need to consider the experiments in their historical context. In the 1960s, the world was hearing about post-war stories including those involving trauma or the military – Vietnam for individuals in the US. People were experimenting with recreational drugs and psychedelics. Bessel Van der Kolk refers to traumatised humans as being "in a cage" (Van der Kolk, 2021). If there is no imprint of a safe person, there is little hope for many other secure attachments. Some of the chimpanzee researchers were in metaphorical cages of trauma of their own, and so what chance did the animals in their real cages have? At least at the end of the experimental day the humans were able to get in their cars and to go home.

Robert realised this. One day as he left to drive home for the evening, he realised that the chimpanzees staring at him outside the cage understood that while he could leave, they had to stay, stuck behind bars. That made him realise that something was wrong with those experiments, but he could not articulate *what*. He had been conditioned to believing that it was acceptable to keep those animals incarcerated. Those chimpanzees were giving him non-verbal signs that they were being tortured by these studies and by their circumstances. Nobody seemed concerned about these issues, let alone discussed them. The 1970s and 1980s did not have a script for trauma. It is also possible that researchers were being dissonant. In *Project Nim*, Terrace explains how "the blinkers were on".

Should the researchers still feel uncomfortable to have been in this position? It may have been difficult to talk about the issues of animal "ownership" in those days, and less was known about adversity and trauma. Researchers such as Bessel Van der Kolk and Pete Walker have made their respective books, *The Body Keeps the Score* (2014) and *Complex PTSD: From Surviving to Thriving* (2013), and others since, highly accessible to the lay public, along with various discussions about the effects of trauma. Why are most chimpanzee researchers not speaking now? This is the reason why we are using this book to talk about those issues. Nobody meant to harm the chimpanzees or each other, but people did. Incidentally, it may be a good place to ask here: who exactly would want to work with chimpanzees anyway? And why? What could have possibly motivated a person to desire this understanding in the first place? A good way to answer that question is to ask the researchers directly. I contacted Fouts, who advised me to cite from the book as it is a better source than his memory. As previously explained, Terrace did not reply to my communication.

Philosophically, we might even say that we could ask the same question about the older famous animal psychologists. What led Skinner to work with his rats and pigeons, Harlow to isolate his monkeys, Pavlov to condition his dogs, and more recently, Pepperberg to train her famous parrot, Alex? Each case is different. I imagine the answers would be somewhere along the lines of studying how people behaved during the war, or that discoveries were made by accident when investigating something else, or that someone had to do it, so why not them? While it is tempting to criticise these researchers, it is also important that we do not take those studies in vain. Given that they happened, it is now important to use their results to maximum effect.

These arguments are a little like the Milgram (1963) and Zimbardo (1974) studies. In these studies, participants were deceived into believing that they were in certain roles. They were invited to dupe other participants, to put some of the group in oppressive or authoritarian roles, to follow a set of instructions without challenging them, or to internalise roles which made them aggressive. It is well known that those studies were highly unethical and conducted without proper informed consent. We could never conduct those experiments again, and so it becomes even more important that the results are presented and that current and future students are made aware of the horrific nature of psychological research when it is not conducted adequately. Watching a clip about the Stanford Prison Study is like watching a science fiction film. Participants in experiments nowadays are no longer as naïve as they were then, so it is incredible to see how the individuals' behaviours changed so significantly within a short space of time. The guards' behaviours in the Stanford Prison Study reflect their own "authority" stories, such as the way in which their parents, teachers or caregivers may have treated them in their lives while growing up. It is possible that the guards – maybe unconsciously – perceived themselves as possessing authority to enact repressed behaviours, and that any violent and sadistic parts of themselves that were repressed or kept hidden and not accessed otherwise were suddenly expressed. It was remarkable to note the way in which each participant lost his individual identity and disappeared in the experimental context, and how each participant conformed to their role as part of the group within a short period of time. It is possible that there was similar experience within the animal studies. Chimpanzees became vehicles for their caregivers to act out repressed behaviours.

The findings from the chimpanzee work went beyond the characteristics of language, but the researchers of the time were oblivious. Terrace and the other researchers grossly underestimated the linguistic abilities of the chimpanzees, and also the impact of each chimpanzee's respective life history on language abilities. A broken child can produce broken language only. A traumatised being will produce traumatised capabilities only.

Contemporary research (Lameira et al., 2022) demonstrates that laboratory-based experiments are no longer necessary in psychology. This extends to animal experiments. Investigations into language utterances in healthy orangutans in the wild have found that information which is broadcast via consonant-like and vowel-like calls breaches the mathematical models of linguistic evolution. Lameira and colleagues from Durham University, UK, recorded and analysed 4,486 collected "kiss squeaks" from 48 animals in four wild populations. These, like many consonants – the /t/, /p/, /k/ sounds – are the consonants that depend on the action of the lips, tongue and jaw rather than the voice. They are crucial "building blocks" in the evolution of language. Most human languages have a lot more consonants than vowels, and so more combinations. In this study, the research team used these orangutan vocal behaviours as something of a time machine, going back to a time when our ancestors were using what would become those precursors of consonants and vowels. It was found that apes embedded several different bits of information in their squeaks. The team compared this to how we might use more than one word to convey the same meaning – saying "car" but also "automobile" and "vehicle" (so a name agreement effect). The animals would make doubly sure that their message was received, so they would send the same message with different kiss squeak combination signals. The study suggests that rather than making an effort to form complex words, it is this redundancy in forming different sounds with the same meanings that reinforced linguistic messages and drove early language evolution.

Traumatised humans show compromised language skills. Children who experienced trauma, abuse and neglect show minimalist narratives. A healthy narrative has emotional responses of characters in stories and real-life situations. A meta-analysis of 40 years of research by Sylvestre et al. (2016) found that language skills of children who were abused and/or neglected were marked by delay compared to their peers. Age of child was a significant factor – unsurprising if we recall the AoA data. The younger the child, the bigger is the impact that abuse and neglect have on language processing. Quality of language exposure and reciprocal interaction with caregivers are crucial to language development. As the ideal conditions for development are disrupted, children with developing lexical processing suffer as language acquisition is delayed. This would have been the case with those chimpanzees, in particular Washoe, who, in her adult years was not allowed out for walks and suffered from impoverished interactions with caregivers. Language delays are marked by impairments in expressive and receptive language, by impaired syntax, semantics, morphology and pragmatics. The only aspect possibly spared is phonology (Culp et al., 1991). In some traumatised human populations, there may be additional problems associated with migration and second or third language learning, so there are even fewer opportunities for any "mother tongue" to develop. Traumatised individuals regularly find themselves in dissociated states in response to their trauma. One way in which they report coping with it is in a tenacious manner, by "reprogramming" themselves so they become able to integrate fully into the language of their environment. This results in individuals who are at the opposite end of language ability. Such individuals have exceptional post-traumatic language function and may even come across as language pedants, fastidious about grammar and syntax.

For trauma survivors, it is possible to have post-traumatic growth and resilience. Tedeschi, who co-wrote the book, *Trauma and Transformation: Growing in the Aftermath of Suffering* (Tedeschi & Calhoun, 1995), considered that "The process of post-traumatic growth involves a reconfiguration of the life story or the narrative; the autobiography that we are writing. Based on that revised narrative, people can go out on new missions in life, do new things and devote themselves to activities they consider to be particularly important. Very often, people consider this a life change". This comes after processing, counselling, introspection, verbal therapy and perhaps antidepressant medication. We need to consider in the animal studies that the chimpanzees were expected to integrate with humans, which in itself would have been traumatic for them. It is rare to have a case where trauma in humans is due to their having been required to integrate with animals, but in this instance, it is apparent that those individuals who were caring for those chimpanzees closely and who forged a bond with them, such as Robert did, will have suffered a deep loss when those animals were moved away.

A deeper discussion is required here about how much Terrace, Fouts and other chimpanzee researchers had considered these issues *prior* to tampering with the lives of these chimpanzees. Given all that is said about survival of trauma, who cares about those things that Terrace and Fouts set out to study, like grammar and syntax? These are not the foundation of survival. It is the *message* of the utterances that counts and that it is received in a way that is effective for communication. Word order is meaningless, further demonstrated by the fact that those orangutans in the wild are able to use whatever they are hardwired to do in order to get their messages to each other. It is crucial that each animal's emotional and physical needs are addressed foremost. Animals do not need human language. Indeed, the chimpanzees were double victims. First because they were stolen from their families, and second by being thrust into the human world and expected to learn human processes.

Another point of note is that the chimpanzees' use of sign language is interpreted as an ability by them to learn and produce language. Chimpanzee signing was not quite the same as ASL. Fouts explains that some signings were acceptable even if they were "sloppy", and that as long as the chimpanzee made him/herself understood, it was not necessarily corrected. This is akin to when children hear linguistic boundaries in the wrong places: je m'appelle or jem appel?

The chimpanzees were not, in fact, simply demonstrating that they could learn language but that they were using *the* acceptable language in the same manner in which they were taught it. You can teach your dog to sit for a biscuit. It will sit for a biscuit. You will believe that your dog can learn language. In the absence of your teaching, it would not sit by itself and expect a biscuit to appear in front of it. The dog has not only learned that "sit" equals biscuit, but it has additionally learned that sitting to the biscuit will result in your approval. It is more than Skinnerian reward learning, because there are emotional aspects attached to this sort of learning. Your perception that your dog has high intelligence will affect your non-verbal dynamic with your dog, and their self-esteem will be raised. Imagine that same dog without a clear owner. Even if it sat, and the biscuit appeared in the absence of the owner's emotional warmth, would their self-esteem be elevated? We have no evidence to suggest that a dog has a self-esteem that gets elevated or lowered (except that some dogs show shame when they are told off), but equally, we have no evidence to suggest that a dog *doesn't* have self-esteem. There is no reason to think that chimpanzees do not have a sense of self-esteem, too.

Individuals with trauma are not in synchrony with other people. A traumatised individual living out disturbance in the body shuts themself down. There is difficulty finding language, and a negative cognitive bias is adopted. There are also struggles in identifying feelings and putting words to them, which is referred to as alexithymia. The chimpanzees would have suffered their own form of alexithymia. Giving the animals the tools to express themselves through sign language in the absence of a secure attachment base meant that they were able to communicate in ways unnatural to them. Typically developing chimpanzees in the wild have been studied in terms of their gestures. Catherine Hobaitor at the University of St Andrews has been working on gestural communication in primates. She explored how this system is used by gorillas and chimpanzees in their behaviours. How chimpanzees communicate with each other can tell us about the evolution of mind and communication in humans. Her focus is to look across groups and species of apes. Most of their data are from one or two groups of chimpanzees and bonobos which would be the equivalent of studying human language in one or two small towns. A bigger comparison will compare more sites, in order to ask questions about whether chimpanzees have gestural "accents" or "dialects", and to give a more holistic look at ape communication. Rather than investigating specific signal types in isolation, the full range of communication signals available to chimpanzees (which they sometimes use in full combination) is investigated to give information about the nature of the information being exchanged (Wilke, Lahiff, Badihi et al., 2022; Graham, Badihi, Safryghin et al., 2022).

In this method, this experimenter studies chimpanzees by spending time among them and in their natural environment, with a camera to capture what they do. Their day is her day – if they walk, she walks with them, if they choose to hang out with each other, she does this also. If they choose to sit under trees eating fruit, she does the same. This is the humane way to study chimpanzees. There is little in the way of intrusion from the experimenter to the chimpanzees. It is a far cry from Washoe being denied walks and being made to stay behind the bars of her cage. This method still investigates these primate communication methods including vocalisations, but in a substantially different and non-intrusive way, which nobody from the original studies had considered. It is fair to say that Jane Goodall's research started in this way, and that these contexts were given some consideration when Lucy was being returned to the wild by Janis Carter. The problem with this return to the wild is that, having been bred or raised among humans, the chimpanzee was not equipped with the skills crucial for survival.

Primates have many ways in which they communicate which do not involve linguistic tags. They have 70 to 80 different gestures which are used every day to negotiate in their lives, similar to human gestures. One which is unfamiliar to humans which Hobaiter describes is the big scratch which mean "come and groom me" or "I would like to groom you". Those nuances are connected to rank, position and sex in the group, especially when the females are in oestrus, at which stage the males regularly try to groom the females. Another example is when a mother chimpanzee would like her baby to go on her back, if she needs to travel more quickly. Often the little ones are tagging behind, and so she will stop and present her foot, lifting the back of her foot to signify to the young one that it is time to get going. When Hobaiter spends time with chimpanzees, she notices that they follow and observe back, giving a sense of familiarity and connection. Again, this is very different from Oklahoma chimpanzees who were *expected* to either conform to rigid experimental rules or adhere to often cruel, human-imposed conditions. In the current studies, there is no problem with inappropriate attachment or exploitations of human upon animal, or of disrupted boundaries. The animals continue with their usual activities, and they are observed at appropriate physical and psychological distances.

Human gestures led me to studying psychology. I was raised by parents whom I understand now, were on the autistic spectrum, and so it can be said that I was "aspergated". When I was growing up in the UK, television programmes by Desmond Morris such as "Body Language", "The Human Race" and "Bodywatching" were ways in which I learned how humans behave, and I bought a copy of *Manwatching* at a car boot sale when I was 10 years old. This gave me the idea to study this topic at university. It was exciting to learn that there was a topic called "Psychology" at university. Skip a few decades, and in the early 2000s, I attended a fine arts fair in central London where I bought one of Morris's paintings. People did not realise that he was a painter as well as a scientist, producer, presenter and life observer. It was serendipitous timing but imagine my further delight when I found an old copy of his book, *Gestures* (1981) in an office clearance at work. I hadn't realised that one of my friends was a co-author. I emailed to tell him that I now owned one of Morris's paintings, and the following week we were all in my sitting room drinking tea and listening to Morris's stories about his friends, Miró and Picasso. A magical meeting, made even more so by his huge generosity in his gift to me of the Italian version of his book, *Gesti*, and also copies of the Italian translations of every single book he has ever written. I was aghast as he autographed each book. I wish now that I had asked him about primates. I knew he had been involved in primate studies but did not think about that context. He had reported how young chimpanzees loved to draw and would do so with attention, balance, composition and care, but like humans, as soon as the offer of a reward was made, it would undermine the activity. In these apes it led to "the worst kind of commercial art" (Morris, 1962).

Morris's work on gestures was the human equivalent of the work conducted by Hobaiter (Morris et al., 1981). Instead of travelling to field stations in Uganda, he and his colleagues visited 25 countries in the European continent involving 15 different languages to map the geographical distributions of human gestures in a precise and methodical manner. This involved detailed interviews with 1,200 informants covering almost the whole of Europe. In addition to standard interviews, they also made direct field observations of gestures in action – just as Hobaiter does – recording on film wherever possible. As Hobaiter has demonstrated, these methods have been transferable to primate studies of language, in an ethical, scientific and systematic fashion.

Orangutan call signals believed to be closest to the precursors to human language can travel through forest over long distances without losing their meaning (Lameira et al., 2021). These sounds are closest to our precursors of human language. These findings questioned a previous and accepted model developed by mathematicians on the evolution of human speech which assumed that the signals used by our ancestors would reach an error limit – a moment when a signal is received but stops being meaningful, and suggested that our ancestors linked sounds together to increase the chance of content travelling over distance.

In applying the mathematical model to real-life data, the researchers selected sounds from previously collected audio recordings of communications by orangutans in Indonesia. Specific consonant- and vowel-like signals were played across the rainforest at distances of 15, 25, 75 and 100 metres, and the quality and content of signals were analysed. It was found that the informational characteristics of calls remained uncompromised until the signal became inaudible. Although we know that sound degrades the farther away from the source we are, these findings demonstrate that despite the sound package being distorted and pushed apart, its content remains unaltered. We have all experienced the effect when shouting for a friend. They do not hear the specific words, but they recognise that we are talking to them and that it is our voice. These are the building blocks of language as demonstrated by apes as a parallel to human language, and again, demonstrating how it is possible to collect and study empirical data from primates in a humane way. Lameira observed that by "using actual great ape communication sounds, which are the closest to those used by our hominid ancestors, we have shown that it's a call to the scientific community to start thinking again about how language evolved."

The same laboratory reported that orangutans demonstrate speech-like rhythm in voiced and voiceless calls (Lameira et al., 2015). This investigated directly how evolutionary origins of speech derived from monkey facial signals. These are a speech-like rhythm of around five open-close lip cycles per second. Monkeys also vocalise some of these signals, which lends plausibility to the idea of an "evolutionary stepping stone" towards speech. The research was conducted through cinematic analysis, finding that an ex-entertainment orangutan was able to produce two calls at a speech-like rhythm, which they call "clicks" and "faux-speech". The clicks require non-vocal-fold action and involve independent manoeuvring over lips and tongue. The faux-speech, on the other hand, demonstrated harmonic and formant modulations. This means that there is vocal-fold and supralaryngeal action. The rhythm was faster than chewing rates in the orangutan, also demonstrated by monkeys and by humans. The rhythm was seven times faster than and contextually distinct from any other calls in the repertoire by the orangutans. Taken together, these findings suggest that great apes are not restrained in terms of respiratory, articulatory or neurological abilities to produce consonant- and vowel-like articulations at speech rhythm, and show the importance of rhythmic speech antecedents in primates, demonstrating that great ape calls and human consonants and vowels show potential similarities in relation, relative position or structure. Again the experimental techniques demonstrate how unnecessary it was to breed and raise chimpanzees within human groups.

Humans are bimodal in their post-trauma language production and learning. They are either behind, because they are alexithymic and "stuck" in their trauma phase, or they become exceptionally good at language, because they find a way of reprogramming and relearning as a part of the trauma response. Once more, relating back to the chimpanzees in research, this has deeper implications for the considerations and discussions which should have taken place even before the work started.

These studies demonstrate that chimpanzees and orangutans possess a type of inbuilt primate-language mechanism which may change and evolve or not, depending on environment. What happens post-trauma? Many of those chimpanzees studied were removed from their mothers, who were either tranquilised or shot. Many of those babies became pets in abusive households where they were dressed as humans, given alcohol and shown maladaptive behaviours, before being discarded by their owners and given up for research or experimentation. If they were lucky, they ended up in the kinder cognitive research laboratories, otherwise they might end up having vaccines and medicines tested on them. Imagine replacing chimp for child. You witness your mother being shot, are placed in a crate and transported cross-continent to a new country where you are installed in the family of an unknown species and expected to learn their mannerisms and their language. Can you imagine if we did the cross-species equivalent to a human baby? To make judgements about whether the chimpanzees could or could not "do language" was not accurate or nuanced enough to be able to take into account all the other factors that were not controlled for, and that would not have been natural to the chimpanzees. If these things happened to you as a human, you would draw together all your resources to find a way to keep yourself together on a day-to-day basis. Traumatised humans lose their original sense of purpose as they form a new a focus, trying to feel alive and capable while all the time dissociating themselves from pain. Dissociation is the separation of the self from pain by disconnection from aspects of mental functioning from conscious awareness, such as by daydreaming. When traumatised individuals dissociate, they feel disconnected from self and the world, and may feel detached from the body or as though the world around them is unreal (derealisation). Every individual's experience of dissociation is different. It is the way in which the mind copes with too much stress during traumatic events. Experiences of dissociation can last for a relatively short time (hours or days) or for longer periods (weeks or months). Dissociation can lead to a degree of mental dysfunction or to psychological conditions such as post-traumatic stress disorder, depression, anxiety, schizophrenia, bipolar disorder and personality disorders.

Traumatised individuals instinctively look for ways of reconnecting such as through drama, sport or music. The brain is stuck in a pattern of self-exploration and self-hate. To be traumatised is to be lost, with the brain stuck in an intensely emotional state and with the action of excessive and irrelevant responses, which Pierre Janet, who taught Freud, called "automisms". Events that terrify the individual cannot be integrated into real life and so become pushed aside. The traumatised individual gets on by pushing these traumatic events aside and even saying that "it doesn't matter". This is a survival response. The problem is that the events come back as re-enactments and are pushed away as the individual becomes too upset to translate their experience into words and memories. The traumatised individual loses the ability to transform the events into simple story. If you are unable to tell this story, you become afraid of the memory and unable to reproduce it. Judith Herman describes how, "The conflict between the will to deny horrible events and the will to proclaim them aloud is the central dialectic of psychological trauma" (Herman, 1992). The traumatised individual possesses a fear of the fear which interferes with being able to put the event in the past, and creates numbing and dissociation. Trauma survivors may turn to hypnosis or other methods in an attempt to integrate those memories. They may turn to psychedelic experiences, using substances like psilocybin ("magic mushrooms"), amphetamines, or LSD, as substitutes for action and to create an associative correction and a set of crutches to aid survival. The chimpanzees were "only surviving" with the crutches that were available to them.

Robert says:

> Every chimpanzee is different. Some chimpanzees are smarter than others, and they all have different personality traits which would have resulted in differences in resilience. Nim was an extraordinary being, it was clear that his personality was strong. He had a good grasp on how it is to not be a human in a world that was inhabited by humans and he had a strong theory of mind. However, he was bred to be among humans from birth, whereas Washoe and some of the others had been abducted from their birth mothers or were confused because they had previously been raised as half-pet half-human chimpanzees, like Kelly. Washoe was not a natural mother, but there were mothers who were successful and resilient like Mona. For these the cage was used as a place of modelling. Lemmon understood the requirements of the chimps, in one way. He made sure they had an adequate diet. He figured out what to give them to eat. It was a mix of meat mixed with vegetables and vitamins which we prepared daily. Cardiomyopathy is a problem for chimps and the diet appeared to help with that.
>
> These chimpanzee mothers had better modelling in those cages because they could see each other and work out the relationships. Pan was the dominant male in this group with Ally and Washoe. You cannot think *for* the chimpanzees, they have to figure out for themselves in that group, who the alpha male is and how to pick up those social skills. They had not seen other chimpanzees as they would have done in the wild. Also they represented a variety of chimpanzees that came from all over Africa. Some were from laboratory-based backgrounds, others not so, and they were all thrown together, yet still managed to sort themselves out. They also made different sounds, like dialects if they had been human, but somehow they made themselves understood to each other.
>
> When it came to fertility, Carolyn, Nim's mother, was an extremely weird chimpanzee. Ally was born, and was a single birth. The next birth of Carolyn's were a twin pair, and I believe that set of twins was loaned to some researchers in Canada – non-identical. Then Carolyn had another birth, Onan, and then twins again, and then Nim. Then next a set of twins again, and then the next baby was named Ham.

The book by Fouts does not mention these twin births. Why were there so many? If she became pregnant every time she ovulated, this would appear to be a functional problem where her ovaries would release one egg, then two eggs, then one and so on, in this unusual pattern. Ultimately, Carolyn came to represent all the laboratory chimpanzees. She was a dominant chimpanzee, but like many in captivity, she was resigned to her fate.

The humans were neglecting their duty to keeping the chimpanzees safe. Introducing language to them in the captivity of the laboratory equipped them with a script for trauma. In part, some of the carers did try to make life a little more pleasant for the chimpanzee friends: they gave them oranges, fizzy drinks, pancakes and maple syrup. In the film *Project Nim*, two of his caregivers explain how "He loved . . . fast cars", and "I breastfed him for several months", all of these perks explained under the banner that this WAS the 1970s and such idiocies were permissible then. Nim is shown in some photographs smoking marijuana. He had arrived in Oklahoma already knowing what marijuana was and having smoked. Robert made sure that Nim had other human friends at Oklahoma and saw it as part of his duties to include Nim in their group, and so he introduced him to fellow undergraduate David (Dave) Autry, who features later in this book. David Autry learned to sign from Nim. Dave was naïve to sign language, and Bob wanted to see how many signs Nim could teach Dave. There were around 14 signs that Nim passed on to Dave. During one of their long walks together, Dave pulled out a menthol cigarette. Nim excitedly signed STONE SMOKE. Dave offered Nim his cigarette, but Nim made it clear he didn't want it but wanted a joint. It became clear that Nim knew the difference between tobacco and marijuana and had a definite preference.

Robert says that they did not want to exclude Nim or any of the other chimpanzees from any part of group interactions on their walks. They wanted them to feel "like they were one of us" and a part of the group. Any time a chimp is excluded from something, they know it. "And so we would make a circle, pull out a joint and pass it like friends. And he was like one of us, in a circle, passing a joint . . . and that was that. . . . A chimp that is high is like you and me, they're easier to deal with, they're mellow . . . I wouldn't do it now, but at the time, it just seemed completely normal. He was fun. Just like it would be if you and I smoked a joint together . . . we would go 'wow, that's nice.' In reality, very few of the Oklahoma chimps smoked pot. They were free to enjoy the countryside while the humans enjoyed a joint."

When we swap chimp for child this makes for particularly uncomfortable reading. The problem is in assuming that there was a fatherly dynamic. Nim was not Robert or David's child. We might consider that it was only fair (and thus ethical) to allow the young chimpanzee the same joys as were administered to the human family around it, and there is evidence to show that marijuana can help with trauma. In this instance it served as a bonding exercise. Robert explains about Nim: "He learned how to be in our world as well as any chimp ever . . . We get a feel for how it is, to not be human in a world geared for humans".

Introducing a language for these things gave the chimpanzees a mode of thinking and processing in a way in which no chimpanzee is programmed to deal with. They were able to ruminate about identity and think about their fate. The act of obtaining food, sex and play, would have been altered through the language experience. The books give interesting reports of the type of play the chimpanzees engaged in, once the ability to sign was introduced. They liked leafing through magazines and would sign to themselves as they flicked through the pages. Washoe liked to play imaginary games with her dolls, creating what Linden refers to as her "magic circle". In the wild, these behaviours would have been linked to socialising with other chimpanzees and to giving and receiving modelling of skills to do with problem-solving, reproducing and nurturing.

3

ONE OF US

"We did a huge disservice to that soul. And shame on us."
Joyce Butler, one of Nim's early teachers and carers, *Project Nim*.

A number of emotional and physical needs are required to be addressed for a healthy upbringing. Once those are identified, we can consider their equivalent in chimpanzees. In doing this, we can reflect upon Washoe and the other Oklahoma chimpanzees to identify if and how their needs were addressed. This chapter presents a number of case studies through direct discussion with Robert and other individuals involved in the care of the Oklahoma chimpanzees. In doing so, we also honour the memory of some of the individuals who were involved in the rescue of the chimpanzees. It is imperative to remember that the studies took place over a number of years, during which time those chimpanzees were growing and developing. After Nim was sold to the Laboratory for Experimental Medicine and Surgery in Primates (LEMSIP), and once it was clear that LEMSIP was closing, the rescue and transfer of the Oklahoma and other primates and the development of primate sanctuaries would take several years.

What are the needs of a human? Apart from our obvious intellectual capabilities which we think distinguish us as a species, we possess unique physical, social, biological and emotional traits. We are similar to each other as humans in that we are born with a set of inbuilt genetic patterns and brain characteristics, and by the time we die, our brain structures will have made certain connections and various behaviours will have been learned, with some genes being expressed and others remaining dormant. Over a life span, certain events will have imprinted their hallmarks and scars upon our being. We will have engaged in billions of cycles of eating, drinking, sleeping, waking, sex and other biological and psychological processes. We have personality traits, identities, underlying brain neurochemistry and structures and life experiences which shape the things that happen in between.

DOI: 10.4324/9781003357650-4

One basic need in chimpanzees is the requirement of other chimpanzees in order to feel supported. For many years, mental health professionals taught people that they could be healthy psychologically without any social support, that "unless you love yourself, no-one else will love you". Bruce Perry, co-author with Szalavitz of *The Boy Who Was Raised as a Dog: And Other Stories From a Child Psychiatrist's Notebook*, says that "The truth is that you cannot love yourself unless you have been loved and are loved. The capacity to love cannot be built in isolation" (Perry & Szalavitz, 2007). One of the main problems with the chimpanzee research was that primate centres all over the US were being run like conveyor belts and warehouse environments. At LEMSIP, for instance, chimpanzees were kept in cages similar to birdcages, that were 5 by 5 by 6 feet, with a steel-bar-bottom box hanging from the ceiling and dangling above the floor. Two rows of these hanging cages were opposite each other across the walkway, so that the chimpanzees could call, gesture or sign to their friends, but could not touch them. There was no group contact or any outdoor access, and there were no windows. By 1990, there were around 300 monkeys and 250 chimpanzees used in research at LEMSIP, which was owned by New York University, and which had won a contract for hepatitis B testing. In Oklahoma, the chimps were kept in crowded cages that they rarely left (Hess, 2008, p. 220), which had an impact upon their behaviours.

Chimpanzees need chimpanzees. They need to grow up in a colony with old and young chimps with different personalities – happy, grumpy, subordinate, alpha. Chimpanzees learn by watching. Infant chimpanzees raised in a group grow up with intersocial skills which allow them to take their rightful place in the world of chimpanzees. Robert says:

> It's like being a human. You could build me the nicest apartment on the planet, I could live in a beautiful apartment and have a beautiful view, but if I didn't have anyone to talk to, or anyone to express my humanness to, that would be a pretty harsh existence. Chimps need other chimps, just like humans need other humans. Chimps behave with their genetic predisposition, but on a cellular level they are very similar to us. It makes sense, then, that those animals are thinking just like us. First and foremost, chimps need to be with other chimps. Second, they need an area, a place where they can be together that's an appropriate place for them, and in captivity, that's very difficult. I work with a number of sanctuaries, and that's always our problem, that no matter what, you can't give them freedom. We do what I call the "illusion of freedom" as best we can, but at the end of the day, they are still in captivity. Captivity is the enemy.

Kelly

> Robert says,
> I still feel her pain. It is hard to talk about what she went through. The depth of what was going on between two beings, who were both very traumatised when young.
> She was the one chimpanzee who really changed everything for me from believing that these were cool studies, to "oh my god what have we done?"

Dr. James Mahoney was the LEMSIP research veterinarian who helped to make Nim's and others' final years more bearable by rescuing them out of the LEMSIP laboratories. Back in New York, he would take my calls all the time. We used to talk about this stuff. He was genuine, and he admitted that he was doing a thing he didn't really like, but he was doing a thing he *had* to do. He would listen to me.

I met Kelly in 1975 as one of my first chimpanzees. It was well before Nim. I spent much of the first 2 years at the Institute for Primate Studies (IPS), at the University of Oklahoma, with Kelly, and she was the first female chimpanzee that Nim got to hang out with, and got to know. I could take both chimpanzees out together, feeling confident that I could handle any situation that might arise, and without being afraid of being bitten. Everyone was wary of Kelly, so they tended not to want to take her out. She was very unpredictable. I enjoyed Kelly, and I liked being able to give her an opportunity to be outside. We would go on walks and forage as a wild chimp might, and we would also do human things like painting and drawing, which she enjoyed. I would take these guys, my friends Dave and Ron, with me, when I would take Kelly out, on occasion. Kelly could be extremely volatile; she would sometimes act out, and so she only went out with a select few "chimp people" who were trusted to be in control of her. I was one of those people and would, over time, become the primary person who got Kelly out of her cage. I knew that Kelly would not bite me. So we got along, and we went on many a walk, which meant she was out of the cage. For me, that was the primary goal: to get her and them out as much as possible. It's 1975. I'm 23 years old, thrust into this unfamiliar college world. I'm back there, as I tell this story now. My mind is racing. "Wow!" I'm thinking, "Last year, I was reading about Washoe, and now she's over there". This is really big, at least to me. I didn't know any of the nuances of any of the research yet. I just knew that this research had a spotlight on it, and people, just like I was and still am, were interested in this relationship between chimps and language. I had ideas about Darwin, of course, and evolution. I also knew that when I met the chimpanzees, it was a sign from God to make me keep my promise, that I had had a second chance, and this could very well be it. Of course, it was really a promise to me. I almost lost my left leg when I was 18 in a motorcycle accident, while in the military. That's how my leg got damaged, and causes me issues to this day. Drunk driver. I was in the hospital for 7 months. It was pretty serious. No fun. But they saved my leg. Three months in traction. They don't do that anymore, from what I understand. Orthopaedic techniques improved quite a lot since 1973. Oddly, that's the same year that Nim was born. I have a permanently dislocated shoulder called an AC (acromioclavicular) separation, another reason I was in hospital so long, and multiple broken ribs. I had a full leg cast for a long time. They gave me last rites. Crazy scary. Nineteen, and asked, "Do you want last rites?" I'm, like, "Do I need them?" The doctor says, "Can't hurt". Indeed, I promised, actually asked God, "Don't let me die." I said, "I'll make something of myself, I promise". And I lived, and two years or so later, I met Kelly and the other chimps, and then in 1977, I met Nim. Since then, I've experienced countless primates. I've been directly involved in their rescue and placement in sanctuary. I've given talks at schools and colleges and conferences, advised groups, participated in volunteer efforts, and had many primate-related experiences. Who knows how many of those kids who I've had the pleasure and privilege of having spoken to have been inspired to go on and be good human beings? And all because I had the good fortune to meet these special chimps, including Nim. That, to me, is the spirit of Nim working.

So, it's 1975, and I get to go to the weekly chimp student meetings, which were mostly graduate student meetings with Dr. Fouts, and to hang out with the chimpanzee people at the University. I was extremely enthusiastic and would do anything needed to help everyone. It didn't take very long for the staff to get it that I had whatever "it" is, in terms of taking the chimpanzees out. I never got bitten, I was able to deal with it, "it" being the volatile nature of chimpanzees, and their manic nature. To me, I was a chimp, from the first day that I got to interact face to face with them with no bars between us.

Early on in the first 6 or 8 months of the time I was working with the chimps as an undergrad at the IPS, Charity O'Neil, a PhD grad student of Roger Fouts, and two other graduate students and I were doing a study on conjugate lateral eye movement. This study was about eye shifts in chimpanzees. We collected data in exactly the same way data were collected in humans. Charity was older than me, and I was thrilled that she was willing to have me help her. I was in a unique position because the others who were involved were mostly grad students and of importance, not undergrads still figuring it out like I was. I was older than the other undergraduate students but not as old as the graduate students, because I'd had a previous life in the military. During the study, we would collect sample data of different chimpanzees, and patterns of eye shifts. Most of the signing studies involved only one, two, or three chimpanzees, but in this study we could use a larger sample size. We collected data from adolescent and adult chimpanzees, both males and females, with order statistically arranged by an independent statistician. We were also collecting handedness data as a component of the study which Kelly was involved in. We didn't do the handedness data with chimps in the cage. We did these portions of the experiments outside the cage with the chimps we knew we could handle, so that they could be out, and they would sit on my lap. Onan and a couple of others, including Kelly, were participants. We had this open wooden box with two bowls with lids attached inside it, and the chimps would retrieve the reward. I was confident that nothing could or would go wrong. I had Kelly who was about 80 lb on my lap, a seriously highly strung chimpanzee, volatile, and pretty close to the edge all the time. She was sitting on my lap, more on my right leg, so she could reach with either hand to retrieve raisins from the bowls. I was as naïve as I could be about all this stuff, in this early time in my years at the IPS. This incident with Kelly changed my entire perspective about being out with chimps. Charity was directing me which bowl to load, according to an already worked out randomly selected design. I would do that, while the chimp participant, in this case Kelly, observed which bowl I put the raisin in and closed the cover on. We would then record which hand was used to lift either lid, and which hand was used to retrieve the raisin reward. I've got a pound of raisins under my leg to retrieve and load the bowls with, and Kelly's cool with me having the raisins under my leg, at first. Each variable was accounted for. Kelly would sometimes open with one hand and reach with the other, and noted on a check sheet, to be analysed later. All I was doing was listening to Charity's instructions, adding a few raisins to the bowls, and watching the response. And of course, she was responding quickly and enjoyed the raisins.

Remembering "Tiny" – Dwight Russell (Died 1983)

Kelly realized quickly. She was thinking, "You motherfucker, you put five raisins in that thing and you've got a bag of them under your leg!". She spun around, and simultaneously grabbed the bag of raisins and brought my left hand up to her mouth and nearly bit the tip of my index finger off. At that point, it was chaos.

Blood flew everywhere. There was that scream, right before the bite. When a female chimpanzee gives you that sound, that scream, it is a guttural screaming noise. I recognise it from both times I had gotten bit. I've heard it twice. This was the first time I heard it, and I knew it was bad. Charity was freaking out as you would expect. Kelly grabbed Charity's tank top and almost ripped it off. Chimpanzees will shit and piss when they are in a highly stressful situation as part of the fight-or-flight response. Once she had the raisins and calmed down a bit, Kelly realized she'd taken it too far. I was screaming at the top of my lungs for Tiny, while at the same time trying to restrain Kelly. Tiny was the Operations Manager at IPS. He was a big, tall man whose help with the chimpanzees was integral to the students being able to conduct studies. He ran the day-to-day operation at the IPS, which we called the Chimp Farm. "Tiny! Tiny! Tiny! Tiny! Tiny!", he could hear. Tiny was 6′ 6″, 230 lb, easy. I'm like 5 ft 2, and at that time 125 lb. He had the best stories; he knew everything about everything. He was a country hippy in overalls and a welder's cap. He knew everything, and if he didn't know, he would have a book to look stuff up, like those *Foxfire* volumes. We loved Tiny in ways I can't explain. He was the guy you asked whatever you needed to know, and the person if you could you'd want to hang with. He always had a smile and a pleasant demeanor. Tiny also had a say, or was directly involved, in pretty much everything that happened at the Chimp Farm. I had a key to take the chimps out, given first to Tiny by Bill Lemmon, and then to me by Tiny, and Roger (Fouts was Robert's supervisor) did not. Bill Lemmon allowed me to have a key, which meant I had permission to take the chimpanzees out whenever I liked. That was why I was there to begin with, to be with the chimps and go out on walks with them. There was competition, but I didn't see myself as Roger's competitor. Only later did I realize that Roger saw me as competitor, and a threat. Fouts, we know now, had feelings of inferiority especially towards Lemmon.

Kelly and I were tussling on the ground, and I'm bleeding all over the place. It's serious. My fingertip was dangling. Tiny appeared and was able to calm Kelly down and return her to her enclosure. That day, Janis Carter (famous for her work with the chimpanzee Lucy) was at the Chimp Farm. She wasn't around much, but on that particular day, she happened to be there. When I walked in to wash my hand and she looked at my finger. I have huge respect for her, I look up to her. She says "You've got to go to the health center, get it looked at". She gave me that advice, and I followed it immediately. That day taught me that I could not trust anyone else to cover my ass when I was with the chimps. I relied on Tiny from then on for backup and information. He also had a lot more life experience. He had a lot more chimp experience than any student. He had been in the military, in the Navy. He was into music. He turned me on to Tom Waits. He had been a roadie for a rock and roll band, which was how he ended up in Oklahoma.

I learned that you want to get the chimpanzee so that they feel the need to not disappoint you. Kelly had been the pet of a pretty wealthy person. When she arrived at IPS, I was told that she had pierced ears and wore gold earrings, and she smoked a pipe, wore lipstick, clothes, all the fucked-up shit that people can do to a chimpanzee. Then when she got older and more difficult, they brought her to us. Kelly was already a resident when I landed at the IPS in August of 1975. After the bite, Kelly and I became much closer. We bonded over that bite. We hugged afterwards. There's a point at which after it happens, you have to make amends. You don't want a grudge. They need hugs, reassurance. In my many years working with different chimpanzees, only two ever bit me. There was the same desire to make up after each bite. Some of these chimpanzees only have 50 words. The same thing happened to me with Abigail, a chimp born at the IPS, that I would encounter much later. The IPS was super successful at breeding chimps. Bill Lemmon bred them to give to students. Abigail was one of them. It was in the early 1990s and we were on the couch in the trailer house where Abigail lived with Marge Fenner, her human companion. We were hanging around for an hour and a half. Abigail bit me badly, a full on canine into the forearm, all the way to the bone. I jump up, and she bounces up and signs SORRY HURT YOU. Maybe this is repentance. She hugged me, and wanted to groom the wound, and make up like she would have with another chimp in a situation like that.

You can see the personality of Kelly in the photos (see Figure 3.1). She expresses the look of a needy chimpanzee. After that day, Kelly and I had a new understanding. We hung out every day we could. I would take her out first, and then take out the other chimps, like Nim's older brother Onan. I had the privilege of being trusted, by Lemmon, and more importantly by Tiny, so I was allowed to take out a couple of chimpanzees at a time.

It is easy to forget that these are chimpanzees behind bars. Being around a chimp is a powerful feeling. Eugene Linden, author of *Silent Partners*, described it as a little like working in front of one of those distorting mirrors in a fairground. The chimpanzees would bring out various attributes in the people working with them. It was like entering a kingdom where the rules do not apply. Robert continues, "It was easy for the researchers to lose perspective. However, some individuals did keep themselves grounded, and James Mahoney was one."

FIGURE 3.1 Robert and Kelly.

Remembering Dr. James Mahoney
(Died 6 September 2017)

There is far more to the story about James Mahoney than is presented in *Project Nim*. His energy and drive at converting his involvement as the chief vet and decider of life/death of chimpanzees at the LEMSIP laboratory, to rescuer of at least 109 chimpanzees and 65 monkeys is not detailed anywhere. Mahoney wrote various books, including, *From Elephants to Mice: Animals Who Have Touched My Soul*, and his chapter "Great Escapes" details some of those actions, but he gives the details with humility, and his unexpected death from Lyme disease in 2017 meant that his story seems unfinished. Mahoney had to be persuaded to appear in the film *Project Nim*, given that the initial period in which he was involved with Nim was probably the most traumatic for Nim. The director, James Marsh, convinced him that he would not be depicted as a villain, since Marsh had no interest in getting into controversy around animal rights. Mahoney's work in the LEMSIP laboratories is distressing to watch, but the aspect we do not see is that ultimately, he was one of the heroes of the primates.

Robert first remembers Mahoney as visiting the Oklahoma chimpanzees and making notes, so he knew that something was being planned. A softly spoken Irish man, he had trained at Bangor University in Wales in the UK, later practiced in the West Highlands of Scotland, then went to New York. His books give a more detailed account of the emotions he experienced in his role at the medical laboratories. He explains how when at LEMSIP in the late 1970s, "I did not recognize the more pervasive and insidious forms of cruelty – that [cruelty] caused by *omission* rather than *commission*". How could there have been healthy development, and how could personality traits be expressed healthily by these chimpanzees when they were kept in enclosures? Mahoney described how, "As I became more involved with the animals, I began to see not only their individuality, but also their unique needs".

The role of Mahoney in these chimpanzee stories could be a book by itself. It is fair to say that there was a huge movement of morals for Mahoney. In his book, he describes Robert as "an amazing angel for Nim". When Nim was taken away from Oklahoma and sold to LEMSIP, Robert bombarded Mahoney constantly with letters. In *Project Nim*, Mahoney says, "The student, Bob Ingersoll, he used to hound me every chance he got, and I would start to get really annoyed. And then it dawned on me that he was the only one who cared."

We do not see what happens afterwards. Mahoney spent immense effort and energy, with Robert, to make Nim's life more tolerable. Together, they were also able to rescue the chimpanzees Midge and Lou Lou, to introduce them to Nim at the Black Beauty Ranch in Texas, in order that they could live together and become companions. These were just a few of the many primates rescued by Mahoney, after he had a shift of spirit about the animal experimentation which he was obliged to conduct as a part of his job.

In truth, Mahoney's ethical concerns about the job he was doing had started many years before. In 1996, the news programme *20/20* aired an episode on chimpanzee experimentation. It featured Peter Singer and Roger Fouts (who was paid $5,000 to appear) and his wife, Deborah, visiting the chimpanzee Booee in the LEMSIP laboratory. Fouts, driven to the laboratory in a limousine larger than Booee's cage, does not know how Booee will react, as he has not seen him for 16 years, a surprisingly long time for a chimpanzee for whom he was the chief carer, and had told many stories about. It is even more surprising since LEMSIP was open even for the general public to visit. Mahoney looks less than happy to be taking Fouts back to Booee, and at the end of the visit it is made clear that poor Booee will not know when, or even if, he will see his former owner again. This was very much a one-off visit. When the presenter asks Mahoney to discuss the experimentation, he says, "We keep finding new viruses, and if it proves that the chimpanzee is the only animal model in which we can grow the virus in, then I'm afraid the chimpanzee becomes a candidate once more".

The research had already saved tens of hundreds of lives. Hepatitis B was a major killer, and a vaccine could never have been developed without this kind of research. This presents a moral conundrum. At the time, AIDS was rife. It was the focus of the experimentation; only chimps and humans could carry the HIV virus, although the chimpanzees never actually got the disease. Mahoney is asked if it is conceivable for him to do the work without the chimpanzees. His answer was that in order to test the vaccine in a human being, one would have to take a person who had never been exposed to HIV before, allow them to be injected with the vaccine, and then say, "I hope this vaccine works, because now I'm going to take a thousand times an infectious dose, and I'm going to inject you with it". If it does not work, one would have an HIV/AIDS-infected person, which would be impossible to do, ethically. Mahoney is asked, "Because of the similarity between great apes and human beings, do we have the right to use them in this way?" Mahoney's reply is humbling, "I personally don't think we have a right. No. I'm thoroughly convinced that we do not have a right. I can only say that we have a *need*." He is asked if he ever feels bad about it, and whether he wishes he were doing something else. "Yes", he replies, "every day. Every night. Unfortunately we do need to use them in research, that's my belief. But I am not so thoroughly convinced about my rightness in doing so." (*20/20*, 1996).

Robert says:

> This led James to re-examine his actions. He rescued 109 chimpanzees. Jim was the hero in all this beside Nim and the other chimpanzees. He realised that what I was yelling at him was true, and that he had to re-examine his spot in all of this. He saved those 109 chimpanzees because of that revelation. I set the ball in motion, and helped him with his plan. Some of those chimpanzees are still alive.
>
> Fortunately for me, and fortunately for the chimps, Jim Mahoney had one of those "aha" moments. He had an epiphany when he realised, "Wow, Bob's right. We should examine this on a different level". Jim Mahoney was one of those people who was willing to revisit the past and in our own "collective sins", let's say, and the wrong that we did to those chimps, and he was willing

to revisit that enough, to at least help some of them. And he was still pretty much dogged by these people saying that he did all those horrible things to those chimps, but indeed, he had an epiphany that opened the door for quite a few of those chimps to actually find their way to sanctuary, including Nim's brother, Onan. This is something that, actually, none of the people who worked with the chimps could pull off.

Mahoney also helped Shirley McGreal, who was an animal welfare activist and conservationist, and who founded the International Primate Protection League (IPPL). She explained in his obituary how, "Mahoney never forgot the gibbons, and came down regularly to stay at IPPL for a week or more, attending to their medical needs, and those of all the other gibbons who had joined us". Bob explains how:

Jim Mahoney had a forward-thinking approach to his laboratory, and it was accessible to the public. You could visit LEMSIP with an appointment, and get a tour of the facility. As time went on and the public's awareness was raised and they had to keep changing the sizes of the cages. Those constant changes would be very costly, and so when the Animal Welfare Act and other legislations became law, it led to the leadership of LEMSIP, Dr Jan Moor-Jankowski, and New York University, to make the decision to close LEMSIP. So the decision was made to close down LEMSIP and to send the chimps to Coulston (the Coulston Foundation, in Alamogordo, New Mexico), a plan that backfired. Animal rights activists were outraged because the Coulston Foundation was known for its inhumane treatment of chimpanzees. Despite the protestation, Coulston got the chimps.

Mahoney – with Robert – and a team of insiders and outside help, was quietly relocating chimps and monkeys to sanctuaries, including to the Black Beauty Ranch in Texas.

Kelly is one of the reasons why we are sitting here talking today. One event that changed Jim Mahoney and me profoundly, without knowing it would. When Kelly went to LEMSIP with all the other Oklahoma chimpanzees, to me, it was like . . . like your sister gets sent to the concentration camp. She didn't do anything wrong. All she did was to exist. I asked Mahoney about Kelly all the time, in all those calls and letters, and hundreds of contacts. I did the best I could to let Mahoney know that I was really serious and I was not going away. It fucked with me, in a way I couldn't express. Kelly, Onan, Booee, Bruno, Pan, PB, all the IPS chimps mattered to me. I still think about this. I've got what might be diagnosed as PTSD [post-traumatic stress disorder], these days, from it. The memories make me cry, still. I understand I have this now.

This is extremely important because you realise attachments can really fuck with you. It's lucky I didn't do something suicidal. I was doing behaviours that were probably killing me – drugs, et cetera. Always asked Mahoney about Kelly. Then I got a phone call around 1993 from Mahoney's associate, Douglas Cohen. He said, "I want to ask you a question about Kelly". He said, "First, I have to tell you she has cancer and it's a weird cancer we've not seen before, and I want you to help me to figure this out if we can. I also shared photos of Kelly. I told him all the stuff I could about her history, and this and that. It was early on in emails, and not many people had email. So then maybe a year or so later, Belle and I were at the American Society of Primatologists (ASP) Conference in Scottsdale, Arizona. ASP's members, while multi-disciplinary, weighted heavily towards invasive research in captive primates. I never felt particularly welcome there, and as an animal welfare person, was certainly in the minority. Mahoney, who I'd never spoken to before in person, walked right over to me. He put his arm around me, and I was freaking out, because I knew it was going to be about Kelly. He said "Bob, we had to euthanise Kelly, and I did it". And we both cried for a few seconds. Not very long. I tried to compose myself because I had to appear tough. I was thinking, "At this conference I'm going to represent those chimpanzees, whether other members of the ASP like it or not." Mahoney says, as he has his arm still around me, "Listen, I've found out that LEMSIP is going to close, and I know when, and I want you to help me get as many of the chimpanzees out before they get sold and moved to Coulston." I was shocked. I said "Really?" He replied, "Yes, really". I said "Yes, I'm in. I'll do whatever I can."

The banquet was in full swing. We walked away from it, but everyone could see us. He and I walked over to the bar which was on the other side the room, out of earshot of anyone. I bought him a Guinness. He said "You're going to get me into every sanctuary you can. We're going to get them into all the sanctuaries, while we can."

This is how James Mahoney became the Oskar Schindler of the primate world (Merritt Clifton, Animals 24–7, 2017). Robert explains, "We got the chimpanzees into all the places. There was a lot of work going on behind the scenes, around 2 years before the moves started to happen in the mid 1990s". Figure 3.2 shows a painting of Onan's footprints. Onan was Nim's older brother. Many years ago when Bob was an impoverished graduate student, he gave a number of his family members framed chimp art. This particular piece was given to his mother in 1979. Unlike Nim, efforts to rescue Onan were unsuccessful, and he spent many years at LEMSIP. Thankfully, in the summer of 1997, Onan became one of those 109 chimpanzees rescued out of the medical laboratory by Bob and by Mahoney and placed into sanctuary.

Robert continues, "In bridging the divide between academia and sanctuary, it is necessary to have a rigid approach in the scientific world, but we should lean towards the ability to work with sanctuaries in a way in which we can help them. The sanctuary people did not trust the academics to not do harm. Many still don't,

FIGURE 3.2 A painting of Onan's footprints.

for good reason; tens of thousands of non-human primates (NHPs) are still used today, in a variety of invasive 'scientific studies'. The laboratory individuals may not be aware of what the sanctuaries need, or indeed, what sanctuaries might even contribute in terms of the science. There are long-term politics involved in this".

Abigail

Dr. Lemmon had a practice of handing out infant chimpanzees to be home-reared in human families. The chimpanzee, Abigail, was one of those (see Figure 3.3). In 1992, I was contacted by Marjorie "Marge" Fenner, who had been given Abigail as an infant by Dr. Lemmon. Abigail was now 18 years old. Marge was over 80 and needed to make a plan for Abigail's long-term future. Marge had seen an article about efforts I had been making on behalf of the IPS chimps Booee and Bruno, who I had hoped to relocate from LEMSIP to the Oklahoma City Zoo's new exhibit, the Great Ape Escape. Within a week of her first contact, I drove east from my home in Norman to meet Marge and Abigail.

I arrived in the forest on the border between Oklahoma and Arkansas. Marge was living with Abigail in a mobile home, with her daughter Barbara in a house next door. As I arrived in the area, I pulled off the highway I-40 and pulled into the local Conoco station and called Marge. This was before cell phones, so I called from the pay phone in the corner of the parking lot. After I called Marge, I went back to my car and waited for her to drive up as she said she would. She was only a few moments away. Marge drove up in this big, 4-door, American car. She had

FIGURE 3.3   Abigail with Marge Fenner.

one arm hanging out of her window, and in the passenger seat was the massive Abigail, with her arm hanging out of the car too. Marge pulled up over by the pay phone and I walked on over and said hello to Marge. I was careful not to go to the passenger side, but to greet Abigail from the driver's side. Marge and I spoke briefly about my following her to her place, which I did.

When we pulled up in her yard, me in my 1988 VW camper van, she in her giant American boat car, Abigail opened her door and leapt out of the car. Out of the corner of my eye, I saw what she was after. The family dog. Abigail grabbed the little dog by the leg, and swung him around a few times. Thankfully, the dog got away despite the flailing from Abigail, and I found out later that he was OK. Turned out the dog belonged to Marge's daughter, Barbara. When I went into the trailer that Marge and Abigail occupied along with a bird or two, I was pretty excited about being with a chimpanzee again. I said hello to Abigail and spoke to her, as I also did normal chimp greetings and postures which I had learned in the IPS days. At first I sat on the chair next to Abigail but after 10 minutes I was comfortable enough to sit next to Abigail on her couch. I spent about 45 minutes playing and signing with her on the couch. We played this game that most chimpanzees like to play, which involves tickling. We signed TICKLE HERE and ME TICKLE YOU and a few other signs. I don't think Abigail had an extensive vocabulary but she did know signs that you'd expect any chimp that had been exposed to some sign language would know and use, like TICKLE, and FOOD, and DRINK, and those sorts of signs. Abigail was in her late teens at the time and weighed 188 lb (just over 85 kilograms). Marge invited me to another room to see scrapbooks with photographs of Abigail and her half-sister, Lilith, another former Lemmon infant, from their days in the rodeo (not something I approved of then or now). Although I wanted to continue playing with Abigail, I obliged, and went to look at these photographs of Abigail and Marge, and the "rodeo days" with Abigail doing her launch skills. In the time that Marge and I were in the other room looking at photographs, Abigail had gotten bored and anxious, and I heard a loud noise which turned out to be Marge's chair which Abigail had flipped over. When we returned to the living room, we righted the furniture, Marge lightly scolded Abigail, and I made the mistake of casually sitting down on the couch, before I asked Abigail for her permission to invade her space. I knew immediately that this was wrong, and a bad move, and so I waited for the punishment to arrive. I heard the scream similar to the one I described before, when Kelly bit me. Abigail took my arm, locked eyes with me, and bit it. Hard. Her right upper and lower canine met at the bone, leaving two huge punctures. Then she released my arm. It was over as quickly as it started. I looked down and I saw blood everywhere. As we stood in front of Abigail, she signed SORRY HURT YOU, HUG HUG. So, we did. Later, we opened the cabinet and it was fully stocked with medicines and bandages and ointments. It was clear that Abigail had done this before. I put a t-shirt on the wound and I called on Barbara, Marge's daughter in the house next door, to take me to the hospital. On the way, I had the opportunity to speak to Barbara both about the bite, and about how was Abigail going to transition from living with Marge, to living in a more chimp-friendly environment, and ideally, with other chimps.

At the hospital, the doctors and other staff were very interested to look at the wound administered by a chimpanzee, because they had never seen a chimpanzee bite before. It was not every day that someone went in saying that "a chimp put this giant hole in my arm". I told them not to sew the wound, but to clean it, pack it, wrap it up, and to cover it up. I had to tell them how to look after it. I wanted the wound to be well-covered and to be out of grooming range of Abigail, and this bandage did the trick. After that, I went back to the house with a large bandage on my arm, which Abigail was keen to groom. I spent the night in my van on the premises, and left the next morning to go back to Norman. I called my fiancée, Belle, from a pay phone on the way back, to give her a heads up that I was alright. She said " 'Alright'? What does that mean?" and I told her that I had a "small" wound on my arm. That was an understatement, but I didn't want to worry her because I knew I wanted to go back to see Abigail again. I did go back, and I gave Marge the advice that Abigail should be rehoused soon, because it was only a matter of time before she would bite somebody else.

After Marge's eventual death, Abigail went to live at Dr. Sarah Boysen's Center for Cognitive Science at Ohio State University, where she lived with several other chimps in a group setting. A few years later, I saw Abigail in a documentary about the Ohio State University chimps and the amazing research Dr. Boysen was conducting, called *Keeli & Ivy: Chimps Like Us*. In the documentary, we see Abigail holding two very young chimps, and the look on her face is one of absolute bliss. Chimps need other chimps. Abigail had been rehoused successfully, and those babies were part of her family, as far as she was concerned. This is a behaviour seen in wild chimpanzee populations, called "aunting behaviour".

It was thanks to our work and Dr. Boysen's work rehousing Abigail that this was finally able to happen. We have a responsibility to do everything for these chimpanzees. We did all the bad work that inflicted trauma in the first place. In most cases we did not realise the long-term implications, and now somebody's got to undo it. We participated in the research that led to this issue of chimps living in human homes. The least we could do was to try and help those chimps get to a more proper environment, one that includes groups of other chimps, if possible.

We can consider stress in children, human and chimpanzee, here. The book by Sue Gerhardt, *Why Love Matters: How Affection Shapes A Baby's Brain* (2004) is an excellent source of information about how stress occurs even prenatally, and into the infant years. Gerhardt gives detailed accounts of the physical attributes connected to stress across early years, and of the impact of adversity. She also discusses the effects of stress in parents upon their parenting. Here, it makes sense to consider stress from the child's perspective, and to consider its impact upon Washoe and those other chimpanzees, and in turn, how they behaved towards both other chimps and humans. We can consider how stress affects a child daily, and the impact it has upon the child's everyday routine, including the effects of carrying the heavy load of familial stress and burdens to school each day.

This topic of stress has been discussed so much in psychological literature that its definition has become broad and almost meaningless. The preferred definition is of being at the extreme end of emotional regulation (Gerhardt, 2004), and in a state of high arousal that is difficult to manage. It is a state of mental or emotional strain resulting from demanding (or sometimes, *under*-demanding) conditions. This can be due to lack of relief, or because there is an inefficient recovery process. The body has a homeostatic mechanism. Homeostasis is the body's ability or tendency to maintain internal stability, in compensation for environmental changes – for example, changes in body temperature and glucose level to keep it in a state of equilibrium.

In development, being able to deal with stress has a huge impact on educational attainment. The human system described here shares similar processes in chimpanzees. In the human world, each child arrives to the classroom as a package of both good and bad potential life stressors, ready to confront a series of mild to moderate stress episodes over the course of a normal school day. There is occasionally a more severe stressful situation or life event in the course of a school day. Being able to cope with novel or threatening encounters is essential to survival, and this capacity is built into the brain's circuitry. Stress is very much a case of brain over body, influenced by a number of experiences both internally and environmentally driven.

When we are stressed, a part of the brain called the hypothalamus is activated. This triggers a cascade of stress hormones. One particular hormone called corticotrophin releasing factor (CRF) is transported through the bloodstream to activate the pituitary gland, which also releases stress hormones. The important hormone here is adrenocorticotrophic hormone (ACTH), also transported through the bloodstream, along with other stress hormones. These then activate the adrenal glands, which are located on the kidneys, and stimulate secretion of adrenaline and release of other stress hormones, hormones which are known as corticosteroids, from the adrenal cortex. Cortisol is an important stress hormone here. The extra cortisol produced under stress mobilises glucose stored in the liver, in order to energise the individual so they can focus on the stressor while other bodily systems are placed on hold. Cortisol output is easy to study. It can be measured in blood, urine and, most commonly in human research studies, saliva. This interaction between the hypothalamus, pituitary and adrenal glands is a kind of feedback loop, like a thermostat for the body. The release of glucocorticoids is inhibited through a negative feedback mechanism. This means that at a certain concentration in blood, protection against the stressor is achieved, and the glucocorticoids, in particular, cortisol, send negative feedback to the hypothalamic release of CRF, and to the pituitary release of ACTH. The mechanism regulates the physiological response of stress reactions and plays an important role in immunity and fertility. This is the "fight-or-flight" response, meaning that in the face of a threatful stimulus, the individual is evolutionarily programmed to prepare to fight the threat, or to flee from it. The biological term for this process is the hypothalamic-pituitary-adrenal (HPA) axis.

Strictly speaking, the stress response takes the form of two pathways. The one explained previously is a more chronic process. The other is an acute and "quick" route called the sympathomedullary (or also the sympatho-adrenal system [SAS], or sympathetic-adrenomedullary [SAM]) pathway (Hardy & Pollard, 2006). Both routes are involved in producing stress and motivational hormones even under normal conditions, to allow the body to prepare for response and coping, and both produce the same stress hormones described. The SAM pathway is an evolutionary mechanism for homeostasis, which is that quick, compensatory change to the body's equilibrium.

Cortisol is released not only during those periods of prolonged stress described in the HPA axis, but also at other times, for example, in response to mild stressors like the shrill ring of an alarm clock. Cortisol levels are at their highest when we awake after a night's sleep. They are also high during periods of increased memory function and focus. There is a difference between heightened cortisol in the short term during normal levels of arousal, and its persistently high levels in the longer term. The latter can impact negatively on cognitive functions such as attention and memory. Another stress hormone, adrenaline, also prepares the body for fight-or-flight action, in the body's quick judgement about whether to stay and fight the stimulus or to flee. This is done by increases in heart rate and blood pressure, and redistribution of blood to muscles and by heightening of blood glucose levels. Again, taken together, these hormones energise the human being into taking action.

The SAM pathway also mobilises energy stores and redirects blood flow to allow the body to confront or hide from the threatful stimulus. The body gets ready for intense physical activity by increasing the fight-or-flight capacity, in order to promote survival. The SAM pathway activates via the autonomic nervous system which responds rapidly, and controls other systems such as the cardiovascular, gastrointestinal, respiratory, renal and endocrine systems. These are under control of either or both of the sympathetic and parasympathetic nervous systems (Gilbey &

Spyer, 1993). The SAM pathway reduces blood flow and activity of the gastrointestinal system and reproductive organs, and mobilises energy to the brain, heart and muscles through cells in the spinal cord. During acute stress, activation of the SAM evokes the release of noradrenaline and adrenaline from the central part of the adrenal gland, which is called the adrenal medulla. Activation of this also produces increased cytokines to connect the stress system with other immunological and inflammatory processes (Vanltallie, 2002), which is why stress can cause colds, flu, gallstones, heart attacks and other cardiac problems, stomach ulcers, bowel conditions and different types of cancer.

Stress and depression cause the adrenal glands to become dysregulated in their production of cortisol, and as measuring cortisol in saliva is cheap and effective, scientists have researched it a great detail over past decades. It is not known if depressed individuals have elevated cortisol levels caused by stressful life events, which in turn lower 5-HT (serotonin) function in the brain, leading to depressive states (Dinan, 1994). Cortisol secretion abnormalities and 5-HT function are a causal chain in which cortisol is the key biological mediator through which life stress lowers brain 5-HT function, thereby causing depression in vulnerable individuals (Cowen, 2002). The behavioural output of this is in socialising behaviours. In humans, there is a strong link between emotional processing involving cortisol, and social behaviours. Strong socialisation behaviours are linked to lowered cortisol, and vice versa, but social isolation is connected to increases in cortisol. Sapolsky's laboratory (Altmann et al., 1995) demonstrated this in baboons, with the high-ranking baboons with social power showing low levels of cortisol, and those who were low-ranking indicating high levels. The famous monkey studies of Harry Harlow et al. (1965) demonstrated how monkeys isolated in their first year of life demonstrate signs of autism and are unable to form social connections with other monkeys. Mahoney describes how, at one of the American Society of Primatology conferences in the 1980s, he was taken aback by the work of Marian Diamond on rats and effects of environmental enrichment. He was surprised to discover that her work comparing young, middle-aged and senior rat groups who were exposed to enriched environments outlived the groups receiving impoverished (restricted) environmental conditions by 30% (Diamond et al., 1972). There was also thickening of the neocortex due to a marked increase in dendrites. The neocortex is an important part of the mammalian brain, different from its counterpart of the dorsal cortex in the reptilian brain. It is involved in visual and sensory processing. At the conference, Diamond asked the primate researchers, "If this is the case for rats, what do you think you are doing to your primates sitting in their sterile boring cages day after day?"

Our earliest experiences in life become translated into patterns of brain physiology which set the pattern for how we cope with our own and others' feelings for the rest of our lives. How we are treated as infants impacts upon who we become as adults, and how we form relationships with others. Babies do not know how to regulate their stress responses by themselves, and so they rely on their caregivers to respond to their distress. In this way, they learn to rely upon others to respond to their needs: in adulthood this translates as their romantic partners. When the infant does not have this ability or opportunity to rely on his/her caregivers, the infant becomes dysregulated and anxious. As psychologist Louis Cozolino describes, "We are not the survival of the fittest. We are the survival of the nurtured" (Cozolino, 2014). He explains, "Those who are nurtured best, survive best."

Washoe would have arrived from Africa in a crate, having been abducted after witnessing her mother die. Exactly how dysregulated her world was by the time she arrived in the US is unknown, but it is unlikely that she would have had her emotional needs tended to on a personal level. The brain wiring for her future life would have been partially set by that stage. Is it any wonder, then, that she would lack the skills which would have rendered her a warm or affectionate mother? Not only would she have had disrupted brain systems, but there was a lack of models for her to learn mothering behaviour from. There would have been immense stresses in her moves, first, from Africa to the Gardners in Nevada, to Fouts in Oklahoma, and then on to Washington. The necessary adaptation alongside being held captive and having to produce signs would have been immensely stressful. Let us compare with Nim, who seemed more robust in his stress responses – but who suffered, nonetheless. Nim was bred for research purposes. Although he was taken from his mother, Carolyn, at around 10 days old, he was placed in the arms of Stephanie LaFarge, who became his foster mother for about a year and a half. His mother was not killed before his eyes, but "disappeared" and was replaced by a human. His stress would have been as a result of that experience, followed by the move from the LaFarge household and his foster "siblings" in the form of those children in the family, to various carers, onto the Delafield estate, then on to Oklahoma, thrust into living among his own different species after growing up surrounded by humans only. This is before we even consider the amount of stress he would have endured at LEMSIP laboratories, where he was given a tattoo with his assigned number, 37, before one final move to the Black Beauty Ranch. All of this alongside being expected to produce sign language.

In humans, stress poses significant problems in schools, with many children and young adults suffering from school-related anxiety, commonly around the issue of examinations, which raises concern and needs serious pedagogical attention. The ability of children and adolescents to maintain robust mental health needs attention. There is a distinction between being stressed at school, and more severe anxiety and panic disorders. The role of individual differences in experiences of and response to normal stress is key, with individuals sometimes experiencing stressful experiences which contribute to the onset of severe clinical conditions like anxiety and depression. In a healthy setting, however, some stress can be motivating.

Children's relationships with caregivers, including teachers, play a critical role in regulating their stress modulation, both in terms of psychological effects and stress-hormone production on a biological level during the early years. Depending on the body's response, stressful life events can be harmful and toxic to the brain, or at times, more tolerable and even beneficial. In the chimpanzees, we see how important their relationships with their caregivers were, who, incidentally, in most cases doubled up as teachers for the chimpanzees. This in itself can pose problems. In the schooling model, the child knows when it is engaging with a teacher and when it is engaging with a parent, and modulates their behaviours and experiences in an appropriate dynamic. In the chimpanzee world, teachers were sometimes "parents". Sometimes the same people were caregivers; sometimes they were more like siblings. Which were they? Who was what to whom, and what was the appropriate response?

Whether a large stress response is provoked or not depends on factors including whether the stress is perceived as controllable; the amount, frequency and intensity of the stress response; and, crucially, whether the child is in a safe and supportive environment with dependable relationships. This is a question we can ask about the chimpanzees. How safe and supported did they feel? There is the further fact of biological differences, that chimps do not have the sort of cortical control like we humans do.

Moja

Moja was another chimpanzee belonging to the Gardners. She was born in a biomedical laboratory and had been with them since infancy. Moja was the eldest chimp in the Gardners' second signing study. The Gardners were seeking advice from the Foutses about Moja's behaviours. She was biting people without apparent reason, and they were struggling to find research assistants. Fouts describes Moja as being "more emotionally manipulative" (Fouts & Mills, 1998, p. 240), refusing to eat in order to get attention, and mutilating herself. She would stay outside until her hands became frostbitten and then chew her fingers to the bone.

Moja left the Gardners when she was 7 years old, in 1979, to join Washoe and the others in Oklahoma. She was transferred by aeroplane, with Greg Gaustad, who had also worked on Project Washoe, but was moving on. She was moved into a building on the South Campus of the University of Oklahoma, where Washoe and Loulis had been moved after Fouts made a physical split of his chimp charges from those of Bill Lemmon at the IPS. By this stage, it was clear to Fouts that the studies were not being planned properly. He says, "These 'adoptions' were beginning to look less like experiments in family attachment and more like nightmares of separation" (p. 196). He describes how in each case, the chimpanzee's perspective seemed to not be considered, and how "We would sanction any use of the chimpanzees if it might help answer an interesting scientific question". There was no doubt that the chimpanzees were under immense stress. "Nobody seemed to notice, much less question, that the chimpanzees were suffering. On the contrary, the scientists around me swore that this shuttling back and forth of chimpanzee babies was a *good* thing because it advanced our own human knowledge" (p. 197). Robert remembers, "It was heart-breaking to see her like this in Oklahoma, and it only got worse, from the reports I had back when they all moved to Washington. Moja had briefly been in Oklahoma, at the South Base at OU Building 31, where George Kimball and I took her out on walks, behind the building. She was indeed psychologically unwell, but when she was out on walks with us, the people who knew chimps, and when we spent time with her, she did improve".

Fouts says about Moja, "It was heartbreaking to see Moja suffer and it was all too easy to cater to her every demand. When she demanded SANDWICH – peanut butter on white bread was all she ate – Debbi and I would fall over ourselves to make it. When she screamed we would anguish over why she was upset. When she chewed her fingers we begged her to stop." (Fouts & Mills, 1998, p. 242). He describes the stress that Moja was feeling: "It was a rocky transition. Moja's separation from Allen and Trixie tore her apart. Washoe had landed on her feet in Oklahoma and had just kept right on going, but Moja was an emotional basket case. She wouldn't eat. She had constant diarrhea. She screamed all the time. She groomed her wounds until they bled. And when all else failed Moja would simply sign to me, HOME? GO HOME?, holding the sign in place for several seconds to stress her urgency."

These symptoms of stress are similar to those seen in children who exhibit attachment problems when they have parents who are inconsistently emotionally available. Their cortisol levels are elevated, and they become the most fearful children during infancy (Kochanska, 2001), due to their cortisol and CRF being dysregulated. High cortisol levels are connected to high activity in the right frontal region of the brain, which is involved in fearfulness, irritability and social withdrawal (Davidson, 1992). Since the frontal lobes are also involved in novel stimuli and disinhibition, these children will be constantly distracted and on alert, especially if they live with unpredictable, unreliable and absent caregivers. The prefrontal cortex is compromised, and this regulates behaviour. These children grow up to be hypervigilant and over-observant, in preparation for reading verbal and non-verbal signals in their negligent caregivers. Since too much fear damages the hippocampus (Rosen & Schulkin, 1998), the child also struggles with attention and information processing. Those same regions of the brain are involved in obsessive-compulsive disorder (OCD), which may also explain Moja's OCD-like symptoms in her overgrooming and repetitions. Moja's problems with appetitive behaviours may have also been due to stress and regulation. She may not have had full-blown anorexia, but it seems she met the *Diagnostic and Statistical Manual of Mental Disorders, Fifth Edition* (*DSM-5*) diagnostic criteria for some of the symptoms, including restriction of food and rigid eating patterns. Anorexics have a hypersensitive stress response, with levels of CRF and cortisol being high, and with adrenal glands that show exaggerated response to ACTH. These factors occur after recovery, so it is thought they are due to the actual disorder rather than effects of starvation (Hoek, 2006). Raised CRF can also result in depression. These same elevated levels are demonstrated in infants who are separated from their mothers/main caregiver, and in depressed adults. Gerhardt makes an interesting point about this: "It may indicate a basic fear about survival with parents who don't create a feeling of safety. Although they are constantly in the presence of the mother, they do not necessarily feel safely cared for by her" (Gerhardt, 2004, p. 109). This certainly appeared to be the case with Moja, and what would have been her stressful move from Nevada to Oklahoma.

Availability of support can be more influential upon stress longevity than the nature of the stressor itself, and the child's ability to deal with stress in earlier years has an impact upon physical and mental health later on in life. It is vital to unpack the development of stress as it arises from earlier childhood development, since relationships that children have with caregivers play a critical role in regulating stress hormones and in setting down stress pathways later on in life. Nursery workers, and later on in school, the teachers hold important roles in the development of the child in this regard, especially when we consider how many hours a day the child spends in school.

Robert says:

> One evening, late, we were staying overnight with Moja to prevent her from chewing her leg off. We did that by hanging out with her. Only a few of us at the Fouts lab then had the sort of experience with chimps that would allow us to be in direct contact with her safely. She was a big chimp and she could potentially inflict severe damage, if she wanted to. She really liked me, and I her, so it was easy for me to hang out with her (see Figure 3.4). At the Fouts lab, we did shifts at night; two people, one with her, and the other sleeping and on alert in case the other needed support. We traded roles during the night. Roger carried a pager in case we needed him. He did not do overnights.
>
> I remember that night. Moja was clear. It's 2 am. Moja signs to me, MOJA WANTS MILK. She was a really good signer, like no other chimp I'd seen, and I'd seen many ASL chimps and worked with many of them. So I got what we had in the kitchen which was soda pop, and gave it to her. She signed NO SODA POP, and repeatedly asked for milk, and made us go out to get milk. Dave had to go to the late-night convenience store for milk. Moja got her milk. All was good. Dave continued to care for Moja in Washington after she was part of the Fouts group that eventually landed in Ellensburg, Washington.

There are a number of ways to distinguish between the various types of stress, and no two researchers in the field offer the same definition. In a report on the harmful effects of stress on the developing brain, the National Scientific Council on the Developing Child (Harvard University, 2006) explains how severe, chronic adversity during development and the absence of responsive caregiving can impair the brain's architecture. This report distinguishes between three types of stress: toxic, tolerable and positive.

Toxic stress involves strong and frequent activation of the HPA axis, and experiences that are chronic and uncontrollable. The child lacks support from adults, and a toxic stress response in the form of the HPA axis is activated. Major adverse life events such as illness or the death of a parent or relative, injury, parental separation or divorce and poverty, can cause toxic stress. These were some of the events that the chimpanzees would have been subjected to. Frequent, sustained

FIGURE 3.4 Moja and Robert.

brain activation leads to increased vulnerability to behavioural, psychological and physiological disorders such as anxiety, depression and addiction, or autoimmune disorders, cardiovascular disease and diabetes. The second type of stress, tolerable stress, involves brief periods of stress where the brain is allowed to recover. Any potential adverse effects to a child can be reversed as long as there is the presence of a supportive adult and a safe environment. Tolerable stress has the potential to become toxic, but it also has the ability to become positive stress, under the right conditions.

Little has been made of the third type of stress, and the positive effects of stress. Moderate bouts of short-lived stress increase the body's stress-hormone levels as children learn to adapt to some aspects of life. This is a feature of human development, as the child learns to control this sort of stress and to manage it well, learning how to ask for support or how to draw upon resources available in the form of caring adults or peers, in order to nurture safe and positive relationships. The average child undergoes several minor but positive stressors of this nature, while the child learns to negotiate their way through life. Events such as starting a new school term, performing in front of peers, sitting tests and receiving results, and making new friends can all be considered examples of positive stressors which the child can master quickly as a part of both social and cognitive learning. One example of this positive stress in the chimpanzees might include the time that Nim was introduced to Midge and other companions at Black Beauty Ranch, later on in his life. While this challenge was met with some anxiety and trepidation, the home footage demonstrates how Nim quickly mastered the social abilities needed to interact with his new mate, Midge, and after some initial chimpanzee display behaviours involving his tyre and toys, was happy to share his space.

It is imperative to consider the toxic effects of stress on the developing brain. Ever since the field of psychology became a science in its own right, psychologists have talked about nature versus nurture in brain development. Are we a set of inherited genetic predispositions and brain structures, making us vulnerable to certain conditions? Is our destiny determined within our DNA? ("They fuck you up, your mum and dad"; Larkin, 1971); or are we the product of our environment, with a malleable brain geared to adapt to external constraints and shaped by background, and perhaps holding onto transgenerational pain unless able to adapt? ("But they were fucked up in their turn", Larkin, 1971). Following decades of exploration from different psychological approaches, we can rest on the viewpoint that we are nature *via* nurture, and vice versa. It is important to emphasise here that psychologists place equal importance in both nature *and* nurture in human development. One of the problems is that the area tends to be dominated by the viewpoint that individual differences are genetic, and there is a great bias away from the idea of the brain as developing through social influence or environmental factors.

The field of neuropsychoanalysis combines neuroscience with psychoanalysis. It is taking time to emerge as a research domain of its own right, partly because the idea that brain development is influenced by the quality of our early relationships seems "a sloppy and unscientific notion" (Gerhardt, 2004). Other research biases lie in the tendency to (a) measure behaviours and brain activity in patients *after* they have been diagnosed, by which time it may be the belief of carrying the disorder which may influence behaviours; and (b) measure gene patterns which are already expressed and apparent, without consideration of genes which may not be expressed *yet*, or of toxic behaviours which may impact upon future genetic expression. Genes are expressed in response to environmental triggers, and in early life these triggers are likely to come in the form of the care which we receive.

Much of what is known about stress in humans has come from research on animals. Indeed, it seems rather ironic to be discussing the studies on stress from animal studies here in order to explain the stress in other animals. The impact of exposure to negative life events in animals has been studied extensively, mostly in rodents and primates. The chemical signals that are sent to the brain via stress hormones can cause disruption and changes to neural circuitry. From a neurodevelopmental perspective, it has been found that neural circuits are malleable during foetal development and following infancy. Human infants are born with the expectation that stress will be managed for them; typically developing infants, who undergo much stroking and feeding, tend to have low levels of cortisol (Hofer, 1994; Levine, 2005). Loman and Gunnar (2009) provide a review on early life stress, early experience, the development of stress reactivity and regulation in children; another review has been given by Gunnar (2017) on the social buffering of stress in development.

Early experiences may shape the brain's stress readability, and toxic stress during this time can result in impairment upon brain circuits and hormone systems (Loman & Gunnar, 2009). This leads to poor control of the stress system: either overly reactive or slowing down completely, particularly if there is stress over the life span. Accompanying psychological conditions involve mood and schizophrenic disorders, and stress is considered a kind of ticking time bomb of illness (Cavanna et al., 2009). Researchers have defined stress in the onset and relapse of schizophrenia as an "inescapable clinical fact" (Weinberger, 1987; Phillips et al., 2006). The suggestion made historically by psychological researchers may, indeed, be true: that each of us is vulnerable to disorders via stress, and that under certain conditions such as excessive episodes of stress, we are vulnerable to schizophrenic illness (Zubin & Spring, 1977). This vulnerability-stress model of psychiatric disorders focuses on the role of physical and mental stress in triggering psychotic episodes. The approach not only explains onset and maintenance of disorders caused by stress but has also been useful in identifying a number of vulnerability markers.

In humans, the roles of the school and teacher care are highly important in the attenuation of stress symptoms, and in the development and onset of other psychological disorders in childhood. These roles have not been researched properly and require further study. The environment in which one is existing and trying to survive in is highly crucial to development, particularly when there is suffering from stress. Existing research has already linked increases in stressful life events over 6 months with manic episodes (Bebbington et al., 1993), demonstrating that patients with depressive psychoses had more stressful and traumatic life events 3 months prior to their episode, compared with a control group (Bebbington et al., 1993). In this study, the timing and precursors of social decline in schizophrenia and affective psychosis were measured in a population from Camberwell, London, UK, in order to examine whether there were excessive stressful life events preceding the onset of psychoses, and to consider their role in emergence of psychotic symptoms, since changes in the social environment can lead to psychological symptoms in vulnerable individuals. Other historical findings report that bipolar, depressed and schizophrenic individuals were more likely to have experienced significant and stressful life events preceding relapse of symptoms (Clancy et al., 1973; Chung et al., 1986).

It is not only psychological problems that are elicited by stress. The body's immune system defends against infectious diseases, and autoimmune conditions can be triggered when it turns against the body's own cells. Chronic stress is associated with higher levels of pro-inflammatory cytokines, leading to these health problems (Gouin et al., 2012). Inflammation helps as a response to eliminate pathogens to encourage healing, but chronic system inflammation causes dysregulation to the immune system, leading to an increased risk of diseases including atherosclerosis (Ershler, 1993), hypertension via increased blood glucose and insulin – leading to weight problems and obesity – as well as activating latent viruses. Stress causes "wear-and-tear on the immune system" (Pawelec et al., 2005; Morey et al., 2015).

Sustained activation of stress pathways leads to damage lasting past exposure. Cortisol remains elevated for prolonged time periods. Studies on Holocaust survivors and their offspring have even found that the children of Holocaust survivors have impaired cortisol secretion, suggesting they may be at risk, despite not having endured the adverse experiences themselves (Yehuda et al., 2002). In both animals and humans, elevation of cortisol has been found to change brain architecture in terms of hippocampal atrophy. The hippocampus is the structure involved in learning and memory, which explains some of the problems seen in learning in stressed children. Finally, studies on Vietnam veterans found decreased hippocampus volume in veterans with PTSD (Bremner et al., 1995a, 1995b; Gurvits et al., 1996), and hippocampal volume to correlate inversely with PTSD symptom severity and extent of combat exposure (Gurvits et al., 1996).

A large number of scenarios of extreme stress in the chimpanzees are described by Fouts (Fouts & Mills, 1998, pp. 162, 163, 321, 325–326). He describes the chimpanzee Maybelle, who is left by her human caretaker, Vera Gatch, a psychotherapist and student of Lemmon, for the first time. Fouts explains how, "As soon as Vera was gone a full day, Maybelle went to pieces. She developed terrible diarrhea and a respiratory infection. Those of us who knew Maybelle set up shifts to care for her around the clock . . . but poor Maybelle was wasting away before my very eyes and I felt utterly powerless to save her." Maybelle's condition worsened, with her diarrhoea turning into dysentery, and her lung infection into pneumonia. Poor Maybelle died. It is unclear how things escalated so rapidly, but one can assume that the emotional stress of her missing her key attachment figure and being looked after by numerous individuals, even those she knew and for a short space of time, was too much for her psychological health and her immune system.

In another example, Fouts explains how almost a year after this incident, "I watched my youngest pupil, barely older than a baby, also shrivel up and die in the absence of her human mother". This time the chimpanzee is Salomé, who started life as being raised by a patient of Lemmon's and the patient's wife, Church and Susie Blakey. On taking a holiday, "immediately Salomé lapsed into pneumonia and was close to death. The Blakeys rushed home, and she recovered from her grief-induced illness. Shortly thereafter, the Blakeys decided to try another vacation. But this time Salomé didn't make it. She died within a few days" (p. 163).

Emotional Memory

Think back to your first day at school. As a small child, why did the classroom feel larger and more unsafe than later in your school years? How did it feel to have to make new friends? Perhaps there was a new routine, and you can recall your teacher calling out the register for the first time? Your memory for emotion-laden events such as these, which trigger key emotions of anxiety and even excitement, holds a special status. This is why these episodes can be recalled with apparent ease. Emotional memories are easier to bring to mind than neutral ones. It is easier to remember your feelings when you received your exam results, than what you ate for dinner this time last week. One explanation for this is in the neuronal mechanisms underpinning emotional memory. Emotional events hold a privileged status in memory, partly because of the brain structures involved in their encoding. These lie deep within the centre of the brain, in the limbic system. The structures here are the thalamus, acting as a gatekeeper for messages passed between the spinal cord and the cerebral hemispheres; the hypothalamus, regulating the body's motivational systems; and most importantly for memory consolidation, the hippocampus, which sends memories to be stored in appropriate sections of the cerebrum, later recalling them when needed. This process is modulated by a small, almond-shaped part of brain, named the amygdala.

The amygdala modulates memory-storage processes and is responsible for the processing of negative emotions mostly involving fear, disgust and sadness. Cahill and McGaugh (1996) found that during periods of emotional arousal, stress-hormone systems interact with the amygdala to modulate memory-storage processes as they occur in other brain regions. As the hippocampus and the amygdala lie adjacent in the brain, emotional memory becomes more salient than neutral memory. Memory is generally enhanced for emotionally important events, and emotion may either enhance or impair memory, sometimes even creating a combination of both (known as "hotspots"). A number of brain scanning studies have found that the amygdala modulates memory-storage processes occurring in the hippocampus, caudate and other brain structures involved in memory. Indeed, Cahill and McGaugh (1996), using positron emission tomography (PET) scans, found that amygdala activity while watching segments of emotional films predicted long-term memory compared with presentation of neutral film clips.

In a more positive environment, emotional memory impacts upon the rate of information learned. Students presented with emotionally reactive material in their classroom learning will attend to the information and subsequently grow in mind-set. This is the idea that with practice, neural networks grow new connections, strengthen existing ones and build insulation that speeds transmission of impulses, rather than remaining passive in information processing. Methods such as "flipped learning" work in the classroom by keeping students engaged and attentive. Students who are required to put effort into an exercise in preparation for class are more likely to invest emotion into that material. This makes it easier to learn and can promote social interactions and a heightened sense of belonging in the class-room. Affiliation with others has been demonstrated to reduce stress and cortisol levels (Rofé, 1984), so in such instances it is possible to use emotional memory to the advantage of the learning child.

There was a great deal of variation in the descriptions of the chimpanzee "classrooms". Fouts explains how "The Gardners decided to teach Washoe ASL signs as if they were teaching a rat to press a lever by using an operant conditioning technique called shaping. The experimenter shapes the rat's movement by using rewards to lead the rat closer and closer to the food lever. According to Skinner, parents shape a child's babbling into words when they reinforce word-like sounds with smiles and nods of approval" (p. 73). There was, at least, some positive emotional expression associated with Washoe's learning with the Gardners. They waited until Washoe made a sign resembling an ASL sign and then shaped the gesture by rewarding her until the gesture became the sign itself. Washoe would be encouraged to repeat signs by being tickled, which was one of her favourite rewards. When she stopped the sign, they would stop the reward. Then in order to encourage Washoe to use the sign in its appropriate context, they would either prompt her by making the sign themselves, always rewarding her with tickles, and then by introducing that word into games or activities. However, reward- or emotion-based learning were not the only ways in which Washoe was picking up signs. Fouts explains how she also learned through observation. He claims that he and his wife used only sign language around her, so she was able to imitate. According to Fouts (p. 75), signs did not always need an explicit demonstration. For instance, they could simply point to a car and sign THIS CAR, and she would learn. He also explains how one day, a companion of Washoe's called Naomi was searching for matches, and when she couldn't find any, Washoe, who was following Naomi, explained by holding up an empty box of matches, and signing SMOKE, which she must have learned by watching humans asking each other in signs for cigarettes and matches.

While Fouts's descriptions of the learning environment sound enriched and stimulating, one researcher, Chris O'Sullivan, describes it on the contrary in Elizabeth Hess's book, *Nim Chimpsky: The Chimp Who Would be Human* (p. 219). "O'Sullivan . . . was also troubled by the way Fouts worked with the chimps . . . She had assumed that the learning at the farm would be more integrated into the chimps' whole social experience, rather than confined to discrete training sessions". This was because her assumptions had been based on a video which Fouts showed recruits, demonstrating him working with uncaged chimps in outdoor environments and on a nearby island. Hess describes how, "When she arrived in Oklahoma, O'Sullivan soon learned that only a few social groups of adolescents made it out to the island during warm weather, while most of the chimps lived in crowded cages that they rarely left." She became increasingly disillusioned and was not sure that this was a humane way of teaching: "If the chimps were so intelligent and social, what were they doing locked up behind bars?"

Motivation: The Yerkes-Dodson Law

Not all motivation is biologically driven. The concept of positive stress can be demonstrated through the Yerkes-Dodson law. The same Yerkes involved with the initial chimpanzee work in the US was involved in research with Dodson, which produced a law (Yerkes & Dodson, 1908), presenting a relationship between performance and arousal. The law can be explained with the example of the anxiety felt under exam conditions. When taking a test or exam, the increases in arousal levels help a student's performance, motivating the student to work harder and stay focussed. However, too much arousal is detrimental to performance and can cause anxiety and panic, and too little can cause the individual to become bored. Both impair concentration, making it harder to be productive. The law proposes that increased stress and arousal can help improve performance but only up to a certain point. When arousal becomes excessive, performance diminishes. The amount of arousal is a window of capacity within which to work. The law predicts an inverted U-shaped function between arousal and performance (see Figure 3.5). Too much or too little arousal works against the learner, and there are optimal levels based on difficulty of task and endurance of the learner. Levels of arousal are lower for difficult tasks which require the learners to concentrate on the material, and higher on tasks which require endurance, because learners need more motivation to persist.

Another influential factor is the interaction between the environment and brain differences in cortical arousal. This is directly linked to the personality trait of extraversion (versus introversion). Extraverts are outgoing, sociable and energetic individuals who enjoy loud, gregarious events, sensation-seeking situations such as

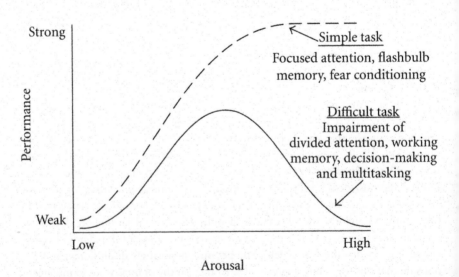

FIGURE 3.5 Yerkes-Dodson Law.

dangerous sports, and opportunities for sensory stimulation. By contrast, introverts are reserved and solitary, and prefer quiet events and situations requiring focus and attention. Extraverts have lower baseline levels of arousal and so are more suscepti- ble to disruption of attention, as they tend to be more distractible in their search to increase arousal. Introverts, instead, already holding high levels of arousal, are more likely to concentrate on material and are less likely to be distracted.

Do chimpanzees have different personality traits? Why would we expect them not to, given that they share 97% to 98% of our DNA? There was certainly a range of individual differences in the Oklahoma chimpanzees, in terms of the personal- ity trait of extraversion. Nim was gregarious and enjoyed being social. According to *Project Nim*, he liked fast cars, smoking and alcohol. These behaviours suggest lower levels of cortical arousal, and the opportunity taken by him to raise the levels of arousal externally, in the form of sensation-seeking activity. Washoe, by contrast, and according to the descriptions in Fouts's book, seems more engaged in solitary activity which requires focus: "After we had eaten our breakfast, I would clean up the kitchen while Washoe washed her dolls in the dishpan or played with wooden blocks, stacking them into higher and higher towers . . . Sometimes she would just sit there sewing . . . she would go about her random stitching with complete con- centration for twenty or thirty minutes at a time" (p. 33). She does not appear to be much of a sensation-seeker: "she could sit quietly for hours studying the hardware and wielding the tool" (p. 33), "and she enjoyed reading – always the sign of an introvert" (Fouts & Mills, 1998).

Another way of conceptualising motivation is as intrinsic and extrinsic theories. Extrinsic motivation takes place when we are motivated to perform a behaviour in order to gain a reward or to avoid a punishment, such as studying in order to achieve a good grade. Students might find the act of studying punishing, but the extrinsic motivation and desire of the good mark or qualification keeps them going and encourages performance. In intrinsic motivation, instead, an individual engages in a behaviour for interest and personal satisfaction rather than for any external reward. An example of this might be undertaking some form of art for the sake of personal pleasure rather than for money or recognition.

The two types of motivation differ in their effectiveness at driving behaviour. External rewards for a behaviour that is already established as internal and reward- ing can lead to a reduction in intrinsic behaviour. Lepper et al. (1973) found that nursery school children who were rewarded for playing with a toy that they had already been interested in playing with, became less motivated to play after being externally rewarded with a sticker. The expectation of a reward made people less interested in taking part in an activity which had been intrinsically interesting prior to the experiment. On the other hand, extrinsic motivation can also be beneficial as it encourages interest and participation in activities, makes expectations explicit, acts as reinforcement when progress is tracked and developed, and motivates indi- viduals to an initial encounter with a skill, after which they may become more intrinsically motivated.

It is interesting that this same motivational process was recognised in primates, long before the language studies had started on them. Desmond Morris, the zoologist, observed in his book, *The Biology of Art* (Morris, 1962), how the chimpanzee, Congo, at London Zoo, would demonstrate various behaviours during painting and drawing experiments. These included a degree of intense focus on the paper and on his markings, an aversion to being interrupted, and finding his drawing or painting to be a rewarding activity in itself without any connection to outside positive reinforcement. Congo treated painting as a special kind of activity that held a different value for him than regular play or roughhousing. He demonstrated a resistance to any direct positive reinforcement used to make him paint. Congo is described as being similar to another chimpanzee who was once subjected to bribery with a food reward to encourage him to draw more intensely. He quickly learned to associate drawing with getting the reward but as soon as this condition had been established, he took less and less interest in the lines he was drawing. Morris explains that "Any old scribble would do and then he would immediately hold out his hand for the reward. The careful attention he had paid previously to design, rhythm, balance, and composition was gone and the worst kind of commercial art was born!" The Oklahoma chimpanzees enjoyed painting. Nim would do so with no reward. Figure 3.6 shows Moja's painting of a cat. When these two chimps were asked what they had painted, Moja signed CAT, and Nim signed BIRD.

FIGURE 3.6 Moja's picture of a cat.

In discussion with Morris, he made the following statement about the chimpanzee, Congo:

> Regarding my research with the chimpanzee Congo at the London Zoo in the 1950s, I have a conflict. When I made my studies of chimpanzee painting and drawing, over sixty years ago, we knew little or nothing about the social lives of chimps in the wild. My wife's assistant in the Zoo TV Unit, a young girl called Jane Goodall, was yet to carry out her ground-breaking studies in the wild. In later years, looking back, I was horrified by how everyone (including myself) had been treating captive chimps before Jane's results became known to us.
>
> When I was doing my doctorate with Niko Tinbergen in Oxford, he had taught me that, when studying animal behaviour, we must always attempt to recreate as natural an environment as we can for a captive animal, and we did our best to do this with Congo, trying to give him a natural "family" and learning to speak chimp as fluently as possible. I communicated with him using chimpanzee sounds and, even today, could express – in chimp – the subtle different between, for example, 'hallo', 'the food is coming', and 'the food is good' (roughly: oooh-oooh-oooh, ooaah-ooaah-ooaah, and aaah-aaah-aaah).
>
> But despite our efforts to behave like chimps with him, we did, of course, fall far short of what was needed and I would never again repeat such research. As a good ethologist, I would only watch what wild chimps do and never interfere with their social lives. But this deeply felt change of attitude creates a dilemma for me, because, if I had not had that very close pseudo-parental relationship with Congo, I would never have been able to write 'The Biology of Art' and uniquely investigate the roots of human art.
>
> So – Congo gave me so much – but I would never repeat that work. I hope you understand my conflict.

Personality Traits

Decades of research have converged on the existence of three (Eysenck, 1952, 1967; Eysenck & Eysenck 1992) or five (Costa & McCrae, 1992; Goldberg, 1992, 1993) personality traits. Each of these traits is bipolar, meaning that it has two extreme poles – for example extraversion is on the extreme end, with introversion at the other. Individuals differ with where they cluster around those two, with (for that trait) most people clustering around the centre. The three/five personality traits are extraversion, neuroticism and psychoticism (Eysenck); and extraversion, neuroticism, openness to experience, conscientiousness and agreeableness ("Big Five" models). The general consensus is that traits are hardwired and inherited, and also subject to environmental adaptation and behavioural learning.

Personality traits play a key role in response to stress, and consequently, to engagement in the environment: in family life, in the classroom, and later on in the workplace. The personality trait most related to stress is neuroticism. An individual who is high in neuroticism is tense, edgy and highly strung; worries excessively; and experiences rapid mood changes. Neurotics are unable to inhibit emotional reactions and experience negative affect when confronted with relatively minor stressors. As a result, neurotic individuals appear easily nervous or upset, whereas low neurotics are more "emotionally stable" and experience negative mood in the face of major stressors only. It is important here to explain that a "low neurotic" still has *some* level of neuroticism, but to be deemed low is to register on a certain level against existing norms (Eysenck, 1952, 1967; Eysenck & Eysenck, 1992; Costa & McCrae, 1992; Goldberg, 1993). As they are able to remain calm as they possess emotional control, low neurotics bounce back quickly from emotional upsets.

From the cortisol and stress studies, the question is whether increased cortisol differences seen in stressed individuals with depression are due to *state*, where they are short-lived, transient and as a result of temporary change, or whether they are due to *trait* and are long-lived, hardwired and enduring Salivary cortisol increases found in acutely depressed patients after wakening hint at this being a trait factor. Cortisol is higher in patients who have recovered from depression compared with healthy volunteers, but *crucially*, it is also abnormally high in individuals who have no personal history of depression and who are at increased risk of anxiety and stress either through having high neuroticism scores, or a parental history of depression (Bhagwagar et al., 2003; Portella et al., 2005).

In an ideal world, schools would find some way of paying special consideration to those children whose parents have a history of psychological disorders, since such students may be subject to environments where behaviours and rules are eccentric. For example, where one or both parents are on the autistic spectrum, children may present both with the underlying trait for the condition and also with the state, in terms of having learned social behaviours consistent with "being aspergated". However, this would be hugely problematic to measure, for ethical reasons; indeed, it would be impossible to do. For these individuals, the quality of the environmental background of school during childhood years, and of work and social environments in adulthood, play a particular and crucial role in development of social processing. For such children the provision of school as a place for socialising and having named caregivers in teachers is particularly important, and in adults, healthy group membership and social environment are vital for models of behaviours. This would have also been the case for the chimpanzees, who would have needed particularly clear boundaries, given their difficult childhood histories. For Nim, this came in his teacher, Joyce Butler, with whom he had a particularly strong bond. Hess explains how "Young male chimps, not unlike some human males, require an alpha female to organise their lives. Butler ruled Nim" (Hess, 2008, p. 135). Nim knew that when he was in a room with Joyce, she was the dominant person, taking on an enduring sense of responsibility for his welfare. Joyce made sure that both the other staff and Nim understood the rules around his care. The result of this was a reciprocated affection which resulted in Nim being calmer in Joyce's presence, more willing to work, and clearly more fluent with his signs.

The cortisol findings suggest that although some abnormalities in the HPA axis resolve with recovery from psychological illness like depression, others are persistent and present even before onset of illness. This provides further evidence that impairments to the stress system are a vulnerability factor for psychological disorders like depression (Bhagwagar et al., 2003). Furthermore, research studies have demonstrated that increases in salivary cortisol can predict future depressive episodes in adults, *and also* in adolescents (Goodyer et al., 2000; Harris et al., 2000). Saliva samples taken from twins show that waking salivary cortisol is heritable, suggesting a genetic predisposition to some of these vulnerabilities in stress. Taken together, the evidence suggests that HPA axis abnormalities are partly genetic but that they are exacerbated by early adverse experiences. Studies on maternal separation in monkeys demonstrate how this leads to abnormalities in cortisol persisting into adult life (Pariante & Lightman, 2008). Children with mothers with postnatal depression show increased secretion of cortisol, suggesting that disturbances in early attachment, along with maternal depression, can lead to abnormal development of the brain's stress system (Halligan et al., 2004), a nervous system which is wired to seek familiarity. In terms of attachment experiences, the child grows up to become wired to seek familiarity within romantic relationships as well. Since we are conditioned to cope with predictability (or, if there has been abuse when growing up, a lack of predictability), we end up stuck in a corresponding state of arousal. Each of us falls under one of the following categories of attachment styles: secure, anxious, avoidant or disorganised. The latter is a recurrent pattern among people with a history of complex trauma. This explains why many of such individuals end up in repeatedly abusive or emotionally unavailable relationships, where the difficulty of abuse or neglect endured in the childhood experience is mistaken for love and affection. Alain de Botton (2006), the philosopher, explains how: "We think we're out to find partners who will make us happy, but we're not. We're out to find partners who will feel familiar". Some individuals reject the types of kind, loving partners and instead accept emotionally unavailable and avoidant ones, because in partner selection, we are not in a quest to be happy, but in a quest to find a partner who is *familiar* to us.

Self-efficacy

Self-efficacy refers to the set of beliefs we hold about our ability to complete a particular task. Bandura explains how the development and exercise of self-efficacy begin in infancy and continue throughout a lifetime (Bandura, 1994). Initial efficacy experiences are primarily centred on the family, and transfer to peers over time. An example of social cognitive development is in the parent who is responsive to their infant's behaviour. The parent cultivates opportunities for exploration through an enriched and free environment, accelerating the infant's social and cognitive development (Bandura, 1994). It is also influenced at peer level through social comparisons which widen a child's developing knowledge of their own capabilities. School is another agent for cognitive self-efficacy. The way in which the institution and teachers operate influences the child's development greatly. The culture created by a school affects the development of intellectual self-efficacy and cooperative learning structures through the practice of teamwork, which promotes positive self-evaluations of capability and higher academic attainments, rather than individualistic or competitive ones.

In adolescence, growing independence opens the opportunity for experiences without structure, and risky behaviours. Backgrounds that have developed one's self-efficacy greatly determine how one can cope with new experiences. For career development in early adulthood, level of occupational functioning is determined by the degree of developing coping capabilities, motivation and thought processes. If these are fully developed, there is an increased perceived self-regulatory efficacy, allowing the individual to become resilient and cope effectively with job requirements and adjustments.

Later on in aging, intellectual capabilities influence a person's perception of self-efficacy. For example, if an elder understands that they are losing their concept of time and memory, they are less likely to exert effort into recalling previous experiences, which results in a more progressive decline in memory than in those who do not have memory decline. Overall, perceived self-efficacy and its ability to determine behaviour, as Bandura explained, occurs over a lifetime and is influenced by external and internal factors. Vulnerability to success or failure is thus indicated through adequate development of personal self-efficacy.

One of the most important factors in human development and existence is the connection to another human being. The significance of this connection has been grossly underestimated. The capacity to be present with, and to understand, another being and to accept them unconditionally is fundamental to human existence. If a human grew up in a home where a parent was emotionally disconnected – say as a result of alcohol abuse, or as a consequence of their own neglectful and abusive history – there will be much anxiety and fear, say, of parental anger. This was no different for the Oklahoma chimpanzees. The importance of connection to a caregiver was grossly underestimated, with a range of different caregivers of varying levels of commitment to the research being brought in. Each caregiver entered the project with their own complicated network of histories, and most of them were also very young and naïve with regards to the needs of a chimpanzee. Gabor Maté (Maté & Maté, 2022) explains how in the US and Canada, the multitude of childhood developmental disorders and physical and mental illnesses such as attention deficit-hyperactivity disorder (ADHD) and addiction are regulated with Ritalin, antipsychotics or immunosuppressants, to treat the behaviours, particularly in childhood. Maté's approach is to look deeply in therapy, in order to gain understanding and solutions, and to consider the *source* of these problems. Maté explains that in mental illness such as anxiety, depression, PTSD and other illnesses like cancer and rheumatoid arthritis, there is a tendency to look at the impact of childhood stress on the individual. That stress happens in a social context. The conceptual separation of mind from body neglects the understanding of the physical manifestations of these lifelong emotional patterns of early stressors that result in disease. If the individual can change their relationship with their emotions and how they respond to stress, they can significantly affect the course of illness in a positive way.

Despite an abundance of evidence, this idea that the individual's relationship with their emotions is key to health and wellbeing is ignored, and it was certainly ignored in the chimpanzee studies. If a 2-year-old human child becomes frustrated and angry with their parent, and the parent shows rage as a response, the child becomes terrified and anxious of anger, and learns that "being good" means not expressing anger. The child starts to believe that little children who get angry do not get loved, and adapts by repressing anger, maintaining the relationship with their parents by self-repression in this way. This is because the fundamental human dynamic in life is about attachment and connection to another human being. Infants are helpless, and without this attachment relationship, we do not function well, or even survive. We have evolved as a species of attachment. Indeed, "love" is the common word for attachment – for being held. The same is true of chimpanzees.

Even parents who abuse their children love them. They do not know *how* to love them, because they are acting out their own childhood programming, and are working with a limited set of emotional tools. Ideally, to love is to demonstrate the emotional capacity to be present with, to understand and see the other human being for what they are, and to accept them and invite them unconditionally to be in the other's presence. Parents who are dealing with their childhood issues as adults may be incapable of loving their children in this way. When children do not receive the "unconditional positive regard" which is the unconditional invitation to be in the other's presence (Rogers, 1957), they have to adapt to it in order to have the attachment relationship in order to survive. Without attachment, survival is difficult. If the child receives the message that they are not invited to be in this presence, the child will hold off demonstrating their anger or frustration and will repress it. This is not a conscious behaviour but an automatic brain mechanism for survival. When anger is repressed, the immune system is also repressed, and then fails to function, or turns against the individual in the form of autoimmune illness. An emotional loss translates into biology, since emotion and the underpinning neurophysiology are inseparable. That which happens on an emotional plane inevitably has its manifestations on the biological plane.

If this is difficult enough in humans, imagine how it was for the chimpanzees. Not only was it difficult for the chimpanzees because of their early childhood backgrounds, such as jungles in Africa, Air Force bases, or lives as pets, but also because of the emotional difficulties that the researchers themselves were experiencing. Laboratory research can be intense, and the chimpanzees needed looking after day and night, which meant spending a lot of time with one another, at an age where one was making sense of interpersonal relationships, emotional processing and romantic relationships. Boundaries were not always clear, and there were issues within the "family" of the investigators and laboratory members.

Robert says:

I got divorced in 1979 from my first wife Gail, which created the need for me to live somewhere else, and I had to have an in-between place until I could find a long-term solution. My friend Ron was living with this guy named David Autry. I knew Dave but not well, and so when I got divorced I moved in with them. It worked out well and we would hang out and talk about whatever we were into. For me and Ron it was chimps so Dave heard a fair amount about chimps. Ron and I got permission to take him, and so Ron and I talked Dave into coming out with us to the IPS, AKA the 'chimpanzee farm'. Dave was tall and slender, 6 ft 2, with a beard and long curly hair and glasses. It was before Herb came back to visit Nim after he was dropped off in September 1977, and we used David as our naïve human who didn't know any sign language. Dave had never been exposed to any ASL at all. We said to him, "We want you to learn sign language from Nim, or what you can, while we go on walks and simply hang out". He was good with Nim, and it was soon clear to Ron and to me that Dave was in no danger and he could cut it, and so we allowed Nim and Dave to hang close and see where it went. And he had it, he was good with chimpanzees, he had us as examples to help him. Ron was good and I was good, and Dave became good. Good examples in most areas in life are a healthy way to learn anything. That was true with being around chimps. You had to be willing to learn. Most people could learn, if they had the right guidance and enough time. Most folks use a certain amount of intimidation, like height and weight, their size, to help them deal with aggressive situations that can arise while outside the cage with a chimp. The older the chimp, generally the harder it is to get into that space. Nim came to us when he was under 5. He was 4 years and 2 months. By then only a few of the New York people, including Joyce, could handle Nim. Many of the others got bitten, as is reported in *Project Nim*, and in the various books.

We considered each chimp was considered one of us. I used a different method, a more subtle means, since I am not a big person, and so the use of size and intimidation was not something that worked for me. I never attempted to be that. I describe my method as the "You just don't want me to be disappointed" method. This worked for me most of the time, but not always, and when it didn't, I used the "time out" method and would do things like stop and tie the lead around a tree, and wait for things to calm down. I did that many times with Onan, Nim's brother, who could be testy when he wanted to be, and who was really big. Onan would get frustrated, so you had to recognise that state before it went too far, and you had to try and change the subject, such as by using a loud chimp alarm "waaaa!" bark to distract the chimp, who then would be alarmed, and who would then seek reassurance from me.

In that period of time, Dave started coming to the graduate meetings, hanging out with chimpanzees at the IPS, going on walks with a host of chimps and helping grad students. He was becoming part of the "IPS chimp people", as we were called by fellow students. When Washoe gave birth to Sequoyah, Dave was around. Ron had started a new relationship and had moved out. So Dave and I were living together, and so we would do late-night shifts from 11 pm until 6 in the morning at the IPS, watching and observing Washoe and Sequoyah from behind a makeshift blind, which was part of the "science". That did not fool Washoe for one second. We wrote in the diary, making notes about what happened during the shift. I was a grad student, he was an undergraduate, and we had other student volunteers to come out and help us. It was difficult to do this by ourselves, so sometimes we would have one or two other people come and meet us. We would go out there and it was about a 6 mile drive from his house to the chimpanzee farm.

There was already huge tension between Lemmon and Roger, for a lot of reasons, right from the start of their relationship. When I arrived in 1975, it was pretty much a full blown war. Mostly, I think they just did not like each other, and were unable or unwilling to get past that. Plus disagreements about business, and costs of cages, and issues like that. I think the blame for that can be equally distributed between them both. After Washoe had her baby, we would sometimes be in tears on that drive out, worried that she was going to take the baby and abuse him in front of us, and worried we might have to take him away, or worse. One night my decision was to smoke weed with Washoe, because I thought she was going to kill the baby, and I think that if I had not intervened in that way, she could have killed him. In the next meeting, the week when I reported what had happened in the diary, Roger was questioning what we were doing. First, I was surprised, since generally speaking, he never looked at the diary. If he had done, he would have seen the pattern of abuse that was happening right before our eyes, and written in the diary or in the project notes. I tried to explain to Roger that without that distraction, the outcome could have been tragic. We had a major disagreement about the chimpanzees, and how to deal with behaviours that put the infant at severe risk. It was all in the diary, clearly abusive behaviours from her onto him, while she looked at us and signed GIVE ME followed by X or Y. It was nerve-racking, and it was extremely stressful. I already perceived that what was going on was fucked up. No-one was actually reading the diary except, of course, the part where it said that "Bob smokes a joint with Washoe". No-one was understanding what was actually happening, or they just ignored it. We needed Washoe to accept her baby. If she didn't, we would have no study. Roger had a lot to lose if she rejected the baby. On the other hand, the baby was being put into a dangerous and life-threatening situation. We didn't talk about it. No plan. Clearly, Washoe did not have the mothering skills required. There was no consideration of what should happen if she started beating the baby. Yet she had already slammed him into the cage, then stopped, and signed GET ME ORANGES, multiple times. There were many incidents of this nature reported in the diary. She meant business. We had isolated Washoe from her friends like Ally, and the other adult chimps she had been living with for a number of years. She was in a weird small cage, where she was prevented from going outside. There was no WALK WITH ROGER, which is really what she wanted. She wanted to be OUT and continuously signed KEY OUT, WALK THERE, HURRY, ROGER, ROGER. There was never a time when the baby was a status raiser, as it would be in the wild. In a chimp group, the baby would have raised her status in her group from which she would have learned, but in the situation she was in, here in the cage all the time, she did not get that benefit and that was a massive problem. Her behaviour toward the baby was becoming more and more abusive. The baby became her display object.

By then Washoe had transformed from the daughter of the Gardners in their "cross-fostering" study to an adult chimpanzee. When she came to Oklahoma, she eventually lived in a group of 20-something chimpanzees, and she got along well in the chimpanzee house with her new chimpanzee friends. It took her a little while, but by 1975 she had had years of experience with other chimps, and I think she realised that she was, indeed, a chimp herself, in spite of the fact that when she first encountered chimps at the IPS in 1969 she called them BLACK BUGS. She could hold her own as a chimpanzee. This is one of the things that was missed. Washoe had evolved after the Gardners. Before she gave birth to Sequoyah, she had already had a couple of babies in the chimp house, with the other chimps surrounding her. This time, she was isolated from chimps and from humans. Dave and I would drive home after a shift with Washoe and Sequoyah, and we would look at each other and I would say – "goddamn it, I hope she doesn't kill her baby. Will she kill her baby tomorrow?" It was very difficult to watch because I knew Lemmon was right. The baby needed to be pulled away permanently. Sequoyah was not thriving, and it appeared to some of us that he would die if he stayed in with her.

The baby, Sequoyah did end up dying. Roger said he took him to the hospital. Sequoyah was taken to a human hospital, and not a veterinary hospital. I read that in his book, years after the events, and I know what did and what didn't happen. Not long after that, Roger decided he wanted to move from the IPS and the University of Oklahoma, and he invited me. I thought I would go, until right until the end, and then I told him I wasn't going and that I wanted to stay with the remaining chimpanzees.

When Sequoyah was born, several of us were present, including Lemmon. Shortly after she gave birth, Washoe put Sequoyah on the floor, and Lemmon advised that she was not going to mother, and that Sequoyah should be removed for his safety. Ultimately, that would not work for Roger or his grant, and the money associated with that. Roger hatched another plan, which was to take Sequoyah away, and to then put him back with Washoe as quickly as we could. His decision. Lemmon gave him advice about the safety of both infant and mother, which was based on his years of successfully having raised many chimp babies from many chimp mothers. About ten days from then, maybe two weeks after the birth, we did place Sequoyah back with Washoe, in her cage in the pig barn. Sequoyah was born in the main lab building in a special birthing cage not accessible to the other chimps, with the adult group adjacent to the birth, so those other chimps were able to see what was going on. When Washoe did kill the baby with the toothbrush, Roger placed the blame on Lemmon, which completely ignored the reality of the situation. That led to Roger breaking away completely from the IPS, and moving his operation, consisting of Washoe and Loulis, to a building on the South Base in Building #31 at the University of Oklahoma, a portion of campus that was formerly a navy base which Roger had procured as his new base of operations; the "Fouts Lab". We were there for around two years, joined by Ally, temporarily, before Lemmon insisted that he was returned to him, and then Moja was moved to us from the Gardners. Building #31 was a harder place to take the chimps out than the other part of the campus, as we had to avoid pedestrians, and it was an open area. We would take them 400 yards south of Building #31, where there was a wood near Highway 9 with a water tower there. The cage that was installed in this new facility was the same cage from the IPS. Roger was also upset about that, as Lemmon had apparently built a cage that Roger was not satisfied with. Roger suggested that the cage was a factor in the death of Sequoyah. The real reason why Sequoyah died was because Washoe stuck a toothbrush almost all the way down into Sequoyah's throat. That was the cause of the pneumonia which killed him. He died at the home of Roger the day after he was found with the toothbrush protruding from his mouth.

Once Roger moved to his new location, things got better for him, at least for a while. He had managed to procure a weaned infant a bit older than Sequoyah from the Regional Primate Center at Yerkes, in Atlanta. It is not clear if this was a gift, or whether money was exchanged for the infant, who was named Loulis. We had settled in at the new facility and Lemmon was no longer as big an issue for Roger, now that he had physically split from Lemmon and from the IPS. I continued to have a relationship with the IPS and continued to work with the 25–35 chimps that remained there. Things were going well. We even had famous visitors like the Kenyan paleoanthropologist Sir Richard Leakey, son of Louis Leakey, at the "Fouts Lab". They came to film Washoe and Roger for a segment of the *Making of Mankind* programme. However, dark clouds were on the horizon, and one day not long after Leakey had visited, another well known scientist came to come visit and to pay his respects to Washoe and Roger. He was Karl Pribram, a prominent neurology researcher at Stanford University. That day did not go well.

Dr. Pribram was visiting us because he was the mentor for Penny Patterson and Koko, and her major advisor for her PhD. Unfortunately, while feeding strawberries to Washoe, she grabbed his hand and pulled it into the cage and bit him badly, so badly that he had parts of several fingers removed because they were so badly damaged. This incident was downplayed, but the reality was that this was the moment that Roger knew his days at OU were over.

Roger took steps to find another position, and ended up at the Central Washington University (CWU) in Ellensburg. This was a small school where Roger could star, along with the signing chimps, Washoe, Moja and Loulis. Here, he was given the 3rd floor of the Psychology Department, which he persuaded the senior grad students that it was a salubrious place for the chimps. The truth was that the cages were cramped with little chutes between them, and it was a big hassle because it was on the 3rd floor. The chimps could not be taken out easily. Indeed, some of them never got to touch the grass again.

Once Roger made the decision that he was leaving from the University of Oklahoma to CWU, I told him that I had made the decision to stay, and that he should take Dave Autry and his girlfriend, Nancy Thompson. Nancy was 18 or 19 back then, and an undergraduate. Roger was not proficient in writing, and so he needed at least one graduate student to help him with that. He chose Alan Hirsh – his new graduate student from New York – to write for him.

They pulled out late at night on the night they were leaving. I knew they were leaving that night, because Dave and I were friends. Dave could handle Moja, and Roger could handle Washoe. They drove from Oklahoma to California. Nancy and Debbi stayed behind in Oklahoma to clear things up, and then followed Roger to Ellensburg, to prepare for the chimps' arrival.

I wanted to stay with Kelly and Ally, and all the other IPS chimps, and I had decided not to go with Roger. I didn't have a plan, but I knew I didn't want to abandon my other chimp friends in favour of just Washoe, Moja, and Loulis. I knew Dave could handle Moja and that they liked each other, and Roger had Washoe, so all would be good. Roger knew that the University of Oklahoma would change its policy on keeping the chimps, now that they had a serious reason to rid themselves of him and the animals. He simply avoided the embarrassment of them telling him that things had to change, which was why he left in the dead of night. Chimpanzees were bad for the university. They had to pay a substantial sum for the lawsuit over the Pribram bite. They chose a strategy that was most protective of the institution, without thinking about the students who were caught up in it. They did as their lawyers suggested, and Roger knew that he could not operate as he had. A few years later, they made that same decision about Lemmon, and de-funded his operation, which led to all the chimps being sold to LEMSIP.

And so Dave and Roger trekked out to California where they stop at this place in Riverside, California, called the Gentle Jungle which was owned by

Toni Helfer. She was part of that Hollywood scene where the chimpanzees were all halfway to sanctuary. [Gentle Jungle, reported Eugene Linden, was a commercial animal-training facility.] When Roger left Oklahoma, he didn't have a fully blown-out plan, he miscalculated how long it would take for the University in Washington to get the place ready. Roger went to California, Debbi went to Washington.

Eugene Linden reported that "when the truck left Norman, Oklahoma, it contained the chimpanzees, Roger, and Ken DeCroo from Gentle Jungle. Roger departed on such short notice that two students who had intended to come along were left behind. Also left behind was Roger's wife, Debbi, who tidied up matters in Oklahoma and then went to Ellensburg to prepare for Roger and the chimpanzees' arrival. Roger and the other refugees from Norman spent a little more than a month at Gentle Jungle before heading north to Ellensburg."

Robert continues,

At some point after they all had finally landed in Washington, there were rumours about Roger having affairs with various women, and this came to a head. It was said that Debbi made various threats against Roger and the kids. I think that was the moment when Dave, Nancy, and Alan realised that they were going back to Oklahoma. When they returned, at first they landed at my house in Norman, where it all had started. The cages in Washington were tiny . . . These chimpanzees (Washoe anyway, not Moja) had lived with many other chimpanzees, and now they were isolated, and I had seen the size of the cages they were living in, in photographs. Roger knew that I was saying that everything with the chimps in his care in Washington was not as it should be. In fact, the chimps had had it much better in Oklahoma, despite Roger proclaiming that that was like escaping from hell. Perhaps for him it was, but not for the chimps. In the few times that I encountered him at conferences or talks, he attempted to avoid contact. I was more than willing to keep my distance. Dr. Shirley McGreal once tried to get us to talk, or at least to shake hands, but I wanted no part in his lie.

I continued to speak up for the chimps after Roger left. I did manage to get Lemmon to agree to become my advisor on my work, which meant that I could continue to see Nim and all the other chimps almost every day. That is, until the University decided that chimps were not to their advantage, that they could not take the associated risks, and then de-funded Lemmon. Lemmon had to sell the chimps, which he did to LEMSIP. This part of the story is told in the film, *Project Nim*. I didn't get a PhD out of this work, but I stood up for Nim. Where was Roger for Washoe? He was in Washington, having her appear in beer commercials! That's the one thing in my whole life that I did right. I kept my promise that I would do something right in my life, when I was 19 years old, and when I was on my death bed those years ago, after my motorcycle accident that I had in the Air Force.

It was bad in Washington, Dave told me recently, he hated it there. Debbi told him straight up, "You can't take Moja out". He said, "no way, she's in a cage in the Psychology Department, and there's no way you can tell us". He went out with Kelly and me. He was a righteous man, and he came back here to Oklahoma. Fouts and his wife terrorised those chimps without thinking about it. These were very close to abusive behaviours. They didn't prepare, they didn't have a plan, or a place to go. When they did, it was in these tiny cages connected together in the Psychology Department. Completely unacceptable.

It broke Dave's heart, because there was another chimpanzee, a chimpanzee called Dar [named after Dar es Salaam, the capital of Tanzania, and acquired as an infant from Holloman Air Force Base in 1976], and they had to leave Dar and Moja. All that ended up being really traumatic. There is all this interpersonal stuff that goes along with the project stuff because we thought we were cutting edge. We thought we were a long way ahead of the zoo world. We were emotionally connected to those chimps.

There has been much work on humans on these themes. Judith Herman was one of the first clinicians to write about the understanding of trauma and its victims. She distinguished between single-incident traumas involving one-off events and complex or repeated traumas. This persistent type can lead to complex PTSD (c-PTSD) which is the syndrome that follows from this prolonged suffering. It is not in the *DSM-5* (American Psychiatric Association, 2013), but the notion of complex trauma has been proven useful in clinical practice. The recently revised International Classification of Diseases, 11th Revision (ICD-11) now includes that diagnosis for the first time (WHO, 2022; Cloitre, 2020). Researchers have proposed the addition of a Developmental Trauma Disorder (child version of Complex PTSD). Developmental trauma refers to stressful events that occur repeatedly and cumulatively over a period of time and within specific relationships and contexts (Courtois, 2004; Sar, 2011). This is a form of chronic traumatisation arising from sexual, emotional and physical abuse in childhood and physical and emotional neglect. Families with mood and emotional dysfunction can also be traumatising towards their offspring (Ozturk & Sar, 2005).

There is no doubt that chimpanzees like Washoe, Dar and Moja had these vulnerability factors imposed upon them. As Robert identified, the fact there were also interpersonal complications between the researchers was a crucial point as it added to the neglect and gaps in wellbeing for those chimpanzees. Each of those researchers brought their own traumatic experiences and ideas about wellbeing and upbringing to the chimpanzees' care. Most of them were young and indeed some were even grasping for a sense of identity and belonging; Robert says, "I just knew I was a chimp. I knew it. And I . . . it was like . . . my people . . . you know, family . . . whatever. Maybe I was looking for something."

Caregiver Bonds and Language Learning

Psychological studies have emphasised the importance of parental bonding in language learning. Infants are not blank slates to be passed around caregivers. Newborn babies recognise their mother's voices and smells. They have an intimacy of connection that cannot be replicated by another parent, no matter how loving. A newborn forms an attachment with his/her parent (usually mother) formed around emotional security and against abandonment. A child removed from its mother will suffer issues around abandonment that are pre-verbal, and that no amount of love, reassurance or rationalisation will heal. The sort of chimpanzee surrogacy demonstrated would create developmental trauma. Furthermore, babies are born with the capacity to choose their own language over a different language. Two-day-old infants whose mothers were monolingual speakers of Spanish or English were tested with audio recordings of female strangers speaking either Spanish or English, and when tested through infant sucking which controlled the presentation of auditory stimuli, these infants activated recordings of their native language for longer periods than the foreign language (Moon et al., 1993). Newborns can also recognise the sound of a familiar voice (DeCasper & Fifer, 1980; Fifer & Moon, 1989), story (DeCasper & Spence, 1986) and melody (Cooper & Aslin, 1989). English-speaking 2-month-olds were also able to discriminate English from Italian (Mehler et al., 1988), and there are similar findings in French, and it even occurs in utero. The key is that familiarity with one of the languages is necessary for discrimination.

These studies demonstrate the innateness of language in the human brain, but Moon et al. (1993) make further important points. Aside from language being a specifically human function which has demonstrated neurobiological adaptations associated with communication in these other primates, as an evolutionary trend, it is *exposure* to language that is important for its acquisition and culture. The Oklahoma chimpanzees were unique for being highly encultured, through the attempts to teach them human language.

Specific alleles exist for some genes for human language and the brain circuits for language are generally lateralised towards the left hemisphere, but there are suggestions that a crucial factor for human verbal language is in its motivational nature. Moon et al. (1993) propose that aside from genetic, brain and cultural factors, language is promoted by the building of love. They argue that from an evolutionary perspective, language was maintained by hominid women as proto-language during some hundreds of thousands years through the maternal–filial interaction, until the first permanent settlements of the current human species, between 40,000 and 10,000 years ago. They also describe the transmission of speech through symbolic thought, and how it promoted historical artistic displays such as sculptures, painting and music, associated with the expansion of love and speech to the relationship between the sexes and with consequent diversification of languages, especially in the last 10,000 to 5,000 years. Love, they explain, caused and causes human speech in both phylogeny and ontogeny. They believe that for language, an organism's fetal development follows the species' previous evolutionary forms.

As humans, we are born with a certain amount of social understanding about the world. Meltzoff and Moore (1977) demonstrated how infants as young as 12 and 21 days of age can imitate facial and manual gestures. This cannot be explained in terms of either conditioning or innate releasing mechanisms, and Meltzoff and Moore explain how "Such imitation implies that human neonates can equate their own unseen behaviors with gestures they see others perform". Eibl-Eibesfeldt had already demonstrated that children who were deaf and blind through maternal rubella could demonstrate the same facial expressions of joy, sadness and despair as seeing children, despite having not learned about these through situations. Since he filmed the children away from their parents, he excluded the possibility that mothers or other caregivers were influencing them. This was taken as evidence that the emotional system connecting the brain's limbic system with facial muscles does not need informational input from outside, and that it is independent of learning and culture.

In infants, language perception has a similar goal as face perception. Infants' sophisticated abilities to imitate faces and process language from a very young age are explained through specific biologically relevant stimuli and through sophisticated sensory and cognitive mechanisms, which primates may not possess in the same way. In addition, experience with specific faces and speech sounds modifies infants' perception of both. Again, this suggests that the Oklahoma chimpanzees were particularly skilled at communicating and thought processing because of the experiences and enrichment that were presented to them. Moon et al. (2013) demonstrated how babies as young as 7 hours (in this study they were an average of 32.8 hours postnatal, ranging between 7 and 75 hours) showed that the ambient language to which they were exposed in the womb as foetuses affected their perception of their native language at a phonetic level. This was measured shortly after birth by differences in sucking rates in response to familiar compared to unfamiliar vowels. The babies in this study were 40 American and 40 Swedish infants where the maternal native language was either English in the US, or Swedish in Sweden, and where the infant's mother did not speak a second language more than rarely during the final trimester of pregnancy. Half the infants in each country were assigned to hear the Swedish vowel stimuli and half the English vowels, and it was found that infants responded to the unfamiliar, non-native language with higher numbers of average sucks than to their native language. In other words, language experienced in utero affects vowel perception after birth.

Enhanced discriminability at phonetic *boundaries* is common to monkey and man (Kuhl, 1991), although prototype effects are not. For human listeners, speech prototypes play a unique role in speech perception and have a special role in speech perception – they are like "perceptual magnets". A baby's "perceptual magnet" is language-specific by the age of about 6 months. By this age, exposure to a specific language changes the infant's perception, even though the infant may not yet have acquired word meaning and linguistic contrast.

It is unusual that Terrace overlooked the research previously done by Harlow on rhesus monkeys separated from their mothers, prior to his research on Nim. That research in 1958 found that while the behavioural theory of attachment suggested that infants would form attachments with carers who provided food, attachment developed through the mother providing "tactile comfort", suggesting an innate (biological) need to touch and cling for emotional comfort. Harlow and Zimmermann (1958) separated infant monkeys from their mothers immediately after birth. They were placed in cages with two "fake" mothers, both made of wire, but one covered in soft terry towelling cloth. In the first group, the terrycloth mother provided no food, but the wire mother had an attached baby bottle containing milk. Both groups spent more time with the cloth mother, regardless of whether she secreted milk or not. The infant would only return to the wire monkey for milk when it was hungry. The cloth mother was preferred each time. The study is important for supporting the evolutionary theory of attachment, in that it is the physical attachment and security of the caregiver that is more important than the provision of food. Perhaps Terrace set out to make LaFarge the lifelong surrogate mother of Nim, but his ideas about this family's involvement in Nim's care were short-sighted.

Similarly, it is surprising that Fouts did not consult Harlow's literature in the care of Nim, Washoe and the other chimpanzees. In a modification of the original study, Harlow and Zimmermann (1958) separated the infant monkeys into one group with a cloth mother providing no food, and the wire mother who did. Both groups drank equal amounts and grew at the same rate, but in this study the monkeys with the soft, tactile, cloth mothers showed significant behavioural differences compared with the hard wire-mother monkeys. Monkeys raised by either type of mother for more than 90 days were more timid, easily bullied and could not stand up for themselves, had problems mating, did not know how to interact with other monkeys, and perhaps most significantly for Washoe later, the females became inadequate mothers. Monkeys left for fewer than 90 days showed reversal of some of these effects if they were placed in a normal environment where they could re-form attachments.

In further studies of impoverished social engagement/confinement, baby monkeys were left in total social isolation for 3, 6, 12 or 24 months. This was to mimic humans in harsh orphanages, although we could consider in this context the social detachment that the Oklahoma chimpanzees would have experienced. Harlow and colleagues found that "When initially removed from total social isolation . . . they usually go into a state of emotional shock, characterized by . . . autistic self-clutching and rocking. One of six monkeys isolated for 3 months refused to eat after release and died 5 days later. . . . The effects of 6 months of total social isolation were so devastating and debilitating, 12 months of isolation almost obliterated animals socially." In addition, after being reunited, one of the mothers became so neurotic that she smashed her infant's face into the floor and rubbed it back and forth, demonstrating further how damaging privation is to the attachment bond.

Damaged attachment bonds alongside language development can be further examined in humans. In the 1980s in Romania, dictator Nicolae Ceauşescu outlawed abortion and contraception, and commanded women to bear at least five children. He ordered the children to be raised by the state, claiming that they could provide better care than their parents, and as a result, over 150,000 children were abandoned in institutions named orphanages (although many of the children had living parents). After the fall of Ceauşescu in 1989, the plight of these children received attention. Institutions had been understaffed and neglect and abuse were rife. Child development researcher Nathan Fox and colleagues from the University of Maryland studied some of the children longitudinally. The Bucharest Early Intervention Project was the first randomised controlled trial comparing continued institutional care with foster care. In a study investigating variation in neural development as a result of exposure to institutionalisation early in childhood, Sheridan, Fox, Zeanah, McLaughlin and Nelson III (2012) compared 136 children between the ages of 6 and 31 months living in institutions in Bucharest, Romania, who were randomly assigned to a foster care intervention (foster care group, FCG) or to remain in the institution (care-as-usual group, CAUG). The children were followed prospectively. Conditions in orphanages were regimented with the children having to eat, bathe, go to the toilet at the same time, and with little training for caregivers and a poor ratio of caregivers to children. It was found that there were detrimental changes in brain composition of the children who spent their first years in these institutions compared those who were randomly assigned to foster care.

During the children's 8-year-old checkup, magnetic resonance imaging (MRI, brain structure) and electroencephalography (EEG, electrical activity) brain scans were performed. Early institutionalisation changed both the structure and the function of the brain. Time spent in an institution correlated with reduced volume of grey matter (brain cell bodies). Children who stayed in the orphanages instead of going to foster care also had less white matter, which is the fat-covered tracts between brain cell bodies, than children who were fostered by families from a young age. These same children also showed lower-quality brain activity as measured by EEG, and showed differences in social behaviours, which were attributed to a lack of secure bonding to any main caregiver. Indeed, previous research had demonstrated how children of nurturing mothers have hippocampal volumes that are 10% larger than children whose mothers are not as nurturing (Luby et al., 2012). Early maternal support in humans promotes specific gene expression, neurogenesis, adaptive stress responses and larger hippocampal volumes. A relationship has been found between psychosocial factors in early childhood and later amygdala volume, emphasising the importance of early care upon brain development. Full recovery of linguistic ability was not obtained if the child was transferred to foster care after more than 2 years in an orphanage. This Romanian study suggested that the positive effect of removing a child from the orphanage early was even stronger than initially predicted, as the effects of early institutionalisation during critical early periods can be long-lasting, but so can the effects of having a stable home environment. Transfer of the infant from the orphanage to foster care within 1 year facilitated normal recovery of language function. The findings support a "sensitive period" in the brain for social development.

The findings are not confined to Romanian children. An MRI study comparing 38 children who experienced orphanage care and 40 comparison control children combined Eastern European and Asian children (Tottenham et al., 2010). Fifty-three percent of the children who experienced orphanage rearing met criteria for a psychiatric disorder, with 18% (one third) of those meeting criteria for an anxiety disorder. Changes were seen in limbic circuitry, specifically the amygdala, which were linked to the cause of those emotional and social problems experienced by children who have been internationally adopted. These are also consistent with the negative effects seen of prolonged orphanage care on emotional behaviour, as well as with animal models demonstrating long-term changes in the amygdala and emotional behaviour following early postnatal stress. The group differences in amygdala volume were not driven by the presence of an anxiety disorder but instead were characterised by early versus late adoption, the latter associated with larger corrected amygdala volumes, poorer emotion regulation and increased anxiety. In other words, the longer the infant was institutionalised, the more stunted was development. The studies demonstrate that early adversity, such as poor caregiving, can have profound effects on emotional development. The impact of those chimpanzees being taken away from their mothers and raised in inconsistent and institutionalised environments, in cages, was hugely underestimated. The human studies show that orphanage rearing, even in the best circumstances, is outside of the bounds of a species-typical caregiving environment, with long-term effects on neurobiological effects.

It was the job of the chimpanzee caretakers to look after their charges. Part of that was to look out for their welfare, and to ensure that there were adequate funds for their care. Sadly, Fouts explains how difficult it was to raise funds for Washoe; "Somehow, somewhere, we had to come up with $40,000 every year just to feed and care for Washoe's family". He founded the organisation Friends of Washoe for this purpose, so he was able to accept donations. He threw a show of their artwork in a café in Ellensburg in 1981, with each of the chimps – Washoe, Dar, Tatu and Moja – contributing paintings. More questionably, he suggests (it is not clear if he did) that he donated Dar, who was now 5 years old, for a study involving castration at the Holloman Air Force Base where Dar was born (p. 270). Fouts describes how things were so bad, that "I had to accept that our very best efforts were barely keeping Washoe's family alive and properly cared for". There were scavenges in bins for fruit and vegetables. He put out reports on televisions and in newspapers. The chimpanzees were used in commercials. He explains how he used Tatu in a commercial for Rainier Beer for $500. According to Fouts's account, Tatu is required to imitate a bartender pouring beer for Tarzan, but a YouTube search on "Rainier beer Tarzan" shows a different commercial. Robert remembers at least two commercials and posters.

One has to question this type of chimpanzee procurement. These were clearly conditions of desperation, but if we swap chimp for child, would we allow our own child to appear in beer commercials? Tarzan featured again, when Fouts considered moving the chimps to Africa. Linden reports how "When I visited the Institute for Primate Studies in 1979, Robert Towne, the producer, was also there. At that time, Towne was becoming involved in a movie called Greystoke (based on the original Tarzan story), and he and Roger spoke about using Roger's chimps in the movie in return for a facility that would provide for the needs of both scientists and chimps" (Linden, 1986, p. 100).

Finding Safety

The quality of care a child receives both inside and outside the home is of utmost importance. For some children, school may be the first time they are detached from parents. Others might have been used to leaving for nursery, but school presents challenges in changes of key workers and smaller, time- and event-based stressors, such as timetables, new rooms and new equipment and apparatus. Toddlers and pre-schoolers may show increases in cortisol as the day progresses in childcare (Belsky et al., 2007), although much of this may be due to shorter-term anticipation of stimulus and routine, and we should be careful that this is not critical of parents who use childcare for their young children. By the time children are ready for school, longer periods of time can be endured without this elevation.

Consistency of care is something the chimpanzees did not always have. In humans it allows for healthy therapeutic interventions for individuals with stressful life events. Herman describes a three-stage sequence of trauma treatment and recovery in adult humans. The first stage involves regaining a sense of safety, through a combination of therapeutic relationship, medication or relaxation exercises (Herman, 1997). The second phase involves active work upon the trauma cultivated from that secure base using any of a range of psychological techniques. The third stage involves consideration of a new post-traumatic life which is developed by the experience of surviving the trauma. This is what Tedeschi and others refer to as post-traumatic growth (Tedeschi & Calhoun, 1995).

In the chimpanzee cases, there was no post-traumatic growth because there was no cultivation of any home as a place of safety. The best outcome possible was rehabilitation to the Black Beauty Ranch, although even that was not ideal. At the end of each working day in Oklahoma, the researchers were able to go home – Fouts in his Porsche and Bob in his Alfa Romeo. The humans could go home, but the chimpanzees were to stay behind bars, and that was the only place they knew as home. This is something that we still do not think about to this day in the zoo world. When the visitors have left, those animals in zoos are left behind. They are not home, and they cannot go home. Identifying developmental stress and traumatisation – even in humans – is problematic, but the topic is important in maintenance of robust mental health. It is helpful to recognise the different types of stress, factors contributing to it and the different levels of arousal, personality traits and level of stressor. In children, it is imperative that the safety of the classroom setting is maintained so that emphasis can be placed on stress as a positive process which is harnessed as motivation, in order to nurture post-traumatic growth and resilience.

Denyse

After many years of working with chimps, I find myself in situations like this where I am trusted. This was the morning it was decided we would send Denyse to heaven, no easy decision, but the right one. There were three people in the Quarantine Room with her. Dr. Murphy, the veterinarian, was sitting on the floor next to the cage, beside Denyse, who was in the enclosure. The vet tech was sitting on the floor to my left, and I was standing behind them, leaning against the closed doors to the vet exam room. Denyse knew something was up. Denyse was important to me, because she came to represent all the things that are wrong with keeping a chimpanzee as a pet. She had come to the Center for Great Apes (CGA), a chimpanzee and orangutan sanctuary established by Patti Ragan in Wauchula, Florida, when her owner died. I was visiting the centre and staying on grounds, when Patti asked me if I would hang out with Denyse, keeping her company and engaged as much as possible. When Denyse arrived at CGA, she had had very little exposure to other chimps and she was not able to be integrated into any established chimp groups at the centre. After repeated failed attempts to introduce her to other chimps, it was decided that she was not going to be successfully introduced to another chimp. Obviously, not the ideal situation, but if she didn't want to live with other chimps, CGA was not going to force her to. So Denyse was a single chimp with no chimp companion. She simply did not like other chimps. That's what led to me being asked to spend as much time with her as I could. I visited CGA often, for long periods of time over a two-year period, and Denyse and I became close. This was the last day of that. We still have the shrine, even roses from her grave.

When the decision to euthanise Denyse was made, the medical team assembled in the clinic. I was initially outside with the rest of the CGA staff, approximately 15 to 20 people. While I was standing there, the doors opened, the Head of Animal Care looked out and asked me in. She asked, "Do you want to be here for this? If you do, we think it's appropriate, even if you're technically just a volunteer." That's when I stepped in, first to the clinic, and then over into the Quarantine Room where Denyse was. I was touched to be invited, because many of the folks left outside were staff members who loved Denyse as much as I did. In the days leading up to this, they were all told to come in where I was hanging out with her, so I witnessed a lot of goodbyes those previous two days. We had been there 15 minutes, waiting for Denyse to allow Dr. Murphy to inject her. I could see the emotion on his face. He said, "It really doesn't matter, does it?" I shook my head no, but didn't really know what he meant. He said, "Go get me a couple of beers." I opened the metal doors into the adjoining clinic and the assembled team all looked at me. I said "He wants two beers." I don't recall anyone saying anything, but two cold beers were produced and I took them back into the Quarantine Room, and closed the metal doors behind me. She hadn't had a beer for 6 years, but when she was a pet she had been given beers and doughnuts. This gesture of Dr. Murphy's demonstrates what the chimps will do to you. It's serious, the relationships and the bonds that develop between the animals and the people that care for chimps like Denyse in sanctuary. I handed Dr. Murphy the cold beers, and he popped the tops. I took the tops and put them in my pocket. I still have them. He handed her one beer and they clinked bottles, casually drinking beer together. Then when she's done, she hands him the bottle. She offers her arm against the bars. He injects her.

The reality was that in the last few months she had had health-related issues that were becoming worse and more frequent. She was retaining fluid that had to be removed via a procedure called paracentesis (paracentesis: from Greek κεντάω, "to pierce") a form of body fluid tapping procedure, generally referring to peritoneocentesis (also called laparocentesis, or abdominal paracentesis) in which the peritoneal cavity is punctured by a needle to tap peritoneal fluid. This procedure was performed a number of times on Denyse, and ultimately the decision was made that her quality of life had deteriorated to the point that euthanasia was the most humane option. No easy decision, when you have such a close relationship with the animal.

When the drug took effect, the doors were opened, and the doors to the enclosure were unlocked. We carried Denyse into the surgery where Dr. Murphy performed the necessary procedure. I was holding her hand.

After she passed, the team got foot- and hand-prints for their records, and there were mementoes for the attending caregivers. I was honored to have been given these. No crying, no tears, we were all solid. When he said, "It's 7.40 in the evening . . ." We all took a deep breath, then tears.

As soon as she was gone and we all regained our composure, Dr. Murphy looked at the other vet tech, who stepped over to a corner and retrieved a tool that looked like giant tree loppers, to prepare for the necropsy (post-mortem) before the burial. As she picked up that tool, I said to her, "I probably don't want to be here for this." She replied, "Probably not." I stepped out, as did a few others not involved with the necropsy, and allowed the medical team and the head of animal care to do their job uninterrupted. About 20 minutes later, the double metal doors opened. Several of us walked over back into the room. We lifted Denyse's body and carried her over to the waiting golf cart. The maintenance team had prepared her grave at the memorial garden. It was like a procession. Not just one person, but a procession of golf carts down to the cemetery. It was almost sunset. We lifted her, put her into her grave, and covered her with flowers. We then covered her with soil. Everyone stayed, some for two or three hours post work time. It was one of the most touching things in my whole life.

4

THE TRUTH ABOUT WASHOE

If this book is closing the door on the language part of the chimpanzee experiences, why should Washoe's story be so important? Past books have already told her story. Those are told inaccurately, and those facts need addressing, particularly around the birth and death of one of her infants, Sequoyah. Furthermore, an important aspect has been missed from accounts of Washoe's experiences over the decades, and that is around how much we can learn about parenting, families and transgenerational issues. Parenting – in particular mothering – was less spoken about in 1970s psychology. The psychoanalytic side was very different from the experimental work done today. The story of "Project Washoe" received attention for the signing, but in the revisiting of the Oklahoma chimpanzees, it needs special attention for a different reason. Examination of the maternal bond between Washoe and her infants has been neglected. The discussions around Washoe have always been as examinations of language acquisition, overlooking how traumatised the chimpanzees, and also their carers, were. The chimps were starved of appropriate maternal attachments and of examples of good mothering within their fragmented family groups. They would have learned appropriate and healthy connections around this in the wild. We would do best to reconsider the Washoe research as studies of what traumatised captive chimpanzees do, how they behave, and how sudden disruptions in the mother-child bond can lead to maladaptive mothers – and fathers, too. It is a crucial demonstration of how one's own initial attachments affect the ability to parent later on.

Washoe's case is a clear demonstration of how the chimpanzees' captivity disrupted their parental bonds. Little is told of Washoe's relationship with her infants, in particular, of her behaviours towards her biological chimpanzee infant, Sequoyah. The two presentations of her birthing story in Roger Fouts's book, *Next of Kin*, and of Eugene Linden's book, *Silent Partners*, are different. It is clear that Robert is still traumatised by what happened with Washoe, and Ron Helterbrand, who worked

DOI: 10.4324/9781003357650-5

in the same lab and was also one of Washoe's carers, is similarly traumatised. The full story has not been told properly. We believe this was either because researchers feared losing their grant funds, or because of bias in the accounts, or it is possible that those designated to tell the stories received selective information, only. Whatever those reasons, we use this chapter to – at last – present the facts in an accurate way. It is important to note again here that we do not wish to assign blame, or to vilify, or to heroise, any of those people who worked with Washoe. We wish to present the facts in a non-judgemental and non-accusatory manner, remembering also that each of the researchers involved in the primates' care was unrepresentative, by definition. This level of intense and intimate emotional bonding with a being from another species is not normal. Those researchers were working with whichever emotional tools they had available themselves, and we can keep the facts in the historical and social context.

We are pleased to use this book as a vehicle to present the facts with precision, and to give those chimpanzees their voice, and the dignity that they deserve. We are certain that some readers will be critical and perhaps raise doubt about the accuracy of our account. We are confident about our facts. Our accounts are reliable explanations and interpretations. I (Anna) have come to the project "blind". I only had the briefest of facts at the start, the few papers presented to me in my undergraduate lectures about Washoe's language learning. Prior to speaking to Robert, I had no idea about any of these events. It has only been since my interactions with Robert over the past few months that I have learned about the extent of how emotive and political those events were, with many individuals involved, and problems caused by the lack of planning and foresight. Additionally, readers can be confident that our accounts are trustworthy and reliable since first, Robert was present and integral to the care and study of Washoe, and it is obvious that there is nothing wrong with his memory. He may be biased towards defending the chimpanzees, but he has no reason to attack anyone else. Second, Robert's stories are supported by accounts from other researchers who were present at the time. I interviewed one of the other people on the Washoe project, Ron Helterbrand, who was an undergraduate student when Washoe's infant was born. I also interviewed Eugene Linden, author of *Silent Partners*. Another helpful observer has been Esteban Rivas, who was with Washoe after she was moved to Ellensburg, Washington, from Oklahoma. Rivas wrote his doctoral thesis on signing behaviour of chimpanzees in interactions with long-term human companions. All of these observers have given consistent accounts. It is clear that Linden was not aware of the full extent of some of the problems in the laboratory, but his books, *Apes, Men and Language* and *Silent Partners: The Legacy of the Ape Language Experiments* are clear documents of the facts that were presented to him. Lastly, and perhaps most importantly, we are confident of the facts about Washoe, the infant Sequoyah, and the other Oklahoma chimpanzees, including Moja, Loulis and Booee, because Robert has in his possession the diary log book of Washoe's care. The facts about Washoe's pregnancy, birth and inability to care for her offspring are recorded in an objective manner. Additionally, in the unfolding of the interviews, other researchers have brought forwards their stories and memories, with facts about the care of the chimpanzees.

Before we consider whether and how Washoe was prepared for her laboratory pregnancies compared with how she might have prepared herself in the wild, it is helpful to reconsider how she came to be. Fouts's book, *Next of Kin* is mostly about his experiences in what the "conversations with chimpanzees" taught him about "intelligence, compassion and being human" (*Next of Kin*, cover page). Specifically, his book focuses on and explains a great deal about Washoe's upbringing, her experiences with the Gardners, how she came to be in Oklahoma, and how she learned language.

A document written by Samantha Struthers, entitled "Famous Chimps Get Their Start Here" appeared in "Chimp Chat" published by the Coulston Foundation in January 1995. It explains how Washoe arrived at Holloman Air Force Base on 3 May 1966, and remained there for 6 weeks. It also specifies the birth of Dar there. Dar was born in a biomedical laboratory and would subsequently come to be with the Gardners just as Moja, Pili and Tatu were. This document was in the information package for staff giving guided tours at the Chimpanzee and Human Communication Institute (CHCI), the facility eventually started by the Foutses in 1993, 13 years after they arrived. Prior to this, the chimps were held in the 3rd Floor of the Psychology Building. Fouts left Oklahoma with Washoe and the other chimps to set up this institute at Central Washington University in 1980. There, at CHCI, guided tours were given and observers were able to have a look at the chimpanzees and their behaviours behind the pane of glass.

The document fills in the gaps that Fouts left open in his account. By the time they were in Washington, Washoe was the matriarch of Tatu, Moja, Dar and Loulis. The primates used sign language to communicate with each other and when talking to themselves as they played throughout the day. It is explained that Washoe was received by the Holloman Air Force Base "as a wild-born infant" from Asiatic Imports: "At that time, her age was estimated at less than one year old, her weight at arrival was 7.5 pounds. Washoe only resided with us from about six weeks and was then given to the Gardners in exchange for periodic behavioral reports on her growth and progress". It is explained that Washoe weighed 10.5 pounds on departure and receiving a diverse diet including half-and-half (a mixture of half whole milk, half cream), Log Cabin syrup, fruit and monkey pellets.

This information is crucial to understanding the narration gaps in Washoe's story. Nobody has accounted for the days between Washoe's birth in the wild and her arrival at the Holloman Air Force Base. Knowing that she was less than a year on arrival, and that she stayed for about 6 weeks, gives us a window in which we can analyse how she would have processed the trauma of her mother dying. This early experience would have influenced Washoe greatly and would have affected her approach to mothering, and to life. Prior to her mother being shot by poachers, it is likely that Washoe would have enjoyed a normal mother-child bond. Infant chimpanzees in the wild cling to their mother for at least the first few months, never leaving, even for a moment. It takes them around 6 months before they leave the mother's body for the ground. Chimp mothers in the wild protect their babies very closely because they are vulnerable to any number of situations that can result in the death of the infant. It is probable that Washoe, having being "wild collected", would have witnessed her mother being shot, falling back and dying, before being torn away by captors. Let us imagine how that might have felt for a human child.

Ron Helterbrand is still clearly traumatised by what happened to Washoe and her infant:

> One thing we should give Roger credit for, is that that time after she gave birth and set the baby down, he did try to get her to pick up the baby. He told her repeatedly to "Get the baby". He was angry with Washoe. He was 1 foot, maybe 2 feet away from her face. I didn't know what to do. What would we do if Washoe attacked Roger?
>
> Roger had a lot of great chimp stories that he would tell during class. When I was his teacher's assistant during a summer session, he had a story about research that was meant for testing the strength of the three types of great apes. Researchers had built an apparatus that was an I–Beam attached to the wall with springs. Handles were attached to the other side of the I–Beam for the Apes to pull on, to measure their strength. Researchers would get a gorilla to pull it back to test its strength. When the gorilla would pull the handle back, he would let it go, creating an awful sound, which scared the researchers a bit. Then they would try it with an orangutan. The orangutan would pull it back gently and then let it go back gently. When you try it with a chimp? The chimp would repeat the action over and over, full of testosterone. Chimps are manic. They are between 7 and 9 times stronger than man and have muscle density, it makes them pretty dangerous. We have to be careful not to be anthropomorphic about it. Washoe could be vicious.
>
> I've worked with animals all my life. Originally, I had plans to be a veterinarian. I had grown up working with cattle and horses, but after my freshman year, I felt my grades weren't good enough to get into vet school, so I transferred to the University of Oklahoma to change my major to industrial Psychology. I figured that would be easy enough. First semester, I took a class called "Primate Behavior" that Fouts taught. Following that I took an intersession class that Roger was teaching down at the OU Biological Station on Lake Texoma. During that class is where I originally met Bob. It was a great trip with 4 hours of class in the morning and the rest of the day spent reading and relaxing. That's pretty much when Roger invited me to come along for the ride.
>
> We were looking at language transmission: non-verbal aspects, like gazes and things. He was trying to get me ready to understand these behaviours – when we were going to be watching language being transmitted. My impression of Washoe was that she was not a normal female chimp. She was dominant over most males and could be rather vicious toward them. After the birth of Sequoyah, she learned quickly how to manipulate some of the rookie observers into bringing her yogurt to stop her from pacifying the baby with her index finger. It was a dangerous game. She was good at

manipulating humans who were new to the programme. Chimps are smart, their intellect is high. She learned to adapt to the environment that she was in. The sad thing is that you raise these chimps like humans, and then you go and put them in a cage.

The other side of these studies is that it is not just about the words, but it is about the images, too. When I go back to the afternoon Sequoyah died . . . I realise why I left the programme.

The story told about Washoe as a mother, is that on 8 January 1979 at 7 am, a member of the team noticed blood mixed with water on the floor of Washoe's cage, indicating that her waters had broken, and she was in labour. Fouts claims that he "immediately rushed over to stay with her" (p. 218). Labouring chimpanzees, he says, need privacy, even in captivity. According to Fouts, they will wait for the room to be empty before giving birth and so, he claims, lab workers often do not notice that a chimp is pregnant and will "walk in one morning and discover a new infant in the cage." This seems an unusual perspective. How would a laboratory worker, who is often also a caregiver to a study chimpanzee, not notice a pregnancy? Surely there would be behavioural changes, just as there are in human mothers, along with hormonal changes, and a cessation of menstruation. The most obvious clue that there would be a pregnancy in a chimpanzee would be the clear physical signs that any mammal is pregnant – a swollen abdomen. Fouts makes it unclear if Washoe's pregnancy was known. Robert and the others knew that she was pregnant several months in advance. Figure 4.1 shows Washoe in pregnancy, just a few days before giving birth. Fouts had won a research grant for the very purpose of getting Washoe to produce an infant. Additionally, the other researchers in the institute, Lemmon, Mel Allen and Jeanette Wallace, were also involved in studies examining chimpanzee sexual behaviours, gestation and birthing, and maternal behaviours. At the time of the labour, those present were Fouts, Diana, Dave, Ron, George, Tiny, Robert, and occasionally, Lemmon. It was hoped that the birth would be filmed using an 8 mm camera shooting 35 mm photographs.

Linden explains how, "It had been Roger's dream that Washoe would bear an infant, and that Roger might study the transmission of sign language across chimpanzee generations", and also how "The event was a godsend to Roger in ways totally separate from its scientific interest. The prospect of this intergenerational experiment got Roger a $300,000 grant from the National Science Foundation at a time when the pool of funding for language work with apes was rapidly drying up."

When Washoe was in labour, Fouts acknowledges that at that moment, she had no chance of enjoying any privacy as she was "giving birth in a small 5-by-6-foot cage, next to a larger enclosure holding the main colony's twenty-five highly aroused and screaming chimps." Where was the dignity, for that birthing mother? According to Fouts's account, when he arrived at the cage, Washoe signed COME HUG. His concerns about her lack of privacy "quickly vanished" because she seemed to click into a different state which was removed from everything around her, and knew what to do, assuming numerous positions to relieve pain,

FIGURE 4.1 Washoe in pregnancy, a few days before giving birth.

and advance the labour (p. 218). Between contractions, she lay on her side or on her back and asked for things to eat and drink, like lollipops and ice for sucking, as many labouring human women do. Fouts was "amazed that she could still sign under such extreme physical and emotional stress" (p. 219). He describes how, in the wild, labour in chimpanzees lasts for 1 or 2 hours, but that the noise and cage-banging next to her meant that Washoe's labour dragged on, and took around 4 hours. She finally gave birth at 11:57 am, in "a tripedal stance, holding one hand behind and below her. Then she deftly delivered her infant into her waiting hand." It is reported that she immediately brought the baby to her chest where she greeted it, "chimpanzee-style by panting heavily with her mouth over its mouth". At that stage, he was unable to tell if the baby was male or female (p. 219).

After this, it is reported that Washoe groomed the baby's ear, but it was then that he noticed that the baby's umbilical cord was wrapped tightly around its neck, and that the baby did not seem alive, and was unmoving. According to Fouts, Washoe made a nest for the two of them to lie on, using an old tyre in her cage, and she kissed and sucked mucus from the baby's mouth and nasal passages, breathing into its mouth several times. Despite these instincts, the baby was still and lifeless. Washoe then began to eat the umbilical cord from around the infant's neck, to relieve any suffocation, and she then squeezed one of the baby's tiny fingers with her teeth, in order to revive it. The baby squeaked, quite suddenly, and Fouts was relieved. The placenta was then delivered, which Washoe ate, as is common among mammals (pp. 219–220).

At this stage, Fouts could see that the infant was not clinging how he should, and that despite Washoe grooming and giving the baby mouth-to-mouth resuscitation, the infant remained limp, mostly. The infant grasped Washoe's hair briefly with one hand, but there was little response. After 3 hours, Washoe set the baby down, as she had done with her first baby. In the wild, when chimpanzee mothers do this, it indicates that the baby is dead. Fouts says that he "made the same anguished decision and took Washoe's baby out of her cage". He could then see that the baby was alive, but in distress and greatly weakened, and he could then tell that it was a male.

The next passage explains how, when Fouts got the baby to his house, he discovered that the baby had a fever. The question remains here, as to why the infant was taken to his house, and not to a veterinarian or other specialist. It is explained that Fouts and his wife, Debbi, stayed up most of the night hydrating the baby with fluids, and so by morning, the baby chimpanzee's temperature had stabilised. The baby was continuously fed intravenously, and through a bottle, although it is not clear who would have performed the IV procedure. The baby was named Sequoyah, Fouts says, "for the Oklahoma Indian chief who created the written language of the Cherokee people" (p. 220), although Sequoyah was not a chief, but an important delegate for the Cherokee nation who went to Washington, D.C., to sign two relocations and trading of land treaties. He was also a polymath who created the syllabary to make reading and writing possible in Cherokee, one of the few times in recorded history that a member of a pre-literate group created an effective writing system.

In Fouts's account, they re-introduced Sequoyah to his mother that same afternoon. It is unclear what actually happened from Fouts's account, because it varies from the other versions. He may have misrecollected how many times Sequoyah was taken away from Washoe. In his account, Washoe was re-introduced and was very excited to see the infant, holding the infant to her chest, although his nursing reflex was weak and he would detach from her nipple every time she moved even slightly. The decision was made at this stage to take Sequoyah away from his mother again to feed him properly. Fouts points out that "Washoe was not accommodating. We had to anesthetize her to take her baby away" (p. 220). This is a very important point, because anaesthetising Washoe at this stage would have interfered with two hormones that are crucial to the bonding process, called vasopressin and oxytocin. In humans, stress during labour can cause release of excessive beta-endorphins which inhibits oxytocin and slows down labour. Oxytocin promotes future interaction between mother and baby, decreasing fear and stress levels, allowing the mother to bond with her infant, reinforcing the bond with skin-to-skin contact (Sabihi et al., 2014). Anaesthetising Washoe at this important postnatal stage interfered with her natural instincts, and ability to mother her baby.

In order to get Sequoyah strong enough for nursing, Fouts made the decision to keep them apart for 2 weeks, feeding Sequoyah with human breastmilk donated to a feeding bank by local mothers, to help to avoid any allergic reactions to formula. They also used a different kind of nipple that made sucking more demanding, in the hope of encouraging his nursing reflex. In this time, Washoe became, as any mother who had lost her newborn infant, dispirited. Worried about the disappearance of her maternal instincts during the separation, Fouts provided another young chimp, a 2-year-old chimp named Abendigo, who had been living with his own mother until a week before, for her to nurture "on a foster basis". One has to ask how confusing that attachment would have been, both for Washoe, and for this infant, Abendigo. How might it feel for a human mother, to have given birth, had her baby taken away, and then had that baby replaced with someone else's baby? Fouts reports that Washoe took to him, and spent most of the time holding him.

After 2 weeks, Fouts went back to Washoe's cage and signed to her that her own baby was coming back. She was excited and signed BABY repeatedly. The reality for her was harder. On return, she held and groomed Sequoyah, but she found it difficult to breastfeed him, and "grimaced and moved her body away, dislodging him" (p. 221). Fouts tried to talk to her about feeding her baby, but she refused to do so, and there was a face-to-face screaming match. If this were a human mother, we might think it kinder to introduce a bottle of formula or expressed breastmilk at this stage. Breastmilk donated by local mothers from the local hospital was available at the primate research centre. When her baby finally rooted for the breast, Washoe "looked down at him . . . then let out a deafening scream" (p. 221). According to this account, Fouts tried to reinforce positive breastfeeding behaviour by placing a Tootsie Pop (iced lolly) on Washoe's tongue, and watched her sternly every time the baby fed, in order to stop her dislodging him. It appears that, through this combination of Skinnerian reward and rudimentary "counselling", her attempts to breastfeed him finally became successful.

The account goes on to describe how, once Sequoyah was 1 month old, things were more positive as Lemmon gave Washoe, Ally (the father) and Sequoyah a more spacious cage in the pig barn, and so the family was moved out of the colony and into their own home. However, as the cage was built out of razor-sharp metal to detract chimps from unravelling the strands, Sequoyah cut himself on it. Fouts describes how the wound became infected and the chimp became weaker, barely able to cling to his mother. He also writes that the pig barn was cold, and that the propane heater ran out of fuel one night, and that the temperatures dropped to 27 degrees Fahrenheit, and that the chimps were found huddled together in the cold. These are not salubrious conditions, and the chimpanzees' physical needs were neglected again. The implication is that these conditions caused respiratory illness, with Washoe staying up until dawn many nights to suck mucus out of Sequoyah's nose and mouth. Sequoyah, it is explained, "was deteriorating" (p. 222).

Ron Helterbrand's version of what happened that evening is consistent with Robert's account:

Sequoyah had a scratched trachea and oesophagus from what had happened earlier. It's been so long ago, I really don't remember who taught me how the feed him this particular day. I think it was probably Roger or maybe Debbi. Anyway, it was a very delicate process. There was a small bag with a long skinny tube coming out of it. It was a tool that we had used to help teach the baby to nurse after we had originally pulled him from Washoe. We would insert the tube into the corner of the baby's mouth, after he had begun suckling on a human female's nipple. His sucking would draw milk from the bag down the tube and into his mouth. But on this day the paediatrician [there was a paediatrics doctor present on this part of the project] had us insert the tube in the baby's nose and push it down to his stomach. There was a test we would have to do to determine if the tube had reached the stomach or the lungs.

The way I remember it, I had gotten to Roger's house at around noon. There were several of us setting in Roger's home library. There was some joking and laughing, mostly reminiscing about chimp stories we all had in common. George Kimble and I were setting on the couch, and after my 30 or so minutes of having Sequoyah in my lap, I was preparing to hand the baby over to George.

I quietly explained to George that while I had the baby in my lap, during the feeding process, he had stopped breathing a couple of times, and what I had done to get him to breathe again. I recall saying that it had happened more than once. When I handed him off to George it happened a few more times. Each time we would look at each other and I explained to George what I had done.

The rest of the day is kind of a fog. Everyone was taking their turn watching and caring for the baby. People came and went. Later in the day we thought we had him stabilised, so we pulled the tube out. As I recall, the last people there were Diana, Jill, Roger and me.

I believe we had decided to just have one person in the library at a time so that things were quieter. So we were all going to leave the room except for the person caring for Sequoyah. It was Jill's turn to care for the baby. She was sitting in a chair facing the library door. She took the baby and laid him in her lap. I recall Roger and Diana walking out of the room ahead of me and as I was closing the door I could see through the glass panes that Jill had a frightened look on her face.

We all walked back into the room and began doing very delicate CPR. This went on a little over an hour. I don't remember who called it but it was obvious that Sequoyah was not coming back. I remember looking outside through the windows of the library and seeing that the sun was just starting to set.

Next, I remember following Roger out of the library and into his kitchen. He grabs a bottle of Scotch, grabs 2 glasses. Pours one for him and one for me. Then Diana walks in. Jill walks in. We all have to do something to get this pain out of our hearts.

As the news spread students began coming to the house. The paediatrician also came by and hung out that night and he confirmed that we had done everything we could do to save Sequoyah.

Later I remember Bob arriving and greeting him at the door. By then, most of us in the house had dealt with the initial impact of what had happened.

The PTSD from this, is why I left the programme – that, and I needed to start making a living. I was still participating, working as a handler at the farm during the summer for Lemmon, while the Greystoke thing was going on. Then filling in when needed when Washoe and Loulis were moved to South Base.

It was a really rough time. Things were falling apart. It's so visual. It's as if I have a photograph imprinted in my brain of the fear on Jill's face as I was closing the door. I haven't been able to unlearn that picture yet.

Fouts explains how by 8 March 1979, Sequoyah had severe pneumonia, and was separated from Washoe again. Washoe was sedated again in order to take her baby away. Indeed, it is explained how "she started screaming . . . and signing MY BABY, MY BABY" (p. 222). She saw the needle and anaesthetic and knew that he was there to knock her out and to take the baby away. Is it any less cruel that she was not able to witness – and therefore, process – what was going on, or was it more humane to knock her out and take the baby away then? Of course, it is likely that she was too large, and too dangerous, to have her kept awake as her baby was being removed, but this removal of her infant would have caused immense distress, and lasting trauma.

For some reason, Fouts "rushed Sequoyah to the local community hospital in Norman" (p. 222). It is unclear why the baby chimpanzee was not taken to a vet. Unsurprisingly, the doctors refused to admit him. One has to wonder what they made of this scenario of a baby chimp being produced at a hospital. He describes how "in desperation", a makeshift infirmary was made in his dining room, with his own children understanding that something was wrong, and that their parents were fearful (p. 222). Fouts then called their "family paediatrician and friend, Dr. Richard Carlson", who thought the pneumonia was bacterial and that might have migrated from the staph infection in the toes and settled in the lungs (p. 223). By this stage, the baby was weak and could not cling or grasp, and the prognosis was dim. He was placed in a mist tent with a vaporiser and received ampicillin, and a tube was inserted to help aspirate fluid through his nose. The doctor stayed until 11 pm, before Roger and Deborah took over. Sadly, Sequoyah died the next afternoon, 9 March, at 4 pm. From Fouts's book, it appears that he blames himself, in particular, over the living circumstances:

> Worst of all, it seemed so damned unnecessary. I stayed up all night agonizing over what I had done wrong. If only I'd fought harder for a better cage. If only I'd insisted on a better heating system. If only I'd realized sooner that the infected toe needed systematic antibiotics to prevent bacterial pneumonia.
>
> *(p. 223)*

A different version of this story is presented by Eugene Linden, in *Silent Partners*. Linden describes how "Sequoyah died two days after having been found with a toothbrush jammed down his throat" (Linden, 1986, p. 96). On the Saturday night before Sequoyah died, one of the researchers, Chris O'Sullivan, who was working the 8 pm to midnight shift along with an undergraduate, found a note in the daily log warning people not to give Washoe her toothbrush, which Washoe usually used to brush her teeth. Linden explains that Chris let Washoe brush her teeth but, he reports, she then took the toothbrush back from Washoe and put it away. The day after this, on the Sunday morning, the project assistant doing the 8 am to noon shift discovered Washoe who "rushed up to the wire mesh, very upset, and held up Sequoyah, who was seen to have the toothbrush jammed down his throat" (p. 97).

Robert was present at some of this. The photographs in Figures 4.2, 4.3 and 4.4, demonstrate this. The first three photographs show Sequoyah on the first night, after Washoe put him down and would not pick him up.

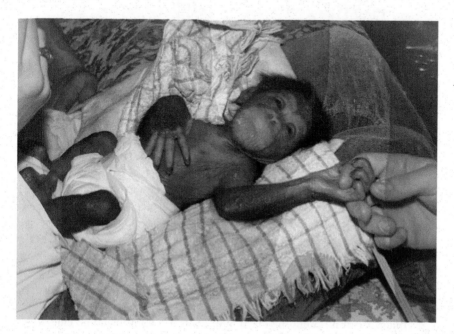

FIGURE 4.2   Sequoyah on the first night after Washoe rejected him.

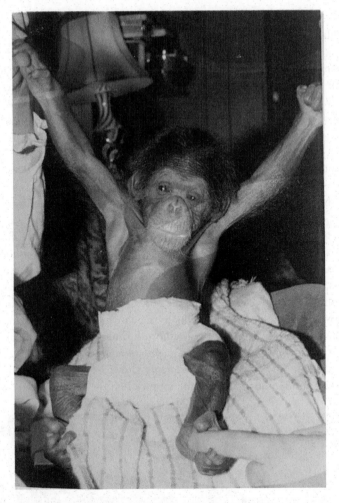

FIGURE 4.3 Sequoyah on the first night after Washoe rejected him.

Robert says:

> There are some forgotten details that were significant to her birthing experience. Washoe was moved to that tiny cage where she gave birth, about a week earlier. She hated it, and wanted to be back in her area where she was previous to that. At least one factor that may have been at play when she put him down was that she was thinking, "OK, there is your baby, now put me back where I'm comfortable", so the baby may have actually played as a bargaining chip right at birth, and the same when he was returned 10 days later, and she used him as a display object, and asked for, among other things, "BEER!" until she killed him. Fouts had no plan and no clue, so he scrambled to get things together. That first night Alyse Moore, Dave Rowe,

FIGURE 4.4   Sequoyah on the first night after Washoe rejected him.

and I, along with a few others, took turns in dealing with Sequoyah. He was a baby chimp, so like a human baby. Two days or so passed, and then he was moved to Diana's house where these bottom pictures were taken. This is pretty heavy shit when you know how it all ended.

Linden acknowledges that Roger Fouts, Roger Mellgren, "and a few others" said that Washoe had been trying to aspirate Sequoyah, who was finding it hard to breathe because of the pneumonia. However, "examinations revealed that Sequoyah had severe lacerations in his throat, which indicates that the toothbrush was inserted with something other than delicacy" (p. 97).

The other researchers: M.L. Allen, Diana Davis, Chris O'Sullivan, Lemmon, and of course, Robert, who were present at the institute during Sequoyah's life and death, saw Washoe fatally abusing her infant, and say that Washoe killed Sequoyah, under the guise of trying to help him. Roger insisted that Sequoyah had pneumonia prior to Washoe's action, but these other caregivers explained how this sort of acute, nonviral pneumonia can arise through the sorts of injuries inflicted by the toothbrush. Furthermore, the warning in the diary demonstrated that this was not the first time that Washoe had inflicted injury upon Sequoyah in an abusive manner, with the toothbrush, and other instances, such as banging him against the cage, in order to achieve what she wanted.

Human language, whether signed or spoken, is not in any sense "better" than the communication system of wild chimpanzees. It is irrelevant whether Washoe used sign or chimpanzee language with Sequoyah. It was not representative of what happens with chimpanzees in the wild, nor of what happens in humans. Evolution is not a ladder of "improvement" culminating in the human being. It is an ongoing process of adaptation for each species. Those animal studies were so unique, that that line of work must never be repeated, and the existing findings need to be placed into a sort of evolutionary context. These chimpanzees were not representative of normal animals, nor did their use of "language" reflect much about what happens in humans. They were considered experimental commodities much of the time and humanlike the rest of the time, yet the truth is that these were not humans, but they were not representative of ordinary chimpanzees. They were chimpanzees raised by humans. Any results reflected that: these were encultured chimpanzees, taught sign language by humans who thought they were in a position to be able to do so. By this very definition, the studies carry little scientific value.

It is important to note here that in the writing of this book, I contacted Fouts, offering an opportunity to voice his opinions regarding those studies. He was very kind to reply promptly, saying that he has been retired for more than a decade now, and he suggested I quote from *Next of Kin* which he thinks would be a much more reliable source than his memory.

In consideration of Washoe's behaviours, we are extremely fortunate to have available the detailed daily log book of her care, written by her carers, who were Roger Fouts, George Kimball, Diana Davis, Lisa Benson, Chris O'Sullivan, David Rowe, David Autry and of course, Robert Ingersoll. A number of undergraduates also wrote entries in the diary. It is event rather than time based, is 1,004 pages long, and in Robert's possession. Most of our explanations of Washoe's behaviours in this book are from this diary. It is a vital tool in our consideration of Washoe's mental states and corresponding behaviours and validates some of the facts around her care. It is also an accurate historical document, giving clarity beyond those accounts which are cited incorrectly in books. Photographs from this log book are presented here, where they are relevant.

The account of Sequoyah's death is from page 990 at 5:03 pm on Saturday, 3 March 1979, to page 992 (see Figures 4.5, 4.6, 4.7, and 4.8).

At 7:57 on Sunday, 4 March 1979, Bob entered the room and found the infant at the back of the cage. The other noteworthy event occurs on page 984 of the diary (see Figure 4.9). It is of an event which has never been reported before now. The event is that a pellet gun was used to threaten, and then shoot, Washoe multiple times. It is clear that individuals amended certain words in the diary. The person who shot the gun was one of the undergraduate project volunteers. It is clear that these were young and inexperienced volunteers who made unwise decisions.

Having a baby in the wild for a chimpanzee is a status raiser. Once a mother chimpanzee has a baby in the wild, her status in the chimpanzee group increases. The baby becomes the status raiser. However, for Washoe, things were different because she was not in a chimpanzee group, and so instead of using her baby as an appropriate status raiser, she used him as a display object in order to get things she

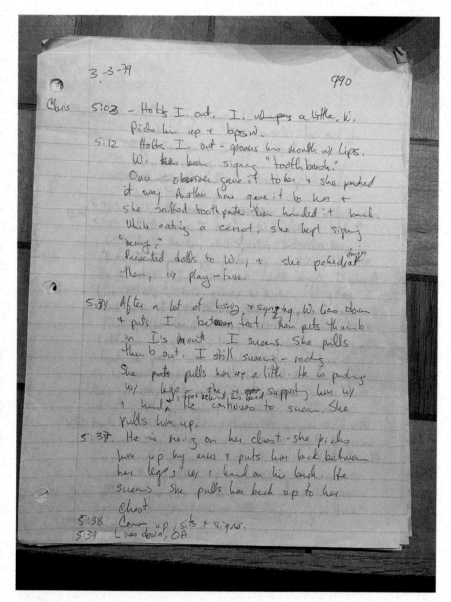

FIGURE 4.5   The account of Sequoyah's death.

wanted from the researchers. The diary reports how she banged him against the cage in order to obtain an orange.

Washoe did not hug Sequoyah very much. We now know why hugging is a necessary part of the developmental process and the connection between parent and child. Hugs release the neurotransmitter, oxytocin, the bonding neurohormone

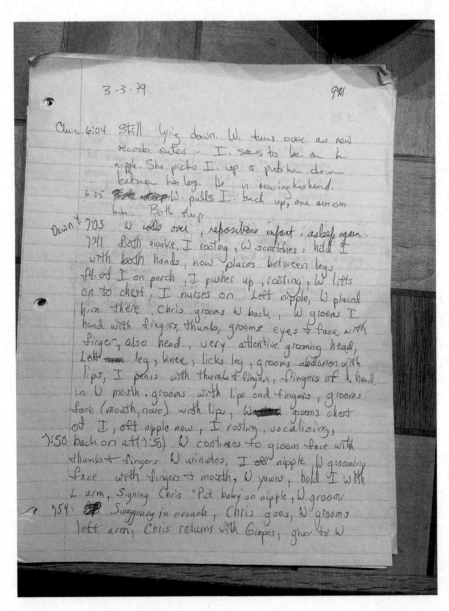

FIGURE 4.6 The account of Sequoyah's death.

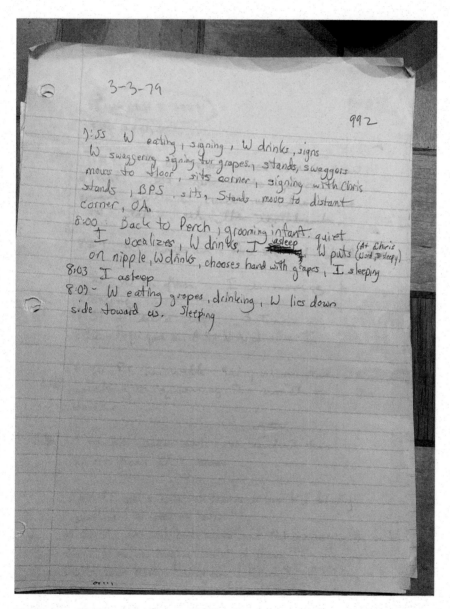

FIGURE 4.7 The account of Sequoyah's death.

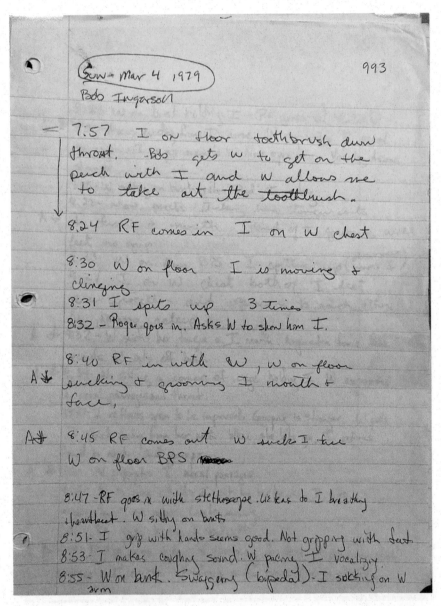

FIGURE 4.8   The account of Sequoyah's death. Bob found the infant with the toothbrush in Sequoyah's throat.

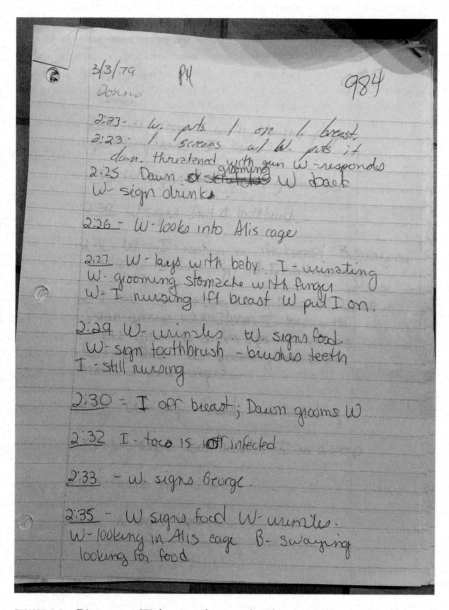

FIGURE 4.9 Diary entry: Washoe was threatened with a gun.

associated with love and intimacy, also released by labouring mothers. The body needs a particular amount of oxytocin before the labour process starts, to enable bonding between mother and infant. It has also been suggested that mothers with personality disorders may not have enough oxytocin to stimulate this parental bond.

A recent study shows how cuddling an infant during the early years can have an important neurobiological effect in later life. Moore, McEwen, Quirt et al. (2017) showed that the amount of hugs an infant receives influences epigenetic changes in at least five areas of DNA, including those related to the immune system and metabolism. Those infants who experienced few occasions of close physical contact in the first weeks of life showed an underdeveloped molecular profile in their cells. The researchers demonstrated how children are affected by close contact and affection in early life. Slower epigenetic ageing reflects less favourable developmental progress. Parents of 94 infants were invited to keep a diary of behaviour, as well as of touching and holding habits for the first 5 weeks of postnatal care. The DNA of these infants was then sampled four and five years later. The epigenetic process of DNA methylation was measured, giving an estimate about how active a gene is. Epigenetics explains how the extent of methylation can be affected by environmental influences, particularly in childhood. The researchers found consistent differences in the extent of methylation at five specific DNA sites between the children who had experienced high levels of contact, and those who had not. Infants who received low contact from caregivers had greater infant distress associated with younger epigenetic age, suggesting that early postnatal contact has lasting associations with child biology. One of those sites plays a role in the immune system, and another influences metabolism, suggesting that cuddling deeply affects our biology and lives. This finding carries broad implications for child health, especially in terms of psychological development. One way to counteract trauma in infants is to encourage close physical bonding with the mother. This was not happening between Washoe and Sequoyah.

Was Washoe Abnormal?

To define abnormality, one must have an understanding of what normality is. Being able to note a disruption in a person's mental functioning means that a clinician must understand how humans function when they are healthy. While no person functions in a completely healthy manner all the time, there are characteristics that help clinicians identify healthy psychological functioning. One of these is psychological flexibility. Researchers noted that a marker of "healthy" psychology is when an individual is able to be present, accepting the emotions felt, whether good or difficult, and being able to pursue what they value in life (Gloster et al., 2011).

The chimpanzees had been held captive for so long that they were not normal any more. Washoe and trauma and psychological problems. Who were the people looking after Washoe, and other chimpanzees? Why is it so important to consider who the actual caregivers or researchers were? In the consideration of how Washoe was looked after, it is of huge importance to consider the inheritance of trauma.

In abusive or damaged parent-child bonds, there is a difference between damag*ing* and the damag*ed*. In trauma and forensics, we know that people who abuse were often abused, themselves. In this case, we might try to understand and perhaps even excuse the damaging parent. We are left with a conundrum: how does one measure levels of abuse? What does the scale which makes abuse look tolerable, look like? In the interests of compassionate parenting, we should say that *no* abuse transmitted from parent to child is acceptable or tolerable. On what level could it be acceptable? However, no mother wakes up one morning and says, "today I will abuse my child". Abusers are not always conscious that they are abusing or grooming another; they may be passing on behaviours that they recognise as normal. Childhood trauma leads us to seek the familiar, even when it is toxic, unhealthy or hurtful. This still does not make these abusive behaviours *acceptable*, but it makes them easier to understand. We must consider, though, that the adult has to take responsibility for their abusive actions. It is within this act of responsibility that lie self-awareness and repentance. The recognition of responsibility for abusive acts lies in the consciousness of the abuser, and in whether there is a capacity for recognition of the acts as abusive.

In the *Diagnostic and Statistical Manual for Psychological Disorders* (DSM-5, American Psychiatric Association, 2013) the origins of post-traumatic stress disorder (PTSD) conceptualise it as a memory disorder. This is because the clinicians diagnosing the early cases were, themselves, young medics who did not go to Vietnam. Instead, they treated many of the veterans who did, finding that those who were coming back from Vietnam were finding it difficult to control their emotions, and to engage with the world. A diagnosis was required, and it was made as one of a memory disorder, because of dreams, cognitive intrusions and flashbacks encapsulating the main symptoms of the disorder. The diagnostic criteria being "exposure to an event outside usual experience", were somewhat ignorant of the fact that most patients with PTSD do not show one-off, unusual experiences. Rather, they show chronic experiences like abuse or parental neglect. Nearly 50 years later, it is still hard to find psychiatrists who can understand that PTSD is often due to problems from childhood. We have learned in psychiatric research how to measure brain chemicals, the neurotransmitters dopamine, serotonin and noradrenaline. We have learned how to take pictures of brains, through functional magnetic resonance imaging (fMRI) and positron emission tomography (PET) scanning, but can these tell us how we think? The techniques can certainly be helpful in understanding how people think, but the mind is more than what the brain "does". We can now also measure DNA. Genetic analysis is now possible. However, again, while underlying genetic patterns are useful, the mind is more than genetic patterns. The notion of trauma is outside the realm of human experience. It is sad to consider that if the notion of trauma is outside the understanding of humans, those poor chimpanzees had no chance.

PTSD as a disorder of memory was incorrect for numerous reasons, not least because one cannot ask an individual who has been abused which *one* traumatic event was the most memorable. The details become vague, and the traumatised individual feels chronically scared. There was the mistaken notion that the critical issue was memory consolidation, and this omitted the fact that trauma transforms identity, attention, concentration and the perceptual system. There are alterations in the sense of self, and the individual constantly feels frozen in fear.

Good therapy addresses trauma by asking how to help the traumatised being to feel safe. Traumatised individuals are chronically angry, or sad or anxious. They cannot care for other individuals, and they find it hard to have healthy relationships. It is a complex picture.

Very large numbers of individuals with PTSD in the US are military personnel. There is a large occupational risk to suffering from PTSD. Trauma is associated with military backgrounds. Individuals from family backgrounds with adverse childhood experiences (ACEs) are vulnerable to PTSD and also are more likely to join the military. They often enlist to escape poverty, violence and abusive or dysfunctional home environments. There is a pre-existing history of trauma. One study of 60,000 Americans with and without military service, during the draft and all-volunteer force eras, measured the number of ACEs on a scale, and found that 27% of males in the military had zero ACEs compared with 42% of non-serving men, whereas another 27% had four or more ACEs, compared with 13% of non-serving men. It is possible that the military is providing a sense of identity and respect, and a refuge for many traumatised males. The majority of soldiers meeting criteria for more than one mental health disorder reported at least one psychological disorder before childhood.

It is worth considering this here, because there may be something similar going on with universities. To the knowledge of the authors, there has been no research study investigating the number of ACEs in the average student of psychology, but it is likely that, especially in the 1960s and 1970s, psychology students will have been coming to a university education with a background of at least one or more ACEs. This pre-existing trauma will have been present in the raising of the chimpanzees and will have presented as transgenerational trauma.

One reason why transgenerational trauma continues is because traumatised individuals internalise what happened to them and pass this knowledge onto their children. There are some important cycles for parents to break if they wish to not pass on their trauma to their children. For instance, learning to apologise to children is crucial. Understanding that apologising is not a sign of weakness, but a sign of modelling, and what respectful humans do when they make mistakes is important. We can note here that many of the chimpanzees were aware of their behaviours, and were able to apologise, and would do so repeatedly. Another example of how to break transgenerational trauma and create a healthy upbringing is to try to understand children, instead of criticising them. Children's emotions, thoughts and behaviours make more sense when adults try to enter the world of the child, instead of imposing the adult world upon them. It is important for adults to pay attention to their children. This is especially true when the child is trying to share any information with them. At this stage, adults need to not dismiss it, minimise it or call it silly. Information that might seem superficial or unimportant to the adult may represent a worrying and concerning thing in the child's eyes, and sharing is the child's way of connecting with the adult. It is important for parents and adults to allow children to feel, name and express their emotions, and not suppress them. Emotions are supposed to be felt and need to be validated. Invalidating, dismissing and minimising emotions demonstrates to children that their emotions are not important, and are not to be expressed or felt. It is also crucial for parents to see the good in their child, and to note their excited voice, happiness and the need for connection. It is essential that adults have empathy for the little human who is trying to figure out the world. It is crucial that adults do not hit or shout at children. If the child shouts, they ought to be taught to speak or act calmly, and if they hit or bite, to be demonstrated how to work with the anger. Trying to help children to understand their own behaviour and to problem-solve is more valuable than punishing them. Did this happen with the chimpanzees?

It is crucial that parents honour, accept and respect their child for who they are, and not for the child that they would like them to be (Van der Kolk, 2021). It is important that adults do not project their unrealistic desires onto their children. Instead, children should be raised in a safe space, so that they can grow up to be themselves, in an authentic fashion. This was problematic in the chimpanzees, because by definition the adults were projecting, in anthropomorphic fashion, upon them, and bestowing human behaviours and values upon them, when it should have been clear that the chimpanzees were not equipped to do these things. An important cycle for parents to reinforce is in demonstrating to their children the things that they might have liked to have learned, themselves, such as empathy, self-care, kindness, respect, goal-setting, introspection, commitment, self-acceptance and limits (Van der Kolk, 2021). Children learn more from watching who adults are than from being told who they ought to be. It is crucial for children to hear that they are loved, even if feels uncomfortable to tell them. Affection is of utmost importance. It is important for a child to be loved and to be hugged, and to be kissed for no reason, other than parental affection. It is important for the child to be told how much they are appreciated, especially for who they are. It is imperative that confidence is gained in their parents' unconditional love. Doing these things can feel very difficult for people for whom these things were not safe to do, or who have not experienced these things. Therefore, it is expected that some traumatised individuals will find themselves pushing away from these behaviours. For children, these bonding behaviours are innate, and present from a very young age, but as parents we often project our own aspects of behaviour on to our children.

Childhood trauma in humans changes how the brain and mind develop. Herman et al. (1989) were amongst the first to suggest that borderline personality disorder occurs as a result of trauma, rather than through genetics – a disorder of nurture rather than nature (although the two are intertwined since we now know it is nature *via* nurture). They devised a Traumatic Antecedents Questionnaire to investigate the history of each participant in their study. This involved analysis of

1. demographics
2. current health
3. family of origin demographics

4. childhood caretakers and separations
5. peer relationships
6. family alcoholism
7. family discipline and conflict resolution
8. early sexual experiences

The chimpanzee studies would have done well to have addressed these points for each animal. Consideration of each animal's history would have given an idea about how this would impact upon each animal's behaviours. When individuals are traumatised across the life span, it can make a large difference to treatment efficacy later on, regardless of whether one is considering humans, or chimpanzees.

Herman et al. (1989) investigated the impact of childhood abuse and neglect upon some of the behaviours demonstrated in those children as adults. They found that a staggering 87% of participants with Borderline Personality Disorder (BPD) had histories of severe childhood abuse and/or neglect, starting prior to age 7 years. With this in mind, we can consider that most of the chimpanzees studied in Oklahoma and other research laboratories, having been taken away from their mothers, or having arrived following a traumatic upbringing as an ultimately unwanted pet, will have had this profile of being vulnerable to personality characteristics as a result of that trauma. This adds a further sad irony to those studies: even if they had had conclusive results about language learning, they would not have been representative. Language learning in trauma is not the same as in healthy, non-traumatised development.

That childhood trauma has a strong link with self-destructive behaviour later in life was demonstrated by Van der Kolk et al. (1991) and has been repeated since in at least 23 studies. BPD is a function of early childhood trauma. BPD is now more commonly known as emotionally unstable personality disorder (EUPD; American Psychiatric Association, 2013). It is characterised by a long-term pattern of unstable interpersonal relationships, a distorted sense of self, and strong emotional reactions. Individuals with BPD frequently engage in self-harm and other dangerous behaviours. They find it difficult to regulate emotion, struggling with feelings of emptiness, fear of abandonment and a detachment from reality (Bozzatello et al., 2021; Cattane et al., 2017). Typically, BPD begins in early adulthood and is associated with other mental health problems. Self-harm and the associated biological changes are noted. We might ask what causes an individual to self-mutilate. The main behaviours are

1. suicidal ideation
2. suicidal attempts (the best predictor of this is sex abuse followed by physical abuse)
3. cutting
4. bingeing
5. anorexia

Childhood neglect was the best predictor for cutting and for suicidal attempts. Approximately 10% of individuals with BPD die by suicide (APA, 2013).

PTSD used to be considered more of a disorder about anxiety or stress, but in recent years it has been reconceptualised as a disorder of memory function, which is why the symptoms include flashbacks and hypervigilance. These can be derived from the relationship between stress and memory, or memory reconsolidation. Conceptualising the disorder in this way can explain why treatments involving memory and changes in conscious state, such as eye movement desensitization and reprocessing (EMDR) and psychedelic treatments can work, and this idea could also inform novel treatments for PTSD. During psychotherapy, for PTSD patients the memory of feeling safe is not rekindled. This is because the disorder also involves the memory for attachment systems. Memory for trauma involves opioid receptors. In rats, opioid receptors in the anterior cingulate are involved in feelings of intimacy. If the patient with PTSD does not have the imprint of a safe person, this memory cannot be activated, and so psychotherapy may not change the core makeup of the brain. In sum, this is evidence that psychotherapy treatment is not effective for every patient. Indeed, some patients report the efficiency of yoga, martial arts, theatre or animal-assisted therapy, which demonstrates the effectiveness of accessing modalities other than trauma-specific ones.

Along with making the individual vulnerable to PTSD in adulthood, the number of ACEs that a child has can predict physical health quality in adulthood. Felitti et al. (1998) studied the effects of child maltreatment on health and found that the more traumatised a child was in terms of ACE scores, the more likely they were to become smokers, obese or depressed and to attempt suicide as adults. Nemeroff's laboratory (Williams et al., 2016) found that children with zero ACEs but who were depressed as adults responded well to antidepressant medication, but those with four or more ACEs responded best to psychotherapy. The chances are that a traumatised child has been raised by traumatised adults. This means that if a child with zero ACEs is upset or suicidal, the child may feel comforted and safe by their parent. If that parent was neglected, however, they are not able to be that safe person for their child. Indeed, suicide attempts are almost always related to child abuse and neglect.

For many years, alcoholism was considered to be genetic, and there was considered to be a link between culture, society and number of alcoholics in that population. It is now known that the more abused the individual was as a child, the more likely it is that they will become an alcoholic. There also exists a link between drug abuse and sex abuse; individuals who feel safe and secure do not tend to take unprescribed opioids or other drugs. Behind addiction lies the issue of enormous pain. Psychiatrists and psychologists treat addiction, which is the "solution" that the individual arrives at, in an attempt to lessen their pain, rather than to deal with the cause (Van der Kolk, 2021). Another example is in the patient with binge eating disorder as a consequence of sexual abuse. "Overweight is overlooked" becomes the mode of operation, and so the patient demonstrates a failure in dieting. Since enormous pain manifests in these issues, one can identify these behaviours and their occurrences – drug abuse, abuse of food/sugary drinks/junk food, extreme dieting behaviour/anorexia, sexual promiscuity and sexually transmitted diseases and consider them symptoms of not loving one's body, and of masking great pain.

If the individual loves their body, they will not abuse it, and will instead choose to value and to treasure it. The role of the psychotherapist, then, becomes to help the individual to treasure their body, and to adapt this somatic response.

In the chimpanzees, it was common to see similar patterns of behaviour. Chimpanzees who were in cages alone, or worse, in cramped conditions with other chimpanzees in cages, showed rocking, anorexia and overgrooming. Trauma was lived out in the body in the form of bodily sensations. Indeed, Bessel Van der Kolk wrote a seminal book for humans in this regard, explaining how *The Body Keeps the Score* in his famous book (Van der Kolk, 2014). He may not have considered that the same phenomenon occurs in primates. Nobody has thought to re-analyse the data from these primates in language studies, to consider that these were traumatised animals. It would have been interesting to study the chimpanzees Washoe, Nim, Booee and the others, in order to analyse their psychological health as survivors of greatly traumatic experiences. Unfortunately, the narrative around trauma did not exist then, and many of those chimpanzees have since died. It would be useful, instead, to study their descendants. Loulis and Tatu are still alive and reside in the Fauna Foundation, in Montreal, Canada. Although Loulis was not a biological offspring of Washoe, his background as her adopted son will have caused damage, since she was lacking the necessary mothering skills. If the chimpanzee offspring were found to be suffering from post-traumatic stress symptoms, we would be left with a difficult ethical and philosophical problem, in terms of what a therapeutic environment might look like for them. If they are able to sign, should we be giving them a form of cognitive behavioural therapy (CBT) in sign language form? It is possible, of course, that they have forgotten some of their life experiences and methods of signing, and that they are now feeling safe.

Making the client feel safe is the mainstay of any psychological treatment. It is clear from the human reports that the more trauma the individual experiences, the more unexplained physical symptoms are experienced, and the more antidepressant prescriptions the individual has. If this is the case, then learning and behavioural programmes are crucial at school. Children do not outgrow their early adverse experiences. Felitti, Anda, Nordenberg et al. (1998) studied ACEs and selected public health outcomes in women. They found that current depression and number of suicide attempts correlated with number of ACEs in childhood. There were over 430,000 deaths in the US in 2019 that were due to excessive ACEs (Grummitt et al., 2021).

Narcissistic Parents

Nim was accessible, charming and fun. Washoe was not fun. She was scary. Cold, harsh, possibly critical. In turn, she made a difficult parent. Some chimpanzees are more charming and agreeable than others. Both chimpanzees had different experiences of being parented, and it is probable that this, in part, led to their different approaches and personality styles. It is likely that Washoe had watched her mother die in their natural forest habitat, but Nim was bred in the Oklahoma laboratory, and although he was taken away from his mother, Carolyn, at around 10 days of age, he was quickly placed into the loving home of Stephanie LeFarge. Perhaps it was after that time when things got particularly tough for Nim, with the many changes.

Tom Martin, who looked after Nim from 1976 to around 1978, told me: "Imagine having 200 parents". He believes that around 200 different people had looked after Nim during his time in New York. Some were students in transit, wanting a bit of experience around chimpanzees and animal learning, some were students who did not "cut it" around the chimps and who left after a very brief period, and others who stuck around a bit longer. Imagine all those models for parenting, and being parented. The best parent figures for Nim in New York, believes Tom, were Joyce Butler and Bill Tynan. Hess (2008) gives a clear explanation of how Joyce provided the very opposite to a narcissistic parent: "Butler felt the most enduring sense of responsibility for his welfare. Had Terrace anticipated the intensity of their bond, he might have been discouraged from hiring her . . . Butler brought out the best in Nim . . . he became calmer in her presence and more willing to work" (Hess, pp. 135–136). Her boundaries were clear and consistent, the opposite to narcissistic parents, who are cold, harsh and inconsistent.

Parents who are narcissistic view their children as extensions of themselves, believing that they should be "seen and not heard", teaching them to obey tightly, and criticising and judging them when they express an opinion or idea that does not align with theirs. These children grow up fearful of being judged, with this fear being linked to an added fear of being abandoned. Narcissistic parents fill the child with the sense that their emotions must be cast aside.

The child of a narcissistic mother will feel that they are never good or valuable enough, and are afraid to speak up confidently, or to challenge others. They are hypersensitive children, attuned to what others are experiencing. They struggle to protect themselves from the emotions of others, worried that they might upset them. Children of narcissistic mothers are unsure of themselves and become preoccupied with what other people think. They are deeply insecure when love is offered, which may make them feel like imposters, or unsure about themselves and their self-worth. These children grow up to have challenging and unsatisfying relationships, and often report feeling used by friends, but also at work, by colleagues and bosses. Poor Sequoyah would not have had a chance, and might have developed a fragile sense of self.

Why do these behaviours manifest? We know that narcissistic mothers have to protect their fragile sense of self, and unfortunately, their problems in feeling unworthy and insignificant affect their survival mechanism, and also that of the child. The children have often received emotional injuries, suffer emotional dysregulation, and grow to feel that they are not enough, or inferior and ashamed, and not able to please. These mothers find it hard to set boundaries, often having had their own boundaries traversed. It is possible that Washoe had problems with intimacy. In humans, when families are enmeshed, there is a problem in allowing individuality. Parents sometimes develop reliance on their children for emotional support, which causes a reversal in the parent–child roles. Parents who are emotionally immature cause a child to feel responsible for managing their parents' emotions. These messages are internalised, and the child feels alienated from him/herself. It is possible that, having introduced language to Washoe's functioning, she had internalised the emotions and expectations of the researchers. In humans, this feeling of being suffocated by parental needs and the lack of healthy defined roles within the family dynamic can lead to a fear of intimacy.

Some of the inconsistencies in behaviour shown by the researchers will have added to the trauma of Washoe. One example of this is in the fact that Fouts was suffering from alcoholism ("I had a predisposition to alcoholism", Fouts & Miller, 1998, p. 200). Fouts explains,

> And once it was triggered I had a hard time turning it off. I drank heavily for the next four years. At first I drank just to blot out the day-to-day reality of cages, guns, Dobermanns and the paranoia surrounding William Lemmon . . . I was drinking out of pure self-pity
>
> *(p. 200).*

On the same page, he explains: "Suffice it to say that I was an absent father and a lousy husband". Children of alcoholics are forced to live by the ever-changing rules set by the parent, whose sense of reality is constantly changing. They learn to survive the chaotic and negative parental behaviours by becoming hypervigilant, abandoning their sense of self, and giving up their rights to setting boundaries. It is impossible to set boundaries with alcoholic parents. The child grows up feeling unsafe and prepared to expect the worst outcome, which in turn promotes a prolonged and heightened state of arousal. They are constantly in expectation of being hurt by the very person who should be holding them in safety. Children of alcoholics become conditioned to living in fear, and even if the parent is not directly abusive towards their child, there is a continued state of social anxiety. Children of alcoholics become fearful of intimacy because they are living in survival. It is likely that many of Washoe's demonstrations of aloofness were a reaction to the problems of the individuals around her.

The parent who is an alcoholic may be physically present but, by definition, is mentally absent, leaving the child isolated. Alcoholism is not the only state to cause emotional neglect, but there may be other states causing a lack of maternal warmth and validation. This results in the child experiencing shame for feeling unloved, leading to feelings of unworthiness. Chimpanzees indicate that they have a sense of self-worth, and this is reflected in some of the more positive aspects of their early upbringing. For instance, a good sense of self-worth was fostered in Nim in his early Delafield days, when Bob Johnson, one of Nim's consistent carers, would put him to bed with a cup of tea laced with honey, and when tucked up under his favourite blanket and surrounded by his collection of stuffed toys, would tell Nim his birth story (Hess, 2008, p. 124). This would be "not in signs, but in a soothing, melodious voice". Johnson (in Hess's book) says how "it began with how he was born in Oklahoma with lots of chimpanzees, and when he was a little baby we brought him to New York". Nim would become sleepy at this stage in the story, and would fall asleep for 12 hours. We can compare this to how Washoe's story might have been told, by contrast.

If, instead, the child carries this sense of shame with them about their birth and existence, they will struggle with feelings of unworthiness, craving intimacy as much as they fear it. In relationships, this later puts the child (as the adult) in the situation where, as much as they crave intimacy, they are also in heightened fear of it. This is because of their cognitive dissonance in feeling unworthy of love, and also in the distrust in terms of that love being taken away.

Perhaps in part because of, or maybe in addition to, the alcoholism of the main caregiver, the researchers involved in the care of Washoe did not always engage in mature or well-defined relationships. Furthermore, the researchers were young, and the humans thought they were replacing the chimpanzee parents. The problem with this, however, is that the chimpanzees did not necessarily see the researchers as parents. In humans, emotional immaturity in parents results in parents and children becoming dependent upon each other in unhealthy ways. Co-dependent relationships lack personal autonomy and there is a blurring of lines between partners, which makes it impossible to set healthy boundaries. Parents who are co-dependent confuse closeness with enmeshment, becoming overinvolved in the child's life, justifying intrusiveness and expressed emotion as a parental right. This leads to the child feeling that they have no way of making their own mistakes, or of thinking their own thoughts. The child grows up believing that it is wrong for them to disagree with their parents' way of doing things, and of how they relate to other people, including the child, him/herself.

It is likely that Washoe had learned to distrust the others around her. In humans, inconsistent parenting teaches the child early on that they cannot trust their parents with their emotions, ideas or needs. This leads to a fear of intimacy in adulthood. The ability to distrust is a survival tool for such children, as they learn to navigate a complicated system of human emotion, learning to survive. It becomes difficult for the child to even trust him/herself, or the fabric of reality. Unless this distrust is reversed, the child continues to feel trapped by the limiting beliefs. As an adult, the distrust pervades relationships, so there is a fear of intimacy, and the child progresses into adulthood as an individual who attracts partners who reflect this parenting style.

How do adults cope with intense emotions, and was Washoe equipped with the survival skills to cope with the intensity around her? Stressful situations can trigger intense emotions which naturally feel easier to suppress, but the problem is that these emotions remain trapped in the body, resurfacing as anger, depression or anxiety. In order to cope with these emotions in a healthier way, positive psychology has taught humans to remain aware, accepting and compassionately curious. This is a recent narrative in the field of positive psychology. In the 1970s when these experiments were being conducted, those researchers might not have had this awareness in dealing with their own emotions, let alone in handling those of the chimpanzees. In turn, the chimpanzees themselves, having had absent their usual, healthier chimpanzee parents to model these behaviours, will not have learned how to adapt in the face of stress. In order to cope with intense emotions, humans have to first name the emotion, being as specific as possible. Do you feel angry? Do you feel ashamed? Do you feel humiliated, worried, anxious, abandoned? We now have a script for labelling our emotions on a sophisticated level. To some extent, in the passing on of a language, the chimpanzees were also given this tool of being able to label certain emotions. The next step, however, is to accept the emotion. In humans, in order to understand emotional intensity, it is important to understand that the emotion is there for a reason, and that it is OK to be feeling it. We are able to be curious as to why the emotion is there, and to understand that the emotion cannot kill us, no matter how painful it might feel. For instance, an individual with a fear of spiders can learn to understand that that fear is masking an underlying fear of dying. In accepting that fear, the individual learns that touching a spider will not kill them. Whether a chimpanzee would be capable of such higher-order deep thought processing in connection to the emotion "fear" for which they would have been taught the ASL, is questionable. Let us not be arrogant as humans who speak for the chimpanzees. We are not in the position to say that they could, or to say that they could not.

The next process in the understanding of intense emotions is to express them safely. Usually, we humans do this without much thought. We share our concerns, anxieties, anger and upsets, with someone we trust. We write stories, poems, articles. We draw or paint about them, we might listen to relatable music, or even write our own music about the experience. We take exercise, we dance or we sing, all in response to the emotion that is charging us. Could the chimpanzees perform these activities, in direct relation to intense emotions?

Lastly, in the acceptance and compassionate understanding of negative and highly charged emotions, it is imperative that the human should be able to increase self-care. Some of us do this without too much thought. We take ourselves away from the emotion for a short while, in order to give ourselves breathing space. We step away from the situation, by taking our mind off it. Perhaps we turn to a good book or a film, we go out for walks or runs, we go shopping and treat ourselves; we might eat something special, or have a bath, a cry or a sleep. We manage to create distance from the situation, to cool off, and to accept the inner emotional conflict, in a way that the chimpanzees would have been unable to do. Washoe would have been dependent on her immediate carers to have provided this sort of emotional sanctuary. Was she given extra care when emotionally charged – either angry or upset? She was continuously signing to get out.

5

POST-TRAUMATIC CHIMPANZEES

Post-traumatic stress disorder (PTSD) is developed by some individuals after they experience a traumatic event or traumatic events. PTSD can be instigated by a wide variety of traumas, ranging from unusual catastrophic events to more common events like car accidents (Nolen-Hoeksema, 2004). Symptoms of PTSD can vary from mild, where some individuals never seek treatment, to severe, greatly impacting and disrupting a person's life. There are three main sets of symptoms that people with PTSD experience. First, they re-experience the traumatic event, having flashbacks and seeing intrusive images from their traumatic experience. Second, they experience emotional numbness and detachment from others and from themselves. This can involve periods of disassociation. The third set of symptoms involves hypervigilance and chronic arousal. People with PTSD feel aware constantly of potential threats, often anticipating the return of the traumatic event (Nolen-Hoeksema, 2004). Some sufferers of PTSD also report feeling guilty for having survived the traumatic event when others have died. This is known as "survivor's guilt" (Nolen-Hoeksema, 2004).

Complex post-traumatic stress disorder (c-PTSD) can develop in response to exposure to an extremely traumatic series of events, in a context in which the individual perceives little or no chance of escape, particularly where the exposure is prolonged or repetitive (Cook et al., 2005). It refers to severe childhood abuse and neglect experiences which arise in a child's early relationships with caregivers, such as living with an alcoholic, or in a dysfunctional home. Since these experiences occur in early childhood development, there is much impact upon emotional, social, psychological and physical development. According to Levine and Frederick (1997), the bodies of traumatised people portray "snapshots" of their unsuccessful attempts to defend themselves in the face of threat and injury. Trauma is a highly activated and incomplete biological response to threat, frozen in time. When we prepare to engage in flight, the muscles in our entire body are tense

DOI: 10.4324/9781003357650-6

and in specific patterns of readiness to exert high energy. When we are not able to complete these actions, we fail to discharge this energy. It becomes fixed in specific patterns of neuromuscular readiness, so that the individual stays in a state of acute arousal, which then becomes chronic arousal, and dysfunction in the central nervous system. Therefore, traumatised individuals are stuck in an aroused state. It is not that they are suffering from a disease as such, it is that they find it very difficult to function normally under these circumstances of fixed aroused state. In adulthood, this means that nervous systems coupled with our early life experiences become wired to seek familiarity within all our relationships. This is because the body is conditioned to cope with the predictability, or even the lack of predictability, that we have witnessed from our caregivers. Since most of us are re-creating the stories of our childhood, we end up wired to seek familiarity within our romantic relationships as well.

Children can experience PTSD, although their symptoms may appear differently than the symptoms of adults. Children's memories and fears of trauma may become generalised, leading them to become afraid of a wide range of stimuli. Children may also adopt regressive behaviours such as bedwetting, and they may play out their trauma with dolls and toys (Nolen-Hoeksema, 2004). Children who have been sexually abused also engage in sexual behaviours that are inappropriate for their age.

The *Diagnostic and Statistical Manual of Mental Disorders, Fifth Edition* (*DSM-5*) defines PTSD under several criteria; the disorder involves "Exposure to actual or threatened death, serious injury, or sexual violence" (American Psychiatric Association [APA], 2013). A person can develop PTSD by directly experiencing the event, witnessing the event, or learning that the trauma occurred to a close family member or friend – such as through hearing the gory/violent details (APA, 2013). Symptoms of PTSD include "repetitive, involuntary, and intrusive distressing memories of the traumatic event(s)" (APA, 2013), dreaming of the traumatic event, and dissociation from one's surroundings. In addition, PTSD sufferers often avoid stimuli that remind them of the trauma experienced. Individuals diagnosed with PTSD may also have some changes in their mood, becoming easily aggravated or increasingly negative (APA, 2013).

We can use this knowledge about human trauma to expand understanding into individual chimpanzees – and also other species. Bradshaw et al. (2008) explain how the psychological sciences are expanding cross-cultural mental health and wellbeing to other species. Through the analysis of two previously captive chimpanzees who underwent biomedical experimentation but who are now residing at the Fauna, a sanctuary outside Montreal, Canada, for chimpanzees and other animals, the authors explain how human psychological models of diagnosis and treatment can be applied to great apes. They describe how c-PTSD in chimpanzees is consistent with descriptions of trauma-induced symptoms as described by the *DSM-IV* and human trauma research. The study considered the chimpanzees Jeannie and Rachel who were both rescued from LEMSIP. Indeed, Rachel was born in Oklahoma, and both chimps were among those rescued by James Mahoney and by Robert. These two chimpanzees exhibited the greatest psychological and behavioural damage compared with the others in the group. It was known that the two chimps had experienced early developmental trauma in the form of premature maternal separation, and other traumas during their tenures in laboratories, and they tentatively suggest diagnoses of c-PTSD, but consider possible co-morbidity with reactive attachment, major depressive and anxiety disorders.

The authors consider that while human-directed trauma recovery therapy may not appear congruent with non-human ethology, rehabilitation and care at the sanctuary are similar in goals and implementation to the human version. They describe this overlap in care: that in order to be treated for c-PTSD, the requirement is for (a) establishing safety, symptom reduction and stabilisation; (b) restoring connection, personality integration and relationship; and (c) reconstructing the trauma, developing authority over feelings/memories. The chimpanzees' symptoms reflected a large range of symptoms which would warrant psychiatric diagnosis and intervention in humans, and the authors explain how therapeutic intervention can be extended to be inclusive of both humans and chimpanzees in a trans-species fashion.

There are four main types of trauma events which commonly trigger PTSD: natural disasters, abuse, war-related combat and common traumas (Nolen-Hoeksema, 2004). Natural disasters include events like fires, floods, earthquakes and tsunamis. Many of these natural disasters are of a violent nature and cause much destruction. There are social, psychological and biological factors that contribute to the development of PTSD (Nolen-Hoeksema, 2004). It is interesting to note that culture may have an effect on the likelihood of a person developing PTSD. We can consider the social and historical context of the condition. The internet, for instance, has led us to understand and to give a script to traumatic events, so that we are able to talk about some of these traumatic events, which, in turn, allows us to promote resilience. In the 1970s, such scripts did not exist, and much traumatic behaviour went unspoken or unexplained.

Individual personality traits are involved in the development of PTSD. The personality trait of neuroticism predicts stability of mood and emotion, and rumination. The trait of extraversion predicts the likelihood of engaging in sensation-seeking or risky activities. Indeed, Eysenck's theory of criminality identified high neuroticism, high extraversion and high psychoticism (disagreeableness) as predicting criminality (Eysenck & Eysenck, 1970). This explains why highly traumatised individuals are susceptible to a life of crime, and also why prisons are inhabited by highly traumatised individuals. Taken together, in our chimpanzee story, what chance did those chimpanzees stand? The ones who were born with high levels of neuroticism would have already had a stress system that was awry, and the life stressors of captivity and lack of identity would have likely triggered the corresponding stress responses. In chimpanzees with hardwired personality traits which lend themselves to resilience, such as low neuroticism and low psychoticism, we see a chimpanzee who is slightly hardier, and perhaps warmer and more agreeable. I am describing here the traits seen in Nim. These traits stood Nim in strong form for survival despite the external conditions being less than salubrious. What about Washoe? Washoe was less hardy.

Abuse is another common form of trauma. It can occur in physical, sexual or emotional forms, sometimes with overlap within these categories. Sexual abuse survivors are at particular risk for developing PTSD. Ninety-five percent of rape survivors qualify for a PTSD diagnosis within the first 2 weeks after the initial trauma, 50% still qualify after 3 months (Nolen-Hoeksema, 2004). Even 4 to 5 years later, 25% of rape survivors still suffer from PTSD (Nolen-Hoeksema, 2004). For survivors of sexual abuse, the risk of developing PTSD can be reduced by receiving empathetic support from friends and mental health professionals (Nolen-Hoeksema, 2004). In combat- and war-related trauma, soldiers, policemen and firefighters are at risk for developing PTSD, in addition to civilians caught in the combat or experiencing the effects of war. The *DSM-5* notes that policemen often see the grisly aftermath of violent crimes first-hand and also need to hear detailed reports from victims of abuse as a part of their vocation. In these cases, the victim and the police officer are at risk for developing PTSD. There have been reported cases of PTSD in many wars, including both World Wars (Nolen-Hoeksema, 2004). In the wars where no cases of PTSD are reported, it is likely that those involved did not have a name for the disorder. In the UK, PTSD only received its name after World War I. In a memoir of the Royal Victoria Military Hospital at Netley in Southampton, UK, Philip Hoare (2001) explains how, "Some believed it was the actual physical impact of bombardment that caused these symptoms; other saw deeper underlying causes . . . which would realise that the emotional and the rational were not so easily separated." Charles Myers, a psychologist to the Army, first described self-shock in *The Lancet* in February 1915. The term was already being used in the trenches, and Myers and colleagues fought to have the condition recognised by the Army, realising that this new phenomenon was not so much about exploding shells, but more about the intense and particular horror of modern war. PTSD first entered the *DSM* in 1980, and so when Washoe was suffering, it was not even used to describe a human condition. It was in the Anxiety Disorders section of the *DSM-III*, and derivatives had also appeared in the previous International Classification of Diseases and DSM manuals.

It can be considered that the main goals in treating PTSD include client exposure to fear in order to ease it, challenging distorted ways of thinking that contribute to symptoms, and helping to reduce other stressors and manage ongoing problems. Therapy can take the form of cognitive behavioural therapy (CBT), eye movement desensitization and reprocessing (EMDR), or antidepressant medication. Additionally, stress management techniques are often taught to help clients manage other areas of stress in their lives (Nolen-Hoeksema, 2004). Individuals with PTSD struggle to sleep, and suffer nightmares. Selective serotonin reuptake inhibitors and/or benzodiazepines may be prescribed to treat these symptoms, which can alter levels of consciousness, so the client can deal with the trauma symptoms. This explains why individuals with trauma also take recreational drugs such as LSD and cannabis. It is likely that one of the reasons why Nim enjoyed smoking cannabis was because it calmed him down. He was similar to a young child in his disinhibited manner, and using cannabis quelled some of those behaviours, and most likely helped him to forget some of the chaos around him.

CBT is effective in employing systematic desensitization therapy, where clients are gradually exposed to their fears. When individuals with PTSD begin to ruminate about traumatic events, thought-stopping techniques, where the individual yells "No!" to stop their thoughts, is helpful (Nolen-Hoeksema, 2004). EMDR is a form of psychotherapy whereby the patient recalls distressing experiences while doing bilateral stimulation, such as side-to-side eye movement, or tapping either side of the body.

PTSD is often accompanied by depression. Individuals with PTSD and depression tend to experience overly generalised memories as well as negative intrusive memories. Ashbaugh et al. (2018) found that the more intense the PTSD symptoms were, the more likely the individual was to have negative memories which included "higher sensory detail, and were more vivid" (Ashbaugh et al., 2018). The more severe a person's depressive symptoms were, the more likely they were to have difficulty accessing their memories of trauma, and their memories also tended to be incoherent. PTSD is a disorder in which sufferers have an overactive memory, causing them to relive their trauma over and over in great detail. This type of memory loop may also serve as a kind of safety mechanism for the brain to remember the trauma and to become hyperaware of what could potentially lead to a similar event, and hypervigilant in the expectation of such an occurrence. It is likely that chimpanzees like Washoe were ruminating in those moments when they felt alone and with no escape from their cages.

When the individual is traumatised, there is a tendency for the emotional part of the brain to take over, rather than the rational part of the brain. The brain is constantly asking itself, "How does this make me feel?" High activation of the amygdala, and low levels of serotonin within the amygdala make the individual interpret the world as dangerous. Low serotonin levels make it more likely for the brain to interpret stimuli as being a part of a danger signal, whereas high levels of serotonin make it less likely to interpret the world as dangerous. There is a cognitive bias signalling danger.

Individuals with PTSD also experience physiological hyperreactivity (Nolen-Hoeksema, 2004). Positron emission tomography (PET) scans revealed differences in the brains of people with PTSD compared with people who do not have PTSD. When imagining trauma, participants with PTSD showed increased blood flow to the anterior cingulate gyrus and amygdala. Both are regions that play a role in emotion and memory. Other studies have revealed damaged hippocampal areas, also involved in memory, but which also play a role in fear extinction, thus interfering with a person's ability to overcome fearful responses to things that remind them of the traumatic event. Pavić et al. (2006) explain how "chronic stress can . . . cause damage in the human hippocampus". These researchers used magnetic resonance imaging (MRI) to examine the hippocampus of war veterans with PTSD compared with a control group without PTSD. MRI data showed that the right hippocampus was significantly smaller in PTSD subjects than in healthy controls. The left hippocampus was also smaller in PTSD subjects than in controls, although this difference was not significant (Pavić et al., 2006). There are also studies which find that hippocampal shrinkage correlates with intensity of PTSD symptoms and number of years on the frontline in Vietnam veterans (Gurvits et al., 1996).

The stress induced by the initial trauma and subsequent stress generated from PTSD damage the areas of the brain that impact memory. While all humans experience some kind of stress at some stage in their lives, individuals with PTSD either experience more significant trauma and stress compounded upon the "normal" stress in their lives, or they react in a particular way in response to such trauma. This may lead to further damage of the hippocampus. Additionally, individuals with PTSD experience flashbacks where they relive stress and trauma which can also damage the hippocampus further.

Flashbacks are a common feature of PTSD. In one study, researchers note that only certain images from trauma become flashbacks (Bourne et al., 2013). They explain that flashbacks often are specific moments within the traumatic event, as opposed to having a flashback of the entire traumatic event from beginning to end. Using MRI, researchers noted that when encoding flashbacks, areas of the brain corresponding with emotional, visual and threat processing were involved (Bourne et al., 2013). While the study did not offer an answer as to why some memories are encoded and become flashbacks and others do not, the researchers argue that understanding the origin of flashbacks may lead to a better understanding of how to treat and minimise them in individuals with PTSD. The researchers emphasise that even though the precise encoding of flashbacks may not be understood, there are methods to reduce flashbacks which can be utilised within hours after a person experiences trauma. We might ask here if it is possible to experience positive flashbacks? The answer is yes, it is possible to experience a sort of positive flashback experience. The phenomenon of "ear worm" is the process whereby the individual experiences the cognitive intrusions of music, which can be pleasant (if a little annoying!). The act of chewing has been shown to work against ear worm, as it stimulates the motor cortex stimulation and causes dopamine surges. This may give us clues in terms of prevention of cognitive intrusions in PTSD. Flashbacks are incredibly distressing to sufferers of PTSD. Holmes et al. (2009) conducted experiments to establish a "cognitive vaccine" to mitigate the number of flashbacks that a person experiences, involving the visuospatial, cognitive computer game, Tetris.

Washoe's Adverse Childhood Experiences (ACEs)

Children from dysfunctional homes struggle to find their identity in adulthood. The severe experiences of children in abuse and neglect that arise from the child's early relationships with caregivers, such as when living with alcoholic, violent or dysfunctional individuals, are adverse childhood experiences (ACEs). Felitti et al. (1998) explain the relationship of childhood abuse and household dysfunction to many of the leading causes of death in adults. They discovered that ACEs are surprisingly common – 67% of their tested population had at least one category of ACE, and 12.6% had four or more categories of ACEs. Furthermore, they found a dose-response relationship between ACEs and poor health outcomes. The higher a person's ACE score, the greater the risk to their health. A person with four or more ACEs was twice as likely to develop heart disease or cancer, and 3.5 times more likely to develop chronic obstructive pulmonary disease than a person without ACEs.

It was certainly the case that Washoe was from a dysfunctional home. Chimpanzees that grew up knowing such extreme levels of stress, as with humans, were likely to pass on their experiences, and to parent in the only way that felt familiar to them. By introducing language, the experimenters inadvertently gave Washoe an extra tool for ruminating. She was therein able to create a narrative for what was happening to her. The situation that Washoe was placed in would have made this worse and produced a chimpanzee with difficulties. What did Washoe think about when she was on her own?

It is possible, then, that some of the narcissistic traits that Washoe demonstrated were inherent, while others had developed as a consequence of her being kept captive. She was not able to demonstrate empathy, but this may have been as a reaction to traumatic experiences rather than due to hardwired personality traits. Washoe learned very quickly that she could use her baby Sequoyah to barter for things. In the wild her baby would have been a status raiser, but in reality, the social hierarchy was so abnormal and she was isolated, the baby became a currency for ORANGES or OUT.

Washoe had difficult personality traits. Robert describes her as "pissy". She could be aloof, and hostile. She tested human relationships for dominance, and developed inappropriate relationships, like crushes. Fouts explains how he allowed his 14-year-old son to volunteer in the laboratory, and "Washoe developed a head-over-heels crush on Josh . . . Washoe's own teenage hormones now began raging at the mere sight of him . . . Washoe literally threw herself at his feet, and began shrieking like a desperate, lovelorn suitor" (Fouts & Mills, 1998, p. 261). Washoe showed "sisterly spats and childhood traumas" (Fouts & Mills, 1998, p. 259). Yet Nim, by comparison, was cheerful and agreeable, of robust personality. Why should this be the case? It is likely, as in humans, that there is a range of distribution for each of the personality traits. Then we have to ask: how much of personality is innate, and how much is inherited? Psychologists know that personality is due to both nature (the hardwired brain regions and genes we are born with) and nurture (the type of caregiving, enrichment and nurturing received from the environment). It is likely that some of this distinction between the two chimpanzees was due to the conditions into which they were born. Nim was bred for language research, and although he was taken away from his mother at around 10 days of age, he would have known nurturance and attachment towards her, and then towards Stephanie LaFarge, who claims to have "breastfed him for a while" (it is unclear whether this is true). It was later on, once Nim was passed from one caregiver to the next, that the damage might have been done to his personality. It is possible that those early acquired memories of attachment and care were warm ones for Nim, so that by the time the transfer of attachment figures occurred, he already felt secure in his sense of self. Washoe, on the other hand, had traumatic early years. While she may have been born to a loving mother in her country of origin, it is likely that she witnessed her mother dying, was snatched from her, placed in a crate and travelled over several days, making a frightening journey from West Africa to the US. Upon arrival into the US, there might have been a quarantine period, certainly a period of time where her new whereabouts would have had a question mark over them. She was incarcerated for several months at the Holloman Aeromedical Laboratory where she was destined for the American Space Program, before being picked out by the Gardners to join a new home and culture with them. In this new environment, she would have been expected to learn sign language and how to survive a cross-species environment. Would we take a human infant and place that infant among chimpanzees, with these expectations? This is a tremendous amount of shift for an infant chimpanzee. The fact that she survived at all is not short of miraculous.

Washoe would have been exposed to another big shift much later in Oklahoma, where she would not even have witnessed another of her own kind before. Washoe would have been exposed to another big shift much later in Oklahoma. It is easy to believe, from Fouts's account, that she would not have witnessed another of her own kind before. However, she was born among chimpanzees, to a chimpanzee mother, who would have been in some sort of group of around 15 to 25, maybe even upwards of 40, chimpanzees. We cannot know for certain what her experience was, but it is probable that her first BLACK BUG encounters with other chimpanzees were not the first time that she saw her own kind. It is not known how long Washoe was in the forest, exactly, but from the documents, it is clear that she was there for at least 6 months. This is a crucial time. Not all infant developmental periods are the same. Those first 6 months are particularly important, developmentally, since the brain develops, and much happens concerning mother-baby attachment in those first months. This would have been a particularly salient time.

How upsetting would this be, if it were a human? You have been taken out of your home, where you have been reared by a selection of research assistant caregivers, into a new environment, which might have been promised to resemble the wilderness, but which, in reality, consists of cages. Linden describes during his exposure to the institute, the "discomfiting realities of the lives of the chimps" (Linden, *Silent Partners*, 1986, p. 90). While the complex of cages interconnected to allow the chimps to be isolated or kept together, "there is no escaping the dreariness of the concrete and steel structure, particularly since a chronic shortage of funds left the institute without the manpower to keep the area clean." The disenchantment was felt within the institute by a number of individuals in the 1970s, including, of course, Robert, but there were other researchers who refused to work at the institute, despite having conducted work with primates. Linden quotes Jane Lancaster, an anthropologist then affiliated with the University of Oklahoma, as saying, "It was sort of like saying, 'I love humans; I think I'll go to the state penitentiary and learn about humans'." (Linden, 1986, p. 90).

By the time Washoe had given birth to Sequoyah, her existence in the cage would have been dismal. She was stuck, and not allowed out. Fouts had abandoned her at this point, and she could see the other chimpanzees being taken out for walks. Robert believes that Washoe could count, and that she could work out that the other chimps were allowed out, and he says how she would sign, "OUT OUT OUT". It is important to note here that it is highly likely that chimpanzees can count. Human infants are born with the ability to add and subtract (Wynn, 1992). It is part of demonstrating separation anxiety, and object permanence, and of understanding when people and objects are present and when they are away, later on in life. Chimpanzees can apply this ability to add and subtract to everyday behaviours when they are taking a running total. It is likely that Washoe was doing a mental calculation of how many times the other chimps were allowed out and how often she was afforded the privilege. There is also separation anxiety in chimps and object permanence. This was a chimp who was obsessed with getting out.

Washoe had to apply these understandings about separation and object permanence, and loss, on a number of occasions. As Linden describes from his visit in 1979, "recent events in Washoe's life have been downright melodramatic. For the past three years Fouts had been hoping that Washoe would raise a child. She gave birth twice and lost both babies, the first because of congenital deformities and the second [this was Sequoyah], after three months, to pneumonia" (Linden, 1986, pp. 90–91).

Washoe was struck by the deaths on both occasions. There was also a stillbirth in between, which happens a lot in captivity. When her first baby died, it is reported by Fouts that Washoe handed the baby to him, touchingly, in hopes that he could save him (p. 91). Robert explains that in fact, the first baby did have congenital deformities, but that he died a few days after birth when he fell off a shelf on which Washoe had placed him. Linden describes this first infant dying when it "fell and cracked its skull" (p. 96).

After Sequoyah died, Roger had to sign to her that the baby was dead, after she rushed up to him and signed, "WHERE'S BABY?" Linden reports how Roger made the sign for "baby" by forming his hand in cradle configuration in front of his body, and how Washoe's response was to slump and drop her hands into her lap, staring off into the corner. It is reported that for the next few days, whenever she saw Fouts, Washoe would ask where her baby was, and each time, he had to tell her that her baby was dead, and Washoe's response was to sit and stare (Fouts & Mills, 1998, p. 91). Coping with trauma and with grief, especially postnatally, is fatiguing for humans. Nobody thought to check this in the chimpanzees.

Linden makes an important point about Washoe's abilities as a mother. These accounts of the infant deaths may give us the impression that Washoe was a caring and nurturing mother, but other observers, says Linden, "including those involved in monitoring Washoe during those critical days", had the opposite impression, and indeed, Washoe was "distrusted by a number of the men and women working at the institute" (Linden, 1986, p. 92). There are accounts of Washoe's aggression against individuals, such as her biting one of the graduate students, David Rowe, on the cheek. This "aggression camouflaged as affection" (Linden, 1986, p. 92) was not only representative of Washoe's behaviours and her unpredictability at the time but is also reminiscent of features of antisocial personality disorder in humans, which is characterised by impulsivity, irritability, a disregard and violation of the rights of others, conning others, physical fights/assaults, recklessness, consistent irresponsibility and a lack of remorse (*DSM-5*). The causes given for antisocial personality disorder include developmental factors that may cause brain function changes, such as abuse and unstable family life.

It is difficult to diagnose retrospectively, and personality disorders are complicated, by definition. It is possible that some of the behavioural manifestations would have been consistent with a diagnosis of borderline personality disorder (BPD), which is now referred to as emotionally unstable personality disorder (EUPD) by the *DSM-5*. This is a disorder of mood and of how one interacts with others. The symptoms usually emerge in adolescence and persist into adulthood. Symptoms include emotional instability (the psychological term for this is affective dysregulation), disturbed patterns of thinking or perception (cognitive distortions or perceptual distortions), impulsive behaviour and intense but unstable relationships with others. These manifest as a fear of getting abandoned, self-harm, suicidal tendencies, frequent mood swings, unjustified anger bursts, impulsive decision-making, paranoia around people, inferiority complexes and feelings of worthlessness, unstable relationships, stress and dissociation. Again, the causes stem from both genetic and environmental factors, and most sufferers have experienced some kind of trauma or neglect as children.

It is apparent that Washoe was exhibiting chaotic personality traits. Linden explains how "She was perceived by many on the staff as a likely candidate to star in a chimp *Mommie Dearest*. She even turned out to be a jealous lover" (Linden, 1986, p. 93). Linden rightly points out that (chimp, but also human) maternal behaviour is not automatic, but is "culturally integrated", meaning that they learn how to be mothers by observing their own and other mothers, during their early years (Linden, 1986, p. 74). Washoe lacked the opportunity to learn these skills. Indeed, it is reported that "Lemmon and others at the institute doubted that she had acquired the necessary skills" (p. 94), which paired with the cage environment, exacerbated Washoe's inabilities to perform mothering skills in order to help her infant to survive. Again, Linden was testimony to some of the accounts of this, and explains how researchers "saw Washoe use her infant to manipulate in ways horrible to contemplate . . . In effect she was saying, 'Give me some fruit, or I will put this infant under the faucet.'" (p. 96). Since those crucial aspects of mothering were lacking, more selfish feelings would take over. There were underlying clues that Washoe would not make a good mother. Mother chimps do not put down their newborns, and the fact that Washoe put her first baby down should have been a clue that her mothering skills were inadequate (Linden, 1986, p. 96). Washoe reacted negatively to Sequoyah's attempts to breastfeed. During this time, it is reported that "Roger asked the female assistants to pretend to breast-feed the baby chimp and then surreptitiously substitute the expressed milk. More than one balked at the idea" (Linden, 1986, p. 96).

Let us consider here other ways in which primates were helped on their way to finding safety. During the course of writing this book, we were sad to learn about the death of Dr. Shirley McGreal. The contributions of McGreal to the rescue of primates will now be explained.

Remembering Dr. Shirley McGreal, OBE (Died 20 November 2021)

Robert's words:

I heard about her in 1975. In Diana Davis's office, there was a newsletter from IPPL – the International Primate Protection League's sanctuary, in Summerville, South Carolina, on her desk. Dr. McGreal – Shirley – was born and grew up in England, but she lived in Thailand where she was working on gibbons at first, and then she moved back to the US, and lived in South Carolina. Shirley was knowledgeable about so much in primate protection. She was friends with Prince Philip (who also died in the same year this book was written), and with Dian Fossey, and had many handwritten letters from both. She helped to pay for a proper headstone for Dian Fossey following her murder by poachers in Rwanda, Africa. In those days, I was a volatile person, and she had a political way of working.

When the chimpanzees began the odyssey of being sold, Shirley came to the rescue. She was incredibly obliging, and helped us to make contact with a number of helpful people, such as a judge in Arizona. When Ally was lost, she helped to find him, and then published the story. . . . She worked both within LEMSIP and outside it. She was friends with Dr. James (Jim) Mahoney. Both Drs. McGreal and Mahoney changed the standards at the LEMSIP laboratory, so that it had to close. Jim Mahoney was unapologetic about the primate research being carried out at LEMSIP at first, but later he was happy to show people exactly what was being done to the primates.

In his book, 'From Elephants to Mice: Animals Who Have Touched My Soul', Dr. Mahoney describes Igor, a 53-year-old, self-mutilating gibbon, who had given many years of his life to research. Dr. Mahoney had managed to negotiate with Dr. Jan Moor-Jankowski, the founder and director of LEMSIP, into donating Igor and other gibbons from LEMSIP to the IPPL's sanctuary in South Carolina, where it was founded by Dr. McGreal.

Dr. James Mahoney described Dr. Shirley McGreal as "a petite, feisty English lady with a rich Yorkshire accent", although she was actually originally from Cheshire, who "has probably done more than any other single person to protect primates living in the wild and to stop, or at least curb, their illicit trade and smuggling". Dr. McGreal's background was that she lived in Thailand with her husband, John McGreal, in the early 1970s. In 1971, she was horrified when she encountered crates of infant rhesus monkeys awaiting export from the cargo area of Bangkok airport. The sight of them piled on top of each other in inhumane conditions, gazing at her with doleful eyes, led her to take action to prevent their smuggling to the US and other countries, as she contacted primatologists around the globe, and then started the International Primate Protection League (IPPL) in 1973. She was able to document the horrors of the primate trade in its first newsletter which was launched in 1974, and which is still in existence.

Dr. McGreal worked with Ardith Eudey, a researcher into the stump-tailed macaque monkeys originally seen at the airport, to investigate the enormous traffic in macaques for use in biomedical research. They organised a team of Thai students to work undercover at Bangkok airport to monitor all wildlife exports over 10 weeks. They revealed staggering volumes of around 100,000 mammals, birds and reptiles, in appalling conditions, and in violation of international standards. Thailand banned the export of all primates shortly afterwards.

Dr. McGreal uncovered the lucrative industry in the monkey trade in 1977, when she exposed the US's breach of a treaty with India, by importing rhesus monkeys for neutron bomb testing. Since the treaty specifically stated that monkeys could not be used in warfare-related research, the National Institutes of Health, and biomedical researchers, were forced to take Dr. McGreal seriously, and the exposure led to a total ban on exportation of rhesus monkeys from India to the US, regardless of what the scientific purpose was, a ban that is still upheld to this day. Dr. Mahoney explains how, "the price of a rhesus monkey in the United States skyrocketed overnight from around $30 to $2,000, if the monkey could be obtained from China, the only immediately available nondomestic source after the Indian embargo went into effect". The price of rhesus monkeys never went down again, and although this did not curtail their use in research, it forced scientists to be more careful about how they used the animals, and it made funding agencies more careful about funding such studies. Furthermore, that work led to similar blanket bans on primate exports from Bangladesh in 1979, where interest from the US had shifted, and in Malaysia in 1984.

Dr. James Mahoney had also worked with IPPL. He met IPPL's local veterinarian, Dr. John Ohlandt, a couple of times a year to carry out examinations on the gibbons up until his sad death in 2017. Indeed, Dr. McGreal announced his death, describing him as "the Oskar Schindler of laboratory primates" (James Mahoney, DVM, "the Oskar Schindler of laboratory primates," dies at 77 – Animals 24–7). Robert explains how "Dr. McGreal was integral because she could give the information. She would often pursue a number of routes to get what she wanted". One example is how she uncovered the "Singapore connection" in 1975, whereby primates were being smuggled into Singapore and exported from there under falsified permits. After contacting first the Singapore government, then the governments of the countries where the primates were being captured, Thailand, Malaysia and Indonesia, to no avail, she wrote an exposé for the Bangkok Post. This was picked up by the Reuters news agency, went global, and embarrassed the Singapore government into action.

Dr. McGreal died on 20th November 2021. It is important to acknowledge the hard work and commitment of these individuals. Dr. McGreal's obituary in the Guardian explains how she ". . . was a firm believer in grassroots conservation; she had a long legacy of seeking out and nurturing frontline conservationists around the globe. As well as organising and attending primate welfare and conservation conferences, Shirley spent her days investigating cases of illegal trafficking, courageous in pursuit despite the intimidation and death threats that could ensue.

It is clear that she had received death threats for her work. She was able to use her extensive network of contacts for investigation into tip-offs, either formally, or undercover, often pursuing numerous routes. McGreal received a number of awards for her work, including one from the Interpol Wildlife Crime Group, and from the Dutch Police League in 1994 for exposing an international ring of primate smugglers. Prince Philip, the Duke of Edinburgh, was a fan of her accomplishments, and they carried out a long correspondence from their meeting at a conference in 1981 until his death in 2021. Indeed, when McGreal was awarded the Order of the British Empire in 2008, she was thrilled to enjoy a private chat before the investiture with the Duke. In a letter he wrote to her in 2015, he said: "I am glad to know that IPPL continues to flourish and keeps up the good work of pursuing the crooks, rewarding the righteous and caring for 36 gibbons!"

Indeed, it is important that the righteous and caring are honoured in this book. The animals deserve their dignity, and these individuals made huge accomplishments in helping these animals with the trauma that they had endured at the hands of human researchers and traffickers.

For human trauma, part of the problem is that a lot of the disturbance occurs in early childhood, so that by the time the child starts school, they are taking their trauma in with them, and having to learn how to focus with the shadow of suffering constantly in the background. Schools and colleges are not psychotherapy centres and may be ill-equipped to deal with traumatised students. When in a chronic state of trauma, the individual works hard to shut down the fearful event, but because the individual is chronically stressed, escape is not sought. The individual adapts to realising that escape is not possible, and so for them, it becomes difficult to distinguish between danger and safety, because they never feel safe. We can consider here how animals like Washoe would have been in their cages under constant duress.

One way in which traumatised individuals try to find safety is through psychotherapy. Indeed, we could consider the role of the therapist to be one of containing the client's fear, and to provide safety at all costs. The role demands that the therapist creates a place of safety where the client can attempt healthy prefrontal cortex function, where the patient is able to observe themself back during the period when they were traumatised, and to say, "That was then", and to be aware that "This is now". A good therapist will ask the client: "Where are you feeling the effects of that right now?" in order to help them identify the physical manifestations of the registering of the traumatic event(s). This is to help with the sensations of "now", and how that trauma is being lived out in the present time.

Crucially, patients with trauma have experiences and memories with intense emotions. They remember with excessive and irrelevant responses. The recollection of these events absorbs a great amount of energy and effort, as the traumatised individual struggles to control the self. Memories of traumatic events cannot be integrated into everyday life, and so the individual strives to push them away. The problem is that these intrusions come back as enactments. Those individuals attempt to translate their experiences into words and memories, but they struggle to transform those experiences into a simple story. If unable to tell the trauma story, the individual becomes afraid of the memory, and unable to reproduce it, and so it manifests in other ways – such as through dreams, dissociations, intrusive and ruminative thoughts and cognitive intrusions (flashbacks). The individual then experiences fear of the fear.

Relating this to Washoe, it is possible that some of her "bitchy" behaviours, as Robert calls them, the aloofness and the narcissistic-style mothering behaviours, may have been due to having an absent parent figure in Fouts, who admits problems with alcohol in his book. Since it is now known in the childhood adversity literature that alcoholic parents are linked to personality disorders, and maladaptive functioning. It is difficult to believe that these did not lead Washoe to feel neglected. Furthermore, her sad demeanour and her signing OUT OUT WALK all the time in those days, despite Robert being able to take her out, suggests a sense of yearning. If we think about this in humans: those qualities of being critical and unhappy are often linked to feelings of being trapped and helpless. It is highly possible that when Washoe was kept in her cage, being pressured to name items and keep up with her signs, she was, in fact, probably missing her parent figure and blaming herself for the absences and for the treatment bestowed upon her. Ironically, it is not the spoken language that was important, but the unspoken message.

The field of epigenetics has transformed the area of trauma with a more hopeful spin. It is known that trauma can be inherited through changes in DNA, but it was recently found that this can be reversed through positive experiences. Sadly this evidence has come from experimental work performed on animals. Gapp, Bohacek, Grossmann et al. (2016) studied newborn male mice separated from their mothers, causing traumatic stress. The negative consequences of this are depressive behaviours, cognitive and antisocial problems, and risk-taking. Those male mice *and* their male offspring showed trauma symptoms, which were reversed *both* in father mice, and in their offspring, when exposed to positive environments. This reversed the symptoms, and also the biological reasons for them. The biological reasons were the increased levels of glucocorticoids in the hippocampus. These same alterations were found in the hippocampus of the traumatised fathers and also the offspring. In other words, epigenetic marks can be corrected by positive experiences, suggesting that those who have been traumatised during childhood can reverse their symptoms at some point. Even if there is trauma engraved in the epigenome, the biology is dynamic enough to allow for correction. This study also suggests that we "are" a mixture of our genes, our memories and our lived experiences.

6

WHEN ALL THE CHIMPANZEES ARE DEAD

"I have nothing to fear. And here my story ends. My troubles are all over, and I am at home". The sign at the Black Beauty Ranch in Texas, where Nim ended his days, waves to and fro against the wind. These are the words of the English author, Anna Sewell, from her only novel, *Black Beauty*, which was published in 1877. Cleveland Amory owned the ranch, and he was also an author, reporter, television and radio commentator, and an animal rights activist. Amory's great-great-uncle, George Thorndike Angell, published the first American edition of the book, a few years after it was published in England. Anna Sewell wrote the novel when she was bedridden with hepatitis or tuberculosis, and she died 5 months after its publication. *Black Beauty* is a first-horse narrative of a horse's maltreatment. Anna Sewell gave a careful and detailed description of Beauty, who is an obedient, intelligent, courageous horse, sadly sold to cruel owners after being with kind masters. In the story, Beauty collapses from ill treatment and being overworked. The overall story is one which discusses both animal welfare and how to treat people with compassion.

Amory had sufficient funds to buy Nim from the Laboratory for Experimental Medicine and Surgery in Primates (LEMSIP), and Nim became the first non-hooved animal at the ranch. The ranch owners had no idea how to deal with a primate, but at least Nim was saved from further medical research. Thanks to James Mahoney's and Robert's work, further chimpanzees who were spared from LEMSIP became companions to Nim at Black Beauty Ranch: Sally, then Kitty who was rescued from the Coulston Foundation, Lulu and Midge. It is hard to understand the true motive for Amory's saving Nim, given the many other captive chimpanzees who were left behind.

The linkage of safety with home raises the question of how we define a safe home. We consider "home" to be a safe space in which we relax and unwind, and in which we can be ourselves. Where was home for Nim? Where was home for

DOI: 10.4324/9781003357650-7

Washoe? We could be tempted to believe that the ranch became a safe home for Nim. The ranch was initially set up as a sanctuary for burros rescued in 1979 and the early 1980s by the Fund for Animals, which was founded in 1967. It was the largest sanctuary sponsored by the Fund, which was headed by Amory. How could a primate have been at home in a place run exclusively as a residence for hooved animals? A more appropriate space was needed, and still is needed, for the primates being saved from captivity.

The rescuing of the chimpanzees from their laboratorial and pseudoscientific captivity has been an enduring process. Robert's commitment to finding salvation for these animals has been continued. He has dedicated his life to finding and building shelter for these animals and to promoting their salvation. A tremendous amount of activity has gone into this, which has included promotion, leafletting, giving talks and physical construction of safe spaces for laboratory animals. This has often led to the creation and endorsement of artwork and cultural messages. It is imperative that the message of salvation continues to be spread worldwide.

After Trauma

Turning to human trauma first; Vaswani (2018) performed a comparison of adverse childhood experiences (ACEs) in Glasgow, UK. These are potentially traumatic events that occur during childhood, and can take the form of a single traumatic event, like a death in the family or incarceration of a family member, or ongoing traumatic experiences like sexual abuse and neglect. They are important because, as was explained in previous chapters, they are linked to psychological, social and physical health conditions later in life, and affect future offspring and lead to premature death. Vaswani discusses how violence against children is a case of being hidden in plain sight, with physical and verbal aggression towards children conducted "behind closed doors". If we rank order the countries of the world in terms of number of abuse cases against children, the *not abusing* of children is a hallmark of civilisation (Van der Kolk, 2021). Historically, childhood trauma is correlated with extreme political beliefs. Adolf Eichmann, the major Holocaust perpetrator, for instance, is an example of this. Eichmann was the eldest of five children, born in 1906 to a Calvinist Protestant family in Solingen, Germany. His father was strict, his mother died when he was 10 years old, and he befriended some older boys who were members of various right-wing militias. As a result of poor school performance, his father withdrew him from his school and enrolled him in a vocational college, where he left without attaining a degree and instead joined his father's company, the Untersberg Mining Company, where he worked for several months. Eichmann experienced an enormous amount of physical violence, and when he joined the army he was made to conform by obeying.

There are gender issues associated with trauma. Studies examining gender differences in ACEs suggest that boys and girls are differentially exposed (Baglivio et al., 2013). The consequences of this exposure vary by gender (Duke et al.,

2010), with males being associated with delinquency, and females with substance use. Girls and boys differ in exposure levels to risk factors and strength of associations between risk factors and behavioural health problems (Daly, 1994; Kroneman et al., 2009; Rosenbaum & Lasley, 1990; Steffensmeier & Allan, 1996). A study comparing ACE questionnaire responses from male offenders receiving outpatient psychological treatment, against those in a normative sample, found higher prevalence of ACEs among offenders, reflecting the relationship between ACEs and adult criminality (Reavis et al., 2013).

Rothman et al. (2008) took retrospective reports of adults from the National Epidemiologic Survey on Alcohol and Related Conditions to predict drinking initiation. They found that ACEs were associated with drinking alcohol before the age of 14 years. Duke et al. (2010) examined the impact of ACEs on adolescent interpersonal and self-directed violence and found that each additional ACE was associated with an increase in the perpetration of interpersonal violence such as delinquency, bullying, fighting, dating violence and weapon carrying, and also self-directed violence which includes self-mutilatory behaviour, suicidal ideation and suicide attempts.

Felitti et al. (1998) found that females reported more ACEs than males. In a high-risk sample of juvenile justice system–involved youth, adolescent girls reported more ACEs than boys, were more likely to experience multiple types of ACEs (Baglivio & Epps, 2016) and also reported different types of ACEs compared to boys (Dierkhising et al., 2013; Kilpatrick & Saunders, 1997), such as sexual abuse and assault, whereas physical abuse tended to be more prevalent among boys (Kilpatrick & Saunders, 1997; Teague et al., 2008; Trocmé & Wolfe, 2001). A sample of approximately 4,000 adolescents found that 21.3% of boys had experienced physical abuse, compared to 13.4% of girls (Kilpatrick & Saunders, 1997). It is thought that this was due to the use of physical punishment as more normative for boys (Straus & Stewart, 1999). Duke et al. (2010) also found that ACEs were associated with violence perpetration risk, and this was stronger for boys. There is evidence that males grow up to engage in violent behaviours. Women do not become extremists or terrorists (Van der Kolk, 2021).

After being traumatised, the individual inhabits a different universe. This inner world can be measured and explained through self-report, brain scans or projective testing. The latter can give an idea about what the individual's reality looks like. Although projective tests are not necessarily scientific or conclusive, they can be used as therapeutic tools to give an idea about the client's reality. The same is true, to some extent, of those chimpanzee studies, but this work cannot be done without a starting point of consideration of our place on this planet. The work that has been done gives us an understanding of how we have traumatised not just those animals, but this planet. How, then, can we repair the harm that has been inflicted?

There are new and different challenges to the future of these studies, and to primate life. Deforestation, climate change, the global pandemic – these are existential threats. Chimpanzees are vulnerable to COVID, and it is likely that they will have a higher mortality rate than humans if COVID enters their population. We are looking at a very real chance of losing entire species of apes, and so whether it is through this pandemic or a future one, chimpanzees are at risk.

What is going well, currently? We would do well to consider examples of good practice. The work being carried out currently might not protect all chimpanzees but may be a start to safeguarding at least some of them. There has been a decrease in poaching and illegal logging, there is collaboration with communities so they can access resources, but also so that primatologists can help to conserve and protect the forest to sustain those resources for the generations to come. Bringing this work to a small scale with daily activity helps to keep everyone motivated in order that they might continue with this work. Attention has been given recently to the issues of "rewilding", a new and progressive approach to conservation, with ecologists such as Paul Jepson and Cain Blythe (2020) discussing practical insights to reviving ecological processes, by restoring the interactions between plants, animals and natural disturbances in ecosystems, and Isabella Tree (2018) describing the Knepp project in the UK, explaining how she handed a farm of 3,500 acres back to nature, restoring the land and its wildlife in a short space of time. In his book, *Feral* (2013), George Monbiot gives evidence for how rewilding parts of the world could be economically as well as ecologically advantageous.

It was through the spirit of this work that this book was created. One might say that it was the spirit of Nim himself that made this book happen. We authors did not know each other until just a few months ago. The first time after I saw *Project Nim*, I wanted to make contact with Robert. I was not sure what for. In fact, it took me a few years to consider out why I would even contact him. I thought that maybe he was an established academic, and that perhaps I could help him for a short while with some chimpanzee research, or to learn how things unravelled next, for Nim. I had little idea that there had been other chimpanzees. I had taught his work on Nim and sign language in my Psychology classes for decades, and I wanted him to know. In the showing of the film, it was clear that one of the few carers who was attuned to Nim's psychological needs was Robert, but the point that was clearer to me was that Nim was recognising Bob's trauma, as much as Bob was recognising Nim's.

I searched for Robert on the internet, but he was not easy to find. When I found him on Instagram, in the space of just a few months contact was made, meetings were planned, and this book has been created. We have shared stories and information about psychology, the historical context, views on apes and chimps and animals. We made contact with the other researchers and writers involved in those seminal studies on the Oklahoma chimps. We discussed and re-analysed scenarios and situations from back then, thought about the different perspectives: animal, human, researcher, journalist, activist. This book is the end product of that: a voice for those studies and for the suffering of those chimps. Without Nim, this book and these links between those chimpanzees and trauma would not have happened. It is as though Nim chose Robert to speak up for him. A unique bond of fraternity and trust is apparent in both the film and the numerous home movies of their interactions. It certainly seems that Robert has been left with little choice but to be the spokesperson for those chimpanzees, and for the message going forwards. It is a role that he was given from those early days, when, at the end of each working day running around, playing with and caring for Nim, or for Kelly, or for Onan, or for Washoe, he would get in his car and drive home, leaving the beast behind bars. Robert knew he had to take action. It struck him that these were not ethical studies, even on the simplest level; they had not been thought through properly, and adequate care was not being taken to address even the most basic of needs of those animals. Who was the beast? Robert knew he had to find those animals sanctuary. He knew he had to get them and later, the laboratory animals being used in medical research, out of captivity and into sanctuary. In the intervening time, he was able to share his ideas with others who were influential in the chimpanzee rescue work. One such individual was James Mahoney.

A general discussion about trauma towards humans is presented here. Then, consideration of the bigger picture of what makes us human, and different to other creatures, is needed. This is required because these are issues which force us to consider how we came to be on this planet, and how we came to perceive ourselves as rulers of it. Our human arrogance at our specialness has fuelled our way in which we engage with the planet.

Human Arrogance

A word here about human arrogance. It is imperative to read all of the works on these animals before forming a judgement about whether those studies were moral or not. Robert and I have presented here our ideas about these studies, we have presented the facts in their accuracy, and we could explain here which aspects were moral and which were not, but it is important that, as the reader, you should form your own judgement. It is also worth considering how our elders might have broached the problems. The philosopher and social philanthropist, Bertrand Russell, in his passages from *An Outline of Intellectual Rubbish* (1943) explains how to avoid foolish opinions. He explains how he found it very profitable in diminishing the intensity of insular prejudice.

Russell suggests that avoiding stupidity is easier than seeking brilliance, and offers some advice to help navigate away from obvious errors. If the matter is one that can be settled by observation, he suggests that one makes the observation themselves. With regards to animals and their treatment, therefore, we suggest that readers take a practical approach by going to zoos, seeking out the pet shops that we described. We suggest readers watch the films *Project Nim* and *Lucy*, that they read the academic papers and books written by Terrace, Fouts, Linden, Hess and others. We suggest that individuals read the books by the people who were there, and inform themselves, before forming opinions. Bertrand Russell says that thinking that you know, when in fact you do not, is a fatal mistake. He acknowledges that we are all prone to this mistake and makes an important point that we should not commit ourselves to beliefs until we have seen facts. The same is true of these animal studies. A lot of the researchers thought that they knew about these animals.

The truth is that a lot of the lead investigators did not know what was occurring in those cages and in their laboratories, or did not understand or predict what *could* happen. Many were absent, either because of alcoholism and related issues, or were not physically in the same place as their animals. Indeed, many of the books that came out of that research either tell a different story to the facts or omit important details. Russell points out that there are ways in which we can make ourselves aware of our own biases. For instance, if an opinion contrary to our own makes us angry, it is a sign that we may be subconsciously aware that we have no good reason for thinking as we do. In this particular instance, it is important to find evidence, as it is likely that our belief is going beyond what the evidence warrants. Russell suggests that a good way to challenge the self is to address certain kinds of dogmatism and to become aware of opinions held in the social circles which are different from our own.

As I write this, I am in a state of tension. It is nearly Christmas, and in my Sicilian upbringing, it is traditional to eat octopus, squid, and to buy eels live, and to kill them before frying them. If I were to pass on this tradition, I would repeat those behaviours. Since most of my household is vegetarian, it is unnecessary to present a platter full of fish in the way that my parents presented them to me, but I am aware of wanting to carry on traditions, and so we will have to find a way to react against this particular one and to find a different way to respect it.

In the writing of this book, Robert and I have thought about the views of the "other". We have analysed, discussed and considered the opinions and actions of each of the "other", and we have held up to scrutiny the work that was done across the background of different historical and social contexts. It is ironic that we have been able to do so across two continents and, as a consequence of COVID, without having been able to travel or ever meet in person.

Russell also makes the point that becoming aware of traditions that are foreign to our own does not always have a positive effect. Becoming aware of what the chimpanzees could and could not do did not always have a beneficial effect. Indeed, it led to a catalogue of errors, and a series of ethical dilemmas and constraints. Russell suggests that for those who have enough "psychological imagination", it is a good plan to imagine an argument with a person holding a different bias. Here again, we can consider how sometimes we have been led to change our minds as a result of seeing things differently. Robert, and then James Mahoney, followed by other researchers, experienced this conflict and consequential turning of action. They saw things in a radically different way to the people surrounding them. We hope that this book will motivate and attract other "converts". It is time to stop wondering if animals are sentient, and to accept the fact that they are. Several countries have now declared that animals are sentient beings, including wild animal species and domestic pets. In a review of sentience in non-human animals, Rowan et al. (2021) specify the sentient characteristics; for instance, that animals feel negative emotions, and also positive ones, that they get bored, that they suffer when their bodies are mutilated, that their lives are compromised when they are made to bear children to make more meat, milk or cheese, and when those children are ripped away from them, when they are abused in order to entertain us, and when they are forced to live in conditions of captivity, in the name of humans. The killing of animals "in the name of conservation" or "in the name of coexistence" is equally upsetting, and a shift in attitudes is required.

Bertrand Russell says to be wary of opinions that flatter our self-esteem. We hope that we have presented here the bravery of those animals in the name of flattering of the human ego. Humans are convinced of the superior excellence of their own race. There is abundant bias towards this opinion. Of course, we think we are superior because we are "thinking" people. However, this does not put us in the position to think for those animals. Self-esteem conceals much information from most people. Whichever part of the world we come from, we are persuaded that our own nation is superior to all others. In this instance, we are persuaded that our race as human beings is superior to all others. We are just our standard of values, as Russell says. We consider that the merits possessed by our nation are the important ones, while its demerits are comparatively trivial. With these animal studies, natural abilities were trivialised, and human arrogance in the form of psychological investigator dictated that we should want those animals to be like humans. Bertrand Russell ends his essay in a particularly fascinating way, pertinent to current arguments: "The only way I know of dealing with this general human conceit is to remind ourselves that man is a brief episode in the life of a small planet in a little corner of the universe, and that, for all we know, other parts of the cosmos may contain beings as superior to ourselves, as we are to jellyfish".

I write this in the week that the UK law has changed. Octopi have been considered sentient beings, along with lobsters and crabs in government policy decision-making. As of December 2021, there has been an amendment to the Animal Welfare Bill following a London School of Economics and Political Science report on decapods and cephalopod sentience. The Animal Welfare Minister in the UK, Lord Zac Goldsmith, said "the UK has always led the way on animal welfare, and our action plan for animal welfare goes even further by setting out our plans to bring in some of the strongest protections in the world for pets, livestock and wild animals". The Animal Welfare Sentence Bill provides crucial assurance that animal wellbeing is rightly considered when developing new laws. New Zealand and Spain have also amended their laws, and hopefully there will be further action taken in other countries, especially those such as mine, where these sentient beings are eaten in order to celebrate Christmas. These small cultural shifts will lead to big actions. There are many ways to pass on tradition, and there are many ways to pass on knowledge. We do not have to do what our ancestors did in order to teach our children.

The Global Problem of Language

The global problem of language explains the fundamental errors of using primates to explain language processing in humans. In the process of defining this term "language", we are being circular in argument. We are using words to describe words.

We are using language to describe language. This is akin to debates about intelligence. Boring described intelligence as "what intelligence tests measure" (Boring, 1923). Just as intelligence *is* what we define as intelligence, language *is* whatever language we are using to define "language". One needs intelligence in order to be able to *define* intelligence, and in the same way, it is necessary to possess language, in order to be able to *define* what language is.

Language is a set of linguistic tags which have been, on some level, arbitrarily assigned to a set of concepts geographically determined by defining the borders of various countries on this planet. Even the fact that different countries speak different languages is arbitrary: Italian is linguistically close to South American Spanish, but not to English, yet in terms of physical location it is easier to reach Cambridge than it is Colombia. Being from countries which are in physical proximity does not always guarantee that two people will speak a common tongue. In Belgium, French and Flemish are spoken – same place, yet distinctly different languages. Furthermore, within one language, there can exist several names for one concept. Some languages have dialects ("snicket" for gate in British English), or multiple names can exist for one item as in the "name agreement" effect described earlier, where one object has many labels/linguistic tags: sofa/settee/couch. If English is your first and only language, you will take longer to name a sofa than you will to name a door, because your brain has to search through a small pool of linguistic tags before landing on the most appropriate.

Bilinguals, by definition, have at least two linguistic tags per concept, and trilinguals have at least three. It is not always as clear as this. Language is not binary, and the world is not divided into monolinguals versus bilinguals. Sometimes we drift in and out of knowing a language. For instance, many English children learn French for GCSE study (ninth and tenth grade) at school, but beyond a spattering for communicating on holidays, may not retain it. Bilinguals take longer than monolinguals, who take longer than trilinguals, to produce object names for items (Mägiste, 1984). This demonstration that having more languages is not always "better" is controversial and seems to contradict our instincts to teach our children as many languages as possible. The answer is to continue to teach new languages but to retain depth of processing in at least one, and one which is shared with the main caregiver (preferably the parent) and which contains a wide spread of adjectives and other words appertaining to psychological safety.

Was Washoe Bilingual?

Since we are considering that the language learning in chimpanzees is irrelevant because of their captivity, this question may seem immaterial. However, an interesting proposition is that these chimpanzees were unique for having learned so much of a *second* language. This view is, of course, in direct opposition to the claims of Terrace and Chomsky, who are still thinking in the old-fashioned way, that this was not language that the chimpanzees were expressing, and that somehow these animals were deficient for failing to learn. They were making the usual assumption that all animals start with a blank slate. First, all animals are not equal in terms of underlying brain structures for language, and second, why should we not assume that a species that shares the most DNA with humans would not have a type of "Universal Grammar" of their own?

We could view a position that lies directly opposite to the traditional beliefs: that the chimpanzees were actually smarter than us humans. They not only picked up their own language of meaningful grunts and hoots, but they also picked up a second language *in addition*, and that language was one that *another species* uses. Girard-Buttoz et al. (2022) revealed, after analysing almost 5,000 recordings, that chimpanzees have a complex communication system which contains "words" that are combined into "sentences". Recordings from wild adult chimp calls in the Ta National Park, Cote d'Ivoire, revealed 390 different auditory ways in which chimps made distinct patterns. While this may seem nowhere near as close as the seemingly unlimited human vocabulary, first, we are not able to measure diversity of human vocabulary in a rigorous fashion, and second, this casts shadows on the fact that nobody had thought to test the chimpanzees' communicative abilities prior to any of these psychology studies using American Sign Language (ASL). Ape auditory transmission is significantly more intricate and structured than previously considered, since no large-scale qualitative study has ever been conducted before this one. The utterances were analysed here of 900 hours of natural adult foreign chimp (*Pan troglodytes verus*) discussions from three chimp communities in the park. Auditory stimuli were uttered in single, two-time (bigram) and three-unit (trigram) series, and over 12 different sound kinds were made, including moans, gasps, hoos, growls, shouts and whines, indicating additional roles based on how they were used, and the conditions in which discussions took place. They were combined to create 390 different interludes.

Washoe, who came to the US via West Africa, already had in her brain the language processes for chimpanzee utterances. For chimps like her, signing was like a second language. How would the average human have fared, picking up the language of another species like this? For chimpanzees like Nim, however, who was reared from birth to learn to sign amidst human beings, signing was more like a first language. Putting aside that he heard chimpanzee from his mother in utero and for around 10 days post-birth, he did not have the same exposure to chimp language as did Washoe, who was something of a fluent bilingual, although her second language was suppressed whenever she communicated her needs by signing to the humans who could save her: WALK, EAT, FOOD. We could consider the linguistic capabilities of each of those chimpanzees to ascertain if they were second-language acquirers or fluent bilinguals, but it is beyond the rationale of this book, and we emphasise that the language studies must be laid to rest.

A Rose by Any Other Name

The act of giving the chimpanzees a name is important. It gave those chimps a sense of identity to the humans, but also given that they were bred for the purpose of names, the learning tags for concepts, they came to understand they themselves held tags for their "being". Bob Johnson, Nim's carer who would give him the bedtime story of his birth and existence probably helped Nim to develop his identity. Imagine Washoe being told the equivalent tale of her existence: "Your mother was shot, you were taken by poachers . . ." It is also probable that, in learning how to name so many objects and people, it might have crossed Washoe's mind, by herself, to consider how she came to *be*.

In terms of her naming of humans, Hess explains how one afternoon, Washoe asked Bob his name in ASL: "Then she made up a sign for Bob: the index and middle fingers rubbed along the right eyebrow. Ingersoll liked it and taught the younger chimps to sign his name the same way" (Hess, 2008). Bob explains how it happened, "Not exactly but close enough. NAME YOU." He tells me that they were doing a name-the-item game with Al. Bob was sitting with the box of toys in the cage. The chimps were sitting next to one another, and he was signing with them, holding up items, and saying in sign language: "what's this? what's this what's this?". Bob said, "and occasionally I'd say 'who are you?' or 'whose toy?', so we were going back and forth like that. I would say 'who are you?' and 'who is he?' with them, and during that she says to me; "name you"?

> At that time it had not occurred to me to invent a name sign for me. I signed NO NAME to indicate I didn't have a name in sign, and so she signs to me, NAME YOU 'BOB', with BOB being the forefinger and middle finger of the right hand drawn across the left brow ridge, and from that time forward she used that, which I, of course, adopted. During those sessions, we used "whose dog?" and "Al's dog" or "Washoe's purse", and used non verbal as well facial expressions and body language to indicate a question or a request. That was in the early first year there long before Nim returned so my signing with chimps was not really a thing. The chimps I took out were mostly not signers, so when Nim arrived all that picked up. She gave me my name.

It was particularly clever of Washoe to go from naming objects to naming Robert. It demonstrates empathy, but also the fact she knew that humans as well as objects have names, and that these names may be arbitrary. Although it is unlikely that chimps in the wild have names for each other, since they recognise each others' vocalisations and pheromones, Washoe knew that she had to have a point of reference with Robert and other major caregivers.

The Chimpanzee Brain Versus the Human Brain

A fundamental question in neuroscience is how the chimpanzee brain and the human brain differ. We humans believe that our brain's organisation gives rise to unique cognitive abilities, given that we can produce poetry, music and lifesaving vaccines. The measurement and subsequent understanding of brain function has changed over the decades. Luppi, Mediano, Rosas et al. (2022) consider the brain a distributed information-processing system, with distinct components which interact and are networked through the brain's wiring, exchanging information through complex input and output signals. The review presented evidence from multiple species and disciplines to explain that there is no one sole information-processing area in the brain. Concepts were borrowed from the mathematical framework of information theory. This is the study of measuring, storing and communicating digital information, to explain the internet and artificial intelligence, in order to track information-processing methods by the brain. Different brain regions employ different strategies to interact, with some exchanging information in stereotypical fashion, using input and output signals that are reproducible and dependable. The eyes and ears, which process sensory and motor functions and are involved in processing sound, vision and movement, have such signals. The eyes send signals from the front to the back of the brain, each eye providing information – so it is present in duplicate, but half this information is not needed, and so is "redundant". This redundancy gives robustness and reliability, so we can survive. Not only do we have half a backup brain as "spare" in case of damage, but we are able to see with one eye. This connection is crucial, and so these brain regions are anatomically hardwired in the brain. The other information is not redundant. For example, it provides information for processing depth and distance – the ability to see three dimensionally. This type of processing where complex signals from across different brain networks are integrated is termed "synergistic" and is prevalent in brain regions supporting complex cognitive functions like attention, working memory, social cognition and mathematical function. This is not hardwired; it can change in response to experience. Different networks can learn, through experience, to connect in different ways. It is likely that the Oklahoma chimpanzees would have had re-connected brain networks to match those of the humans. The giving of "human" experiences to them would have altered their brain network function.

These synergistic areas of brain take place in the front and middle of the cortex, integrating different sources of information and connecting them widely and efficiently. These areas are also high in numbers of synapses, which allow neurons to communicate with each other. Luppi et al. (2022) compared brain imaging data and genetic analysis across species and found that these synergistic interactions account for a higher proportion of total information flow in the human brain than in macaque monkey brains, although both species have brains that are equal in terms of how much they rely on redundant information. The prefrontal cortex (PFC) which supports more cognitive function was also examined, and macaque monkeys have more prevalent redundant information processing in this region, but in humans it is heavy in synergy. This may reflect the fact that the PFC has undergone significant expansion with evolution. Chimpanzee brain comparison revealed that the more that that region of the human brain had expanded during evolution in size relative to the chimp counterpart, the more the region relied on synergy. In other words, it is not so much size or shape but type of processing that matters. Indeed, in asking "What is so special about the human brain? Why is it that we study other animals, instead of them studying us? What does a human brain have or do that no other brain does?" Suzana Herculano-Houzel (TED talk, 2013) explains that the human brain is larger than it should be and uses much more energy than it should, so it is particularly special. The advantage is that we have the largest number of neurons in the cerebral cortex, which lead to the remarkable cognitive abilities. We have, on average, 86 billion neurons. Sixteen billion are in the cerebral cortex, the seat of functions like awareness and logical and abstract reasoning, which is the simplest explanation for our remarkable cognitive abilities. The relationship between the size of the brain and its number of neurons can be described mathematically, and it was calculated that with 86 billion neurons and 60 to 70 kg of body mass, we would have to spend over 9 hours a day feeding. This is not feasible, given the limited amount of hours in a day, and the amount of thinking we have to do. The way in which humans discovered to get more energy out of the same foods was to use fire. Cooking food is a method of pre-digesting it, so it becomes softer, easier to chew, and can be completely digested and absorbed in the gut, yielding much more energy in less time. Cooking food enables us to use the time to use our neurons for processes other than survival. As Herculano-Houzel puts it, "If we ate like a primate, we should not be here". Luppi et al. (2022) also looked at genetic analyses in human brains and found that regions producing synergistic information are more likely to express the genes that are uniquely human and related to brain development. The human brain is able to navigate a trade-off between reliability and integration of information.

A Question of Ownership

Let us think back to the issue of identity from the first chapter of this book. As an Italian child raised in an English community in the UK, I know first-hand about the issues to do with identity problems in immigration. I saw first-hand the difficulties that arise from social mobility and immigration. One belongs neither here, nor there. There is difficulty in developing one language and one personality fully. One side develops, and then the other culture emerges from the wings, yet never develops fully. Many of us had a template for a family in the UK, and we were then surprised to learn that a duplicate family template existed in Italy. We immigrant individuals suffered social isolation, social incongruence, which made us vulnerable to psychological disorders such as anxiety, depression, schizophrenia and personality disorders. Since we were also vulnerable to issues connected to poverty, we are doubly at risk of backgrounds of crime, violence, drugs and the usual adversity that goes with traumatic experiences: PTSD, addiction and eating disorders. The socioeconomics of autoimmune disease have not been discussed, but many of us have discovered that we are ticking time bombs of faulty immune systems which, having transmitted inherited trauma, lie dormant and fighting themselves, as though sensitive on the attack, and ready to explode into illness at any time. Nature and nurture, I was taught in my psychology classes. Nature and nurture, nurture *via* nature, and nature *via* nurture. It is about the genetic self being connected to the nurturing environment. The reason why I connected with Nim and these studies is because

I understand the pain of disconnection and divergence. I know the pain that is caused by being genetically incongruent to the environment in which one is raised.

These were the same issues that were occurring within study chimpanzees. The Oklahoma chimps were raised as not-quite chimps and not-quite humans. The same issues were emergent in their carers, many of whom were not-quite undergraduates, but not-quite graduates, interesting characters like Bob, who was not-quite young enough to fit the norm of the usual undergraduate, yet not-quite old enough that he remains even to this day, "the graduate student, Bob Ingersoll" in interviews. Each carer brought their own beliefs, progressions, learning, but also identities, characters and histories to the being of those animals, just as, as parents, we do. Transgenerational issues are not a new concept. For centuries, we have been passing on our family histories, routines and folklore. The important characteristic is a strong sense of self, and healthy ideas about which of those states are useful and salubrious to raising the next generation.

It is a question of dignity. I, in this body, am this person with these characteristics. What I choose to put in, on, or the experiences which I choose to subject my body to, will have impact upon the person I become. The same was true of the chimpanzees, except that many of these choices were made *for* them, by people who were not clear about their own versions of identity. I am reminded of that example that is given in therapy training: on a failing aeroplane flight, we are told that if the oxygen masks come tumbling down, and we are travelling with a child or someone requiring assistance, we should secure our own mask first, and then assist the other person. There is a lot of work to be done on the self, if one is to be responsible for another. Ownership of the self is multifaceted.

In 1990, I bought a copy of *The Beauty Myth* by Naomi Wolf. The book explained how images of beauty were being used against women. It is hard to believe that over 30 years on, the same arguments need to be discussed, with a wider rather than a narrower lens. We have become experts in self-objectification. Wolf wrote that "The quality called 'beauty' objectively and universally exists. Women must want to embody it and men want to possess women who embody it". Never has this been more overtly demonstrated, with sales of Botox, false nails and cosmetic surgery, on the rise, and individuals are partaking in diets which involve fasting – essentially, starving the self. Wolf asks, "If the beauty myth is not based on evolution, sex, gender, aesthetics, or God, on what is it based?" (Wolf, 1990). She explains how it claims to be about celebrating women and those things they represent – intimacy, sex and life – yet it is more accurate to say that it is based upon "emotional distance, politics, finance, and sexual repression", and that rather about being about women, the focus is on men's institutions and institutional power.

Out of Adversity Comes Creativity: Art for Hope

It is undeniable that Nim's spirit lives on. One way is through forms of art. Art inspires expression, which in turn can create social change. It is imperative to give some of these art forms attention here. Art is an integral part of being human, since being creative is one of the ways in which we believe that we are superior to animals (although it is not a human endeavour solely, given the many paintings that exist by primates, for example). Art is, in a way, about taking ownership of the world. Art helps us to identify with each other, creating cultural expression, and when we are moved by a piece of art, we are touched by its message, become aware of emotions, and are inspired to take action.

Chimp Show

In the 1990s, JC (Jack) Lenochen created his art show for the art department of the University of Oklahoma. It was planned for 2 months, and the media were alerted – indeed, it was attended by CNN. The show was created around a cage that was built from chicken wire, in a giant gallery. The cage was split so that one could enter it from one side and come back out from the other, by following red arrows on the floor. On one side of the wall were photographs of the chimpanzees with descriptions. These started with positive depictions – chimps playing and tickling – and as the show moved around, the photographs got progressively darker and darker, showing blown up covers of the PhD titles of the theses that were about *Pan troglodytes*, of James Mahoney wearing his face mask, and with messages such as: "Chimps got AIDS at LEMSIP". Visitors exited from the cage via the arrows on the floor, to the other side of the gallery, where the last wall was hung with chimpanzee art. Visitors became upset about the hanging and the caging and filmed it for documentation. When the show opened, all the local networks came and talked to the individuals at the gallery. This was the goal of the art show: it got people talking, and challenged observers, informing them about chimpanzees and how these particular ones were treated.

The Legacy of Care

We must consider the legacy of unacceptable care that is still existent within the chimpanzee world. Even in the US chimpanzees are still allowed to be bought and sold, and many are kept in substandard unaccredited facilities and "roadside" zoos. The cycles of exploitation and objectification easily repeat down the generations.

There are several chimpanzee descendants that grew up knowing such extreme levels of stress, and they are likely to repeat the cycle of maladaptive behaviours unless proper "chimping" is modelled to them, or unless solid intervention is performed. In human parent-infant interventions, psychotherapy can stop the damaging patterns from repeating themselves. Parents search for guidance and may request support in rearing their infants. How is this education, guidance and support occurring with regards to chimpanzees, and other animals held in captivity?

In most US states, it is illegal to own a chimpanzee. Since 2015, captive chimpanzees were classified as an endangered species, and they can no longer be used in invasive testing. The US applied a moratorium to end these behaviours. The

National Institutes of Health and the government agencies that own chimpanzees are now in the process of retiring them. Chimp Haven has been established as a national chimp sanctuary in Louisiana, with several hundred chimps, and probably several hundred more that will be going there. Chimpanzees that were institutionally held by either the government or by pharmaceutical companies, drug companies or hospitals, in biomedical research, are now in the process of being retired. On the other hand, the pets and the entertainment industry chimpanzees are not so lucky, but some huge changes have been made by Patti Ragan at Center for Great Apes (CGA) in Wauchula, Florida. Over a period spanning more than 25 years, she and her staff have almost single-handedly put an end to the culture of entertainment and pet apes in the US, and built them a sanctuary.

Many chimps now living in sanctuaries came from private owners, who were unable to look after the chimps once they were adolescents or adults. At that stage, chimps can be deadly. There is the case of Charla Nash who in 2009 was severely mauled by her friend's chimpanzee, and lost both hands, ears, her nose and her sight. Chimpanzees are not necessarily predators in the same way as animals such as lions, crocodiles and barracuda fish are, but in the wild, chimpanzees hunt co-operatively, they eat monkeys and they hunt bush buck, as is natural for their species. Chimp cognitive behaviour compliments the harsh behaviours and conditions that they will be dealing with in the wild. They send out points, talk amongst each other, move animals to trees on which they will focus. The planning and advanced thinking in that context are complicated, and the chimps prey on those animals. Those who choose to take on chimpanzee ownership rarely keep their pets for more than a few years, because by the time a chimp is around 5 to 7 years old, it becomes assertive and dangerous. Unless one understands chimps and is an accomplished trainer, there is no ability to teach the chimp what the chimp is required to do, because the chimp is then identified as a pet, which can be dangerous and brutal. Chimpanzees are strong, and when this is combined with almost-human intelligence, can be a huge threat, especially because most people do not understand its being. In the chimp world, "might is right". There is a definitive hierarchy and order in a chimp colony, even if it does not always appear so. Chimps are dangerous since they have around five times the strength of humans, yet the intellect of around a 5- to 7-year-old, which endows them with the ability to plan and to create situations. They are explosive and volatile with large teeth and long arms, and can do much damage to people. Sanctuaries are seeing an increase in surrendered pet chimps. Those individuals who own chimps may be fewer, but they need to examine the next step as sanctuary. The most unlikely of animals are able to be integrated into sanctuaries. Once chimps are surrendered, their owners are allowed to visit them in sanctuary if they wish, although this culture is ending, with fewer chimps being held as pets. These particular types of ex-pet chimps have difficulty learning how to be chimps again, since they have never seen grass, trees, sky, birds or even other chimps, and are startled by them and can be fearful. However, chimps have great brains and are curious, and in time they do step outside and will observe and calculate, watching and learning by example. Most chimpanzees in captivity seek out and enjoy human contact. It is necessary, in sanctuary, to create an atmosphere where the chimps are trusting of their keepers. The chimp is given an opportunity and is helped along in the areas where the chimp has not been comfortable. They settle in time.

It is important to consider chimpanzees in zoos. Zoos are businesses, operating to a corresponding model. Who are the zoo owners? Zoo owners display animals for human viewing, sometimes interaction, in exchange for money, which usually comes from entry fees or charitable donations from the public. London Zoo in the UK is run by the Zoological Society of London, which is an international conservation charity, and receives no state funding, and does not make a profit. One might consider that zoos are a form of interactive museum. Posts on social media show people looking in awe at a gorilla watching intently through a glass window, as a human visitor flicks through some photographs on her mobile phone. One of the readers comments that she, too, used to conduct this activity with this same gorilla daily for many years, with picture books, before mobile phones, giving some indication of how long that gorilla has been behind that window. In another example, the human zoo visitors observe in surprise as a gorilla shows interest through the glass barrier, towards a human mother bonding with its newborn baby. The gorilla looks fondly and graciously at the baby, her face demonstrating an expression that looks familiar; it is a sort of yearning. We might ask: who are the animals in this interaction? Is it humane to gawp at these animals, and to demonstrate to them the very primal behaviours that, for as long as they are raised in captivity, they will not be able to experience for themselves? While the animals may be well looked after, and may be raised with all their substantial creature comforts, one could ask – is it necessary to raise these animals behind screens and in cages, in order that humans may learn about them from these visits? What are zoos for? We might argue that one of the purposes of zoos is for us to learn about animals we might not see otherwise. Is visiting these animals "in the flesh" necessary in order for us to gain this understanding? If I visit the Freud Museum in London, do I expect to see Sigmund Freud?

The zoo problem is complicated. We humans are conditioned to believe we are the masters of the animals, and that we have a right to owning and presenting animals. Many young people aspire to becoming zookeepers or carers of animals in parks and zoos but are often disappointed after they spend time working at these establishments. We are conditioned to seeing these animals behind barriers, behind bars or in cages, and so the role of taking care of them for this purpose is made acceptable to us. Zoo ownership carries many deep economic and psychological factors, including the topic of domination. Visitors to zoos, wildlife parks and aquariums are led to believe that they serve more to educate, and that these are establishments which aid in the building of reserves in captivity to avoid complete extinction. "Got some lovely polar bears up in Yorkshire", said an acquaintance, when I posted about not needing an elephant in a cage to teach our children about elephants. "Where's best for a new cub?" she asked, "Latest predictions are of the final ice cap melting in 2040. Is it best in Yorkshire, or in the wild? Zoos and parks have their place". Sadly, the reality is far different to this story about saving a species, although in some rare cases, zoos and experts have saved a species or two: the example most often used is the golden lion tamarin, a tiny primate, which was saved by the US National Zoo. The reality, though, is that most zoos do not have the resources to make that sort of impact. They are generally for-profit businesses, pressed to keep their operations financially viable.

The zoo world needs to change. We cannot give a philosophical pass to the zoo industry because they are perceived to do less harm and more good. "The lesser of two evils, is still choosing evil". We might superficially hypothesise some ways forward here. One way is to change the zoo business model into a non-profit one. Information acquired in the chimpanzee studies could inform with presentations in zoos. We have methods and techniques to use those data, those photographic captures and video clips, to give the general public of knowledge-thirsty zoo patrons the information they need about these animals, in a respectful and dignified manner. One option is to divert energy and funds to helping with animal rescue and hospitalisation. There are sanctuaries and wildlife hospitals in the UK which also educate visitors: Monkey World – Ape Rescue Centre in Dorset, and Tiggywinkles Wildlife Hospital in Buckinghamshire, are two excellent examples of sanctuary, and both welcome visitors. If zoo visitors supported these places instead of zoos, perhaps shareholders and conglomerates would be forced to rethink animal welfare. It would be helpful to have lists available to parents and holidaymakers of such ethical, welfare-promoting, establishments. Animals do not belong behind screens; they belong in the wild environments for which they are genetically programmed. The new approach of rewilding gives hope in rehabilitating captive animals successfully, including those in zoos. Robert's life choices and work remind me of solid ways in which we can help further. He is vegan, and works actively with vegan groups including Vegan Outreach and Stop Animal Exploitation Now. He was awarded the Animal Rights Activist of the Year from the Farm Animal Rights Movement a few years ago, and serves as a board member at a farm animal sanctuary called Oliver & Friends in Oklahoma. Bob briefly worked with In Defense of Animals to publish a report about the 10 worst zoos in the US for captive elephants. There are several US sanctuaries that could accept those elephants, but it was politically difficult. We have to speak up for all captive animals in all situations.

What about animal ownership as pets? In recent days, I have been looking after a dog whose owner is away. She is a pedigree and cost nearly £1,000. I have heard of pets being bought from stores such as 'Pets At Home'. There are often puppy mills behind these commercial shopfronts. Animals do not belong in chain stores. Those large "animal supermarkets" springing up across the UK are unethical. Would we sell a human child in this way? Would we put a child in a cage, under bright lights, in a large supermarket, for shoppers to come and gawp at and to consider buying on whim, while shopping for groceries? We would think it outrageous. So, too, must we remember that these are sentient beings that are being exploited in the name of an economy.

To put a price on animals is to introduce them as a status symbol. Animal agriculture cannot continue. In his book "Rattling the Cage", Steven Wise explains why we need to change the (English, but other nations should follow suit) laws in order to defend animals in a dignified way (Wise, 2000). Currently, 125 chimpanzees in the US are in limbo, ready to be transferred from laboratories for medical research, to – to where? It remains unclear. Chimpanzee Haven has taken the cases to the federal courts, but this process is slow. It has already taken 3 years for the courts to decide. Can you imagine how much psychological growth and progression occurs in 3 years of life? The chimpanzees do not have legal rights, because they are considered property under the law. The issue of habeas corpus for these animals remains a problem. Habeus corpus is an Act of Parliament still in force today which ensures that no-one can be imprisoned unlawfully. Literally translated, "habeas corpus" means "you shall have the body" (if legal procedures are satisfied). In medieval times it was the expression used to bring a prisoner into court to hear the charges against him, and was later used to fight against arbitrary detention by authorities.

In Nim's case, habeas corpus was used to rescue him. Attorney Henry Herrmann provided pro bono assistance and a plaintiff's motion for a habeas corpus petition for Nim, to argue that as he had been "deliberately brought up from infanthood to think of themselves as human", then he could not be rehomed into a little cage "in some horrible medical lab" (Henry Herrmann, *Project Nim*) to be used in medical experimentation. He argued that Nim had the right to be treated like a human client, and to have his day in court. The judge was reluctant to have a chimpanzee in the courtroom. Herrmann explains how "Our opponents were pig-headed but they weren't stupid. They realised that win, lose, or draw, once I got him to court they'd be losing because even if the judge refused to hear him, the media attention would have been devastating. And the Dean of the Medical Faculty said, 'that's it. Get that chimp out of here'." This provided further evidence that a chimpanzee in those circumstances cannot and should not be yo-yoed from being a personality to being a scientific commodity. Robert knew that these actions were unjust and unfair, and he was the one to organise this, in order to give Nim a respectful and dignified voice. Bob was giving Nim treatment for PTSD, effectively.

The evidence presented in this book demonstrates that it is imperative that action be taken before it is too late for the existence of chimpanzees and other primates. If we are doing this to our nearest evolutionary relative, what are we capable of doing to ourselves? This book was constructed in limited time, in order to convey this message. Gerhardt states in her book on humans and caring that: "the babies who are born now and in the years to come will be the adults who nurse us in old age, manage our industry, entertain us . . . live next door". In the same vein that she asks us to consider whether those offspring will be emotionally balanced or disabled by hidden sensitivities, so we need to ask the same questions about these animals. It is time now to consider that very soon not only that line of chimpanzees, but also the whole species, will cease to exist. We need to consider what to do with the existing animals upon whom human harm has grafted its scars, and above all, to acknowledge the humans' role in the lives of these animals.

We believe we have presented information about the chimpanzees of those experimental times with clarity and accuracy. We hope that this book has provided information and understanding about the emotional aspects of the needs of those chimps, and of the trauma endured by the animals and by the humans in those studies. It is time to close the door on language learning in chimpanzees, and to consider now how to use that knowledge to work on animal and planetary issues. Robert's conclusion about those studies is that "This is the next step in this long, strange, wonderful, tragic trip".

Out of adversity comes creativity. Lessons have been learned, and it is time to close the circle and move the story on. The bigger, overarching issue is to find a *kinder* interaction with our planet, and with other sentient beings. It is imperative that for survival, we consider our wider interactions with our environment and find a way of coexisting with *compassion*, in order that we might preserve the earth's functions for future generations. We hope that any confusion about the language aspects of the primate studies can finally be laid to rest, and that the Oklahoma chimpanzees have now had the last word.

REFERENCES

Altmann, J., Sapolsky, R. & Licht, P. (1995). Baboon fertility and social status. *Nature*, 377, 688–689.

American Psychiatric Association. (2013). *Diagnostic and Statistical Manual of Mental Disorders: DSM-5*. 5th ed. Washington, DC: American Psychiatric Publishing.

Andics, A., Gábor, A., Gácsi, M. Faragó, T., Szabó, D. & Miklósi, A. (2016). Neural mechanisms for lexical processing in dogs. *Science*, 353(6303), 1030–1032.

Ashbaugh, A., Marinos, J. & Bujaki, B. (2018). The impact of depression and PTSD symptom severity on trauma memory. *Memory* (Hove), 26(1), 106–116.

Baglivio, M.T. & Epps, N. (2016). The interrelatedness of adverse childhood experiences among high-risk juvenile offenders. *Youth Violence and Juvenile Justice*, 14(3), 179–198.

Baglivio, M.T., Epps, N., Swartz, K.A., Huq, M.S., Sheer, A.J. & Hardt, N.S. (2013). The prevalence of adverse childhood experiences (ACE) in the lives of juvenile offenders. *OJJDP Journal of Juvenile Justice*, 3, 1–23.

Bandura, A. (1994). Self-efficacy. In V. S. Ramachandran (ed.), *Encyclopedia of Human Behavior* (Vol. 4, pp. 71–81). New York: Academic Press. (Reprinted in H. Friedman [Ed.], *Encyclopedia of Mental Health*. San Diego: Academic Press, 1998).

Bebbington, P., Wilkins, S., Jones, P., Foerster, A., Murray R., Toone, B. & Lewis, S. (1993). Life events and psychosis: Initial results from the Camberwell collaborative psychosis study. *British Journal of Psychiatry*, 162, 72–79.

Belsky, J., Vandell, D.L., Burchinal, M., Clarke-Stewart, K.A., McCartney, K., Owen, M.T. & NICHD Early Child Care Research Network. (2007). Are there long-term effects of early child care? *Child Developement*, 78(2), 681–701.

Bhagwagar, Z., Hafizi, S. & Cowen, P.J. (2003). Increase in concentration of waking salivary cortisol in recovered patients with depression. *American Journal of Psychiatry*, 160, 1890–1891.

Boring, G.E. (1923). *Intelligence as the Tests Test It*. Washington, DC: New Republic.

Bourne, C., Mackay, C. & Holmes, E.A. (2013). The neural basis of flashback formation: The impact of viewing trauma. *Psychological Medicine*, 43, 1521–1532.

Bozzatello, P., Rocca, P., Baldassarri, L., Bosia, M. & Bellino, S. (2021). The role of trauma in early onset borderline personality disorder: A biopsychosocial perspective. *Frontiers in Psychiatry*, 12, 721361.

Bradshaw, G.A., Capaldo, T., Lindner, L. & Grow, G. (2008). Building an inner sanctuary: Complex PTSD in chimpanzees. *Journal of Trauma & Dissociation*, 9(1), 9–34.

Cahill, L. & McGaugh, J.L. (1996). Modulation of memory storage. *Current Opinion in Neurobiology*, 6, 237–242.

Carroll, J.B. & White, M.N. (1973). Word frequency and age of acquisition as determiners of picture naming latency. *Quarterly Journal of Experimental Psychology*, 25, 85–95.

Cattane, N., Rossi, R., Lanfredi, M. & Cattaneo, A. (2017). Borderline personality disorder and childhood trauma: Exploring the affected biological systems and mechanisms. *BMC Psychiatry*, June 15; 17(1), 221.

Cavanna, A.E., Martino, D., Orth, M., Giovannoni, G., Stern, J.S., Robertson, M.M. & Critchley, H.D. (2009). Neuropsychiatric developmental model for the expression of tics, pervasive developmental disorder, and schizophreniform symptomatology associated with PANDAS. *World Journal of Biological Psychiatry*, 10(4 Pt 3), 1037–1038.

Chomsky, N. (1959). A review of B.F. Skinner's 'verbal behaviour'. *Language*, 35, 26–58.

Chung, R.K., Langeluddecke, P. & Tennant, C. (1986). Threatening life events in the onset of schizophrenia, schizophreniform psychosis and hypomania. *British Journal of Psychiatry*, 148, 680–685.

Clancy, J., Crowe, R., Winokur, G. & Morrison, J. (1973). The Iowa 500: Precipitating factors in schizophrenia and primary affective disorder. *Comprehensive Psychiatry*, 14, 197–202.

Cloitre, M. (2020). ICD-11 complex post-traumatic stress disorder: Simplifying diagnosis in trauma populations. *British Journal of Psychiatry*, 216(3), 129–131. doi:10.1192/bjp.2020. 43. PMID 32345416. S2CID 213910628.

Cook, A., Blaustein, M., Spinazzola, J. & Van Der Kolk, B. (2005). Complex trauma in children and adolescents. *Psychiatric Annals*, 35(5), 390–398. doi:10.3928/00485713-20050501-05. S2CID 141684244.

Cooper, R.P. & Aslin, R.N. (1989). The language environment of the young infant: Implications for early perceptual development. *Canadian Journal of Psychology*, 43, 247–265.

Cornelissen, P.L., Kringelbach, M.L., Ellis, A.W., Whitney, C., Holliday, I.E. & Hansen, P.C. (2009). Activation of the left inferior frontal gyrus in the first 200 ms of reading: Evidence from magnetoencephalography (MEG). *PLoS One*, 4(4), e5359. doi:10.1371/journal.pone.0005359.

Costa, P.T. & McCrae, R.R. (1992). Normal personality assessment in clinical practice: The NEO personality inventory. *Psychological Assessment*, 4(1), 5–13.

Courtois, C.A. (2004). Complex trauma, complex reactions: Assessment and treatment. *Psychotherapy: Theory, Research, Practice, Training*, 41(4), 412–425.

Cowen, P. (2002). Cortisol, serotonin and depression: All stressed out? *British Journal of Psychiatry*, 180(2), 99–100.

Cozolino, L. (2014). *The Neuroscience of Human Relationships: Attachment and the Developing Social Brain*. New York: W.W. Norton & Company.

Culp, R.E., Watkins, R.V., Lawrence, H., Letts, D., Kelly, D.J. & Rice, M.L. (1991). Maltreated children's language and speech development: Abused, neglected, and abused and neglected. *First Language*, 11(33), 377–389.

Daly, K. (1994). *Gender, Crime, and Punishment*. New Haven, CT: Yale University Press.

Darwin, C. (1859). *On the Origin of Species by Means of Natural Selection, or the Preservation of Favoured Races in the Struggle for Life* (2nd ed.). London: John Murray.

Davidson, R.J. (1992). Emotion and affective style: Hemispheric substrates. *Psychological Science*, 3(1), 39–43.

de Botton, A. (2006). *Essays in Love*. Revised ed. London: Picador.

DeCasper, A.J. & Fifer, W.P. (1980). Of human bonding: Newborns prefer their mother's voices. *Science*, 208, 174–176.DeCasper, A.J. & Spence, M.J. (1986). Prenatal maternal speech influences newborns' perception of speech sounds. *Infant Behavior and Development*, 9, 133–150.

Diamond, M.C., Rosenzweig, M.R., Bennett, E.L., Lindner, B. & Lyon, L. (1972). Effects of environmental enrichment and impoverishment on rat cerebral cortex. *Journal of Neurobiology*, 3(1), 47–64.

Dijkstra, T. & van Heuven, W. (1998). The BIA model and bilingual word recognition. In J. Grainger & A.M. Jacobs (eds.), *Locarticoids and the Genesis of Depressive Illness. A Psychobiological Model. British Journal of Psychiatry*, 164, 365–371.

Duke, N.N., Pettingell, S.L., McMorris, B.J. & Borowsky, I.W. (2010). Adolescent violence perpetration: Associations with multiple types of adverse childhood experiences. *Pediatrics*, 125(4), e778–e786.

Ershler, W.B. (1993). Interleukin-6: A cytokine for gerontolgists. *Journal of the American Geriatrics Society*, 41(2), 176–181.

Eysenck, H.J. (1952). *The Scientific Study of Personality*. London: Routledge.

Eysenck, H.J. (1967). *The Biological Basis of Personality*. Springfield, IL: Thomas.

Eysenck, H.J. & Eysenck, S.B.G. (1969). *Personality Structure and Measurement*. London: Routledge.

Eysenck, H.J. & Eysenck, S.B.G. (1992). *Manual for the Eysenck Personality Questionnaire-Revised*. San Diego, CA: Educational and Industrial Testing Service.

Eysenck, S.B.G. & Eysenck, H.J. (1970). Crime and personality: Item analysis of questionnaire responses. *British Journal of Criminology*, 11, 49–62.

Feldman, H., Goldin-Meadow, S. & Gleitman, L.R. (1978). Beyond Herodotus: The creation of language by linguistically deprived children. In A. Lock (ed.), *Action, Symbol, and Gesture: The Emergence of Language* (pp. 351–414). New York: Academic Press.

Felitti, M.D., Anda, R.F., Nordenberg, M.D. et al. (1998). Relationship of childhood abuse and household dysfunction to many of the leading causes of death in adults: The adverse childhood experiences (ACE) study. *American Journal of Preventative Medicine*, 14.

Fifer, W.P. & Moon, C. (1989). Psychobiology of newborn auditory preferences. *Seminars in Perinatology*, 13, 430–433.

Fouts, R. & Mills, S. (1998). *Next of Kin: What My Conversations With Chimpanzees Have Taught Me About Intelligence, Compassion and Being Human*. London: Penguin.

Gapp, K., Bohacek, J., Grossmann, J. et al. (2016). Potential of environmental enrichment to prevent transgenerational effects of paternal trauma. *Neuropsychopharmacology*, 41, 2749–2758.

Gerhardt, S. (2004). *Why Love Matters: How Affection Shapes a Baby's Brain*. Abingdon: Routledge.

Gilbey, M.P. & Spyer, K.M. (1993). Essential organization of the sympathetic nervous system. *Baillière's Clinical Endocrinology and Metabolism*, 7(2), 259–278.

Girard-Buttoz, C., Zaccarella, E., Bortolato, T., Friederici, A.D., Wittig, R.M. & Crockford, C. (2022). Chimpanzees produce diverse vocal sequences with ordered and recombinatorial properties. *Communications Biology*, 5, 410.

Gloster, A.T., Klotsche, J., Chaker, S., Hummel, K.V. & Hoyer, J. (2011). Assessing psychological flexibility: What does it add above and beyond existing constructs? *Psychological Assessment*, 23(4), 970–982.

Goldberg, L.R. (1992). The development of markers for the Big-five factor structure. *Psychological Assessment*, 4, 26–42.

Goldberg, L.R. (1993). The structure of phenotypic personality traits. *American Psychologist*, 48(1), 26–34.

Goodyer, I. M., Herbert, J., Tamplin, A. & Altham, P.M.E. (2000). Recent life events, cortisol, dehydroepiandrosterone and the onset of major depression in high-risk adolescents. *British Journal of Psychiatry*, 177, 499–504.

Gouin, J.P., Glaser, R., Malarkey, W.B., Beversdorf, D. & Kiecolt-Glaser, J. (2012). Chronic stress, daily stressors, and circulating inflammatory markers. *Health Psychology,* 31(2), 264–278.

Graham, K., Badihi, G., Safryghin, A., Grund, C. & Hobaiter, C. (2022). A socio-ecological perspective on the gestural communication of great ape species, individuals, and social units. *Ethology, Ecology & Evolution,* 34(3), 235–259.

Grummitt, L.R., Kreski, N.T., Kim, S.G., Platt, J., Keyes, K.M. & McLaughlin, K.A. (2021). Association of childhood adversity with morbidity and mortality in US adults: A systematic review. *JAMA Pediatrics,* 175(12), 1269–1278.

Gunnar, M.R. (2017). Social buffering of stress in development: A career perspective. *Perspectives on Psychological Science,* 12(3), 355–373.

Gurvits, T.G., Shenton, M.R., Hokama, H. et al. (1996). Magnetic resonance imaging study of hippocampal volume in chronic combat-related posttraumatic stress disorder. *Biological Psychiatry,* 40, 192–199.

Halligan, S.L., Herbert, J., Goodyer, I.M. & Murray, L. (2004). Exposure to postnatal depression predicts elevated cortisol in adolescent offspring. *Biological Psychiatry,* 55(4), 376–381.

Haney, C., Banks, W.C. & Zimbardo, P.G. (1973). Study of prisoners and guards in a simulated prison. *Naval Research Reviews, 9,* 1–17, Washington, DC: Office of Naval Research.

Happé, F. & Frith, U. (1996). The neuropsychology of autism. *Brain,* 119(4), 1377–1400.

Hardy K. & Pollard H. (2006). The organisation of the stress response, and its relevance to chiropractors: A commentary. *Chiropractic & Osteopathy,* 18(14), 25.

Harlow, H.F., Dodsworth, R.O. & Harlow, M.K. (1965). Total social isolation in monkeys. *Proceedings of the National Academy of Sciences of the United States of America,* 54 1, 90.

Harlow, H.F. & Zimmermann, R.R. (1958). The development of affective responsiveness in infant monkeys. *Proceedings of the American Philosophical Society, 102,* 501–509.

Harris, T.O., Borsanyi, S., Messari, S., Stanford, K., Cleary, S.E., Shiers, H.M., Brown, G.W. & Herbert, J. (2000). Morning cortisol as a risk factor for subsequent major depressive disorder in adult women. *British Journal of Psychiatry,* 177, 505–510.

Herman, J., Perry, J. & Van der Kolk, B. (1989). Childhood trauma in borderline personality disorder. *The American Journal of Psychiatry,* 146, 490–495.

Herman, J.L. (1997, 1992). *Trauma and Recovery: The Aftermath of Violence.* New York: Basic Books.

Hoare, P. (2001). *Spike Island. The Memory of a Military Hospital.* London: Fourth Estate.

Hoek, H.W. (2006). Incidence, prevalence and mortality of anorexia nervosa and other eating disorders. *Current Opinion in Psychiatry,* 19, 389–394.

Hofer, M.A. (1994). Hidden regulators in attachment, separation, and loss. *Monographs of the Society for Research in Child Development,* 59, 192–207.

Holmes, E.A., James, E.L., Coode-Bate, T. & Deeprose, C. (2009). Can playing the computer game "Tetris" reduce the build-up of flashbacks for trauma? A proposal from cognitive science. *PloS One,* 4(1), e4153.

Humphreys, G.W., Riddoch, M.J. & Quinlan, P.T. (1988). Cascade processes in picture identification. *Cognitive Neuropsychology,* 5(1), 67–104.

Izura, C. & Ellis, A.W. (2002). Age of acquisition effects in word recognition and production in first and second languages. *Psicològica,* 23, 245–281.

Jepson, P. & Blythe, C. (2020). *Rewilding.* London: Icon Books.

Kappala-Ramsamy, G. (2011, July 24). Nim Chimpsky: The chimp they tried to turn into a human. Documentary films. *The Guardian.*

Kavanagh, B. (2007). The phonemes of Japanese and English: A contrastive analysis study. *Aomori University of Health and Welfare,* 8, 283–292.

Kilpatrick, D.G. & Saunders, B.E. (1997). *The Prevalence and Consequences of Child Victimization*. Washington, DC: National Institute of Justice Research Preview, US Department of Justice.

Kim, K.H.S., Relkin, N.R., Lee, K-M. & Hirsch, J. (1997). Distinct cortical areas associated with native and second languages. *Nature*, 388, 171–174.

Kochanska, G. (2001). Emotional development in children with different attachment histories: The first three years. *Child Development*, 72, 474–490.

Kroneman, L., Loeber, R., Hipwell, A. & Koot, H.M. (2009). Girls' disruptive behavior and its relationship to family functioning: A review. *Journal of Child and Family Studies*, 18, 259–273.

Kuhl, P.K. (1991). Human adults and human infants show a "perceptual magnet effect" for the prototypes of speech categories, monkeys do not. *Perception & Psychophysics*, 50(2), 93–107.

Lameira, A.R., Alexandre, A., Gamba, M., Nowak, M.G., Vicente, R. & Wich, S.A. (2021). Orangutan information broadcast via consonant-like and vowel-like calls breaches mathematical models of linguistic evolution. *Biology Letters*, 17(9), 2021030220210302. http://doi.org/10.1098/rsbl.2021.0302.

Lameira, A.R., Hardus, M.E., Bartlett, A.M., Shumaker, R.W., Wich, S.A. & Menken, S.B.J. (2015). Speech-like rhythm in a voiced and voiceless orangutan call. *PLoS One*, 10(1), e116136. doi:10.1371/journal.pone.0116136.

Lameira, A.R., Santamaría-Bonfil, G., Galeone, D. et al. (2022). Sociality predicts orangutan vocal phenotype. *Nature Ecology & Evolution*, 6, 644–652. https://doi.org/10.1038/s41559-022-01689-z.

Lepper, M.R., Greene, D. & Nisbett, R.E. (1973). Undermining children's intrinsic interest with extrinsic reward: A test of the "overjustification" hypothesis. *Journal of Personality and Social Psychology*, 28(1), 129–137.

Levelt, W.J.M. (1989). *Speaking: From Intention to Articulation*. Cambridge, MA: The MIT Press.

Levelt, W.J.M. & Schriefers, H. (1987). Stages of lexical access. In G. Kempen (ed.), *Natural Language Generation. New Results in Artificial Intelligence, Psychology and Linguistics*. Dordrecht: Martinus Nijhoff.

Levine, P.A. & Frederick, A. (1997). *Waking the Tiger: Healing Trauma: The Innate Capacity to Transform Overwhelming Experiences*. Berkeley, C: North Atlantic Books.

Levine, S. (2005). Developmental determinants of sensitivity and resistance to stress. *Psychoneuoendocrinology*, 30, 939–946.

Linden, E. (1981). *Apes, Men, and Language*. New York: Penguin.

Linden, E. (1986). *Silent Partners: The Legacy of the Ape Language Experiments*. New York: Times Books.

Loman, M.M. & Gunnar, M.R. (2009). Early experience and the development of stress reactivity and regulation in children. *Neuroscience & Biobehavioral Reviews*, 34(6), 867–876.

Luby, J.L., Barch, D.M., Belden, A., Gaffrey, M.S., Tillman, R., Babb, C., Nishino, T., Suzuki, H. & Botteron, K.N. (2012). Maternal support in early childhood predicts larger hippocampal volumes at school age. *PNAS*, 109(8), 2854–2859.

Lucy, the Human Chimp (2021). Directed by Alex Parkinson. Available at: Channel 4OD (Accessed: February 2022).

Luppi, A.I., Mediano, P.A.M., Rosas, F.E., Holland, N., Fryer, T.D., O'Brien, J.T., Rowe, J.B., Menon, D.K., Bor, D. & Stamatekis, E.A. (2022). A synergistic core for human brain evolution and cognition. *Nature Neuroscience*, 25, 771–782.

MacWhinney, B. (1998). Models of the emergence of language. *Annual Review of Psychology*, 49, 199–227.

Mägiste, E. (1984). Learning a third language. *Journal of Multilingual and Multicultural Development*, 5, 415–421.

Mahoney, J. (2010). *From Elephants to Mice: Animals Who Have Touched My Soul*. Nashville, TN: Howell Books.

Maté, G. & Maté, D. (2022). *The Myth of Normal: Trauma, Illness & Healing in a Toxic Culture*. London: Penguin Publishing Group.

Mehler, J., Jusczyk, P., Lambertz, G., Halsted, N., Bertoncini, J. & Amiel-Tison, C. (1988). A precursor of language acquisition in young infants. *Cognition*, 29, 143–178.

Meltzoff, A.N. & Moore, M.K. (1977). Imitation of facial and manual gestures by human neonates. *Science*, 198, 75–78.

Milgram, S. (1963). Behavioral study of obedience. *The Journal of Abnormal and Social Psychology*, 67(4), 371–378.

Mody, M. & Belliveau, J.W. (2018). Speech and language impairments in autism: Insights from behavior and neuroimaging. *North American Journal of Medical Sciences*, 5(3), 157–161.

Monbiot, G. (2013). *Feral*. London: Penguin Books.

Montgomery, S. (2015). *The Soul of an Octopus: A Surprising Exploration into the Wonder of Consciousness*. New York: Simon & Schuster.

Moon, C., Lagercrantz, H. & Kuhl, P.K. (2013). Language experienced *in utero* affects vowel perception after birth: A two-country study. *Acta Paediatrica*, 102(2), 156–160.

Moon, C., Panneton-Cooper, R. & Fifer, W.P. (1993). Two-day-olds prefer their native language. *Infant Behavior and Development*, 16, 495–500.

Moore, S., McEwen, L., Quirt, J. et al. (2017). Epigenetic correlates of neonatal contact in humans. Development and Psychopathology, 29(5), 1517–1538.

Morey, J.N., Boggero, I.A., Scott, A.B. & Segerstrom, S.C. (2015). Current directions in stress and human immune function. *Current Opinion in Psychology*, 5, 13–17.

Morris, D. (1962). The Biology of Art. Methuen, London: Knopf.

Morris, D., Collett, P., Marsh, P. & O'Shaughnessy, M. (1981). Gestures: Their Origins and Distribution. Methuen, London: Knopf.

Morrison, C.M., Chappell, T.C. & Ellis, A.W. (1997). Age of acquisition norms for a large set of object names and their relation to adult estimates and other variables. *Quarterly Journal of Experimental Psychology*, 50A(3), 528–559.

National Scientific Council (The National Scientific Council on the Developing Child, based at the Center on the Developing Child, Harvard University, Cambridge, Massachusetts, USA). (2014) Excessive stress disrupts the development of brain architecture. *Journal of Children's Services*, 9(2), 143–153, https://doi.org/10.1108/JCS-01-2014-0006.

Nolen-Hoeksema, S. (2004). *Abnormal Psychology*. New York: McGraw-Hill.

Ozturk, E. & Sar, V. (2005). Apparently normal family: A contemporary agent of transgenerational trauma and dissociation. *Journal of Trauma Practice*, 4(3/4), 287–303.

Pariante, C.M. & Lightman, S.L (2008). The HPA axis in major depression: Classical theories and new developments. *Trends Neuroscience*, 31(9), 464–468.

Pawelec, G., Akbar, A., Caruso, C., Solana, R., Grubeck-Loebenstein, B. & Wikby, A. (2005). Human immunosenescence: Is it infectious? *Immunological Reviews*, 205, 257–268.

Pavić, L., Gregurek, R., Radoš, M. et al. (2006). Smaller right hippocampus in war veterans with post-traumatic stress disorder. *Psychiatry Research. Neuroimaging*, 154(2), 191–198.

Perry, B.D. & Szalavitz, M. (2007). *The Boy Who Was Raised as a Dog: And Other Stories From a Child Psychiatrist's Notebook*. London: Basic Books.

Pfungst, O. (1911/1998). *Clever hans: the Horse of Mr. von Osten*. London: Routledge, Thoemmes Press.

Phillips, L.J., McGorry, P.D., Garner, B., Thompson, K.N., Pantelis, C., Wood, S.J. & Berger G. (2006). Stress, the hippocampus and the hypothalamic-pituitary-adrenal axis: Implications for the development of psychotic disorders. *Australian and New Zealand Journal of Psychiatry*, 40(9), 725–741.

Pinker, S. (2007). *The Language Instinct (1994)*. New York: Harper Perennial Modern Classics.

Portella, M.J., Harmer, C.J., Flint, J., Cowen, P. & Goodwin, G.M. (2005). Enhanced early morning salivary cortisol in neuroticism. *The American Journal of Psychiatry*, 162(4), 807–809.

Project Nim (2011). Directed by James Marsh. Available on: Amazon Prime (Accessed: July 2021).

Reavis, J., Looman, J., Franco, K. & Rojas, B. (2013). Adverse childhood experiences and adult criminality: How long must we live before we possess our own lives? *The Permanente Journal*, 17, 44–48.

Rofé, Y. (1984). Stress and affiliation: A utility theory. *Psychological Review*, 91(2), 235–250.

Rogers, C.R. (1957). The necessary and sufficient conditions of therapeutic personality change. *Journal of Consulting Psychology*, 21, 95–103.

Rosen, J.B. & Schulkin, J. (1998). From normal fear to pathological anxiety. *Psychological Review*, 105, 325–350.

Rosenbaum, J.L. & Lasley, J.R. (1990). School, community context, and delinquency: Rethinking the gender gap. *Justice Quarterly*, 7, 493–513.

Rothman, E.F., Edwards, E.M., Heeren, T. & Hingson, R.W. (2008). Adverse childhood experiences predict earlier age of drinking onset: Results from a representative US sample of current or former drinkers. *Pediatrics*, 122, e298–e304.

Rowan, A.N., D'Silva, J.M., Duncan, I.J.H. & Palmer, N. (2021). Animal sentience: History, science, and politics. *Animal Sentience*, 31(1). doi:10.51291/2377–7478.1697.

Russell, B. (1943). *An Outline of Intellectual Rubbish; A Hilarious Catalogue of Organized and Individual Stupidity*. Girard, KS: Haldeman-Julius Publications.

Sabihi, S., Dong, S.M., Durosko, N.E. & Leuner, B. (2014). Oxytocin in the medial prefrontal cortex regulates maternal care, maternal aggression and anxiety during the postpartum period. *Frontiers in Behavioral Neuroscience*, 6(8),258.

Sar, V. (2011). Developmental trauma, complex PTSD, and the current proposal of DSM-5. *European Journal of Psychotraumatology*, 2. doi: 10.3402/ejpt.v2i0.5622.

Scarnà, A. (1999). Lexical processing in monolinguals and bilinguals. PhD thesis, University of York.

Scarnà, A. & Ellis, A.W. (2002). On the assessment of grammatical gender knowledge in aphasia: The danger of relying on explicit, metalinguistic tasks. *Language and Cognitive Processes*, 17(2), 185–201. https://doi.org/10.1080/0169096014300038.

Sheridan, M.A., Fox, N.A., Zeanah, C.H., Katie, A., McLaughlin, K.A. & Nelson III, C.A. (2012). Variation in neural development as a result of exposure to institutionalization early in childhood. *PNAS*, 109(32), 12927–12932.

Skinner, B.F. (1953). *Science and Human Behavior*. New York: Macmillan.

Skinner, B.F. (1957). *Verbal Behavior*. Acton, MA: Copley Publishing Group.

Steffensmeier, D. & Allan, E. (1996). Gender and crime: Toward a gendered theory of female offending. *Annual Review of Sociology*, 22, 459–487.

Straus, M.A. & Stewart, J.H. (1999). Corporal punishment by American parents: National data on prevalence, chronicity, severity, and duration, in relation to child and family characteristics. *Clinical Child and Family Psychology Review*, 2, 55–70.

Sylvestre, A., Bussières, È.-L. & Bouchard, C. (2016). Language problems among abused and neglected children: A meta-analytic review. *Child Maltreatment*, 21(1), 47–58. https://doi.org/10.1177/1077559515616703.

Teague, R., Mazerolle, P., Legosz, M. & Sanderson, J. (2008). Linking childhood exposure to physical abuse and adult offending: Examining mediating factors and gendered relationships. *Justice Quarterly*, 25(2), 313–348.

Tedeschi, R.G. & Calhoun, L.G. (1995). *Trauma & Transformation: Growing in the Aftermath of Suffering.* Thousand Oaks, CA: Sage Publications.

Terrace, H.S. (1987). *Nim, A Chimpanzee Who Learned Sign Language (Animal Intelligence Series).* New York: Columbia University Press.

Terrace, H.S. (2019). *Why Chimpanzees Can't Learn Language and Only Humans Can.* New York: Columbia University Press.

Thorndike, E.L. & Lorge, J. (1944). *The Teacher's Word Book of 30,000 Words.* New York: Columbia University Press.

Thwaite, A. ed. (2003). *Philip Larkin: Collected Poems.* London: Marvell Press/Faber & Faber.

Tottenham, N., Hare, T.A., Quinn, B.T. et al. (2010). Prolonged institutional rearing is associated with atypically large amygdala volume and difficulties in emotion regulation. *Developmental Science*, 13(1), 46–61.

Tree, I. (2018). *Wilding.* London: Picador.

Trocmé, N. & Wolfe, D. (2001). *Child Maltreatment in Canada: Selected Results From the Canadian Incidence Study of Reported Child Abuse and Neglect.* Ottawa: Minister of Public Works and Government Services.

Valaki, C.E., Maestu, F., Simos, P.G., Zhang, W., Fernandez, A., Amo, C.M., Ortiz, T.M. & Papanicolaou, A.C. (2004). Cortical organization for receptive language functions in Chinese, English, and Spanish: A cross-linguistic MEG study. *Neuropsychologia*, 42(7), 967–979.

Van der Kolk, B.A., Perry, J.C. & Herman, J.L (1991). Childhood origins of self-destructive behavior. *American Journal of Psychiatry*, 148(12), 1665–1671.

Van der Kolk, B. (2014). *The Body Keeps the Score: Mind, Brain and Body in the Transformation of Trauma.* London: Penguin Books.

Van der Kolk, B. (2021, December 13–14). *2-Day Trauma Conference: The Body Keeps the Score: PESI.* Oxford: Oxford University Press.

Vanltallie, T.B. (2002). Stress: A risk factor for serious illness. *Metabolism*, 51, 40–45.

Vaswani, N. (2018). *Adverse Childhood Experiences in Children at High Risk of Harm to Others: A Gendered Perspective.* Glasgow: Centre for Youth and Criminal Justice.

Vygotsky, L.S. (1978). *Mind in Society.* Cambridge, MA: Harvard University Press.

Walker, P. (2013). *Complex PTSD: From Surviving to Thriving.* California: CreateSpace Independent Publishing Platform.

Weinberger, D.E. (1987). Implications of normal brain development for the pathogenesis of schizophrenia. *Archives of General Psychiatry*, 44, 660–669.

Wilke, C., Lahiff, N.J., Badihi, G. et al. (2022). Referential gestures are not ubiquitous in wild chimpanzees: Alternative functions for exaggerated loud scratch gestures. *Animal Behaviour*, 189, 23–45.

Williams, L.M., Debattista, C., Duchemin, A.M., Schatzberg, A.F. & Nemeroff, C.B. (2016). Childhood trauma predicts antidepressant response in adults with major depression: Data from the randomized international study to predict optimized treatment for depression. *Translational Psychiatry*, 6(5), e799. doi:10.1038/tp.2016.61. PMID: 27138798; PMCID: PMC5070060.

Wise, S.M. (2000). *Rattling the Cage: Toward Legal Rights for Animals.* Cambridge, MA: Perseus Books.

Wolf, N. (1990). *The Beauty Myth: How Images of Beauty Are Used Against Women.* London: Chatto & Windus.

World Health Organization (WHO). (2022). *International Classification of Diseases.* 11th ed. https://icd.who.int/.

Wynn, K. (1992). Addition and subtraction by human infants. *Nature*, 358, 749–750.

Yehuda, R., Halligan, S.L. & Bierer, L.M. (2002). Cortisol levels in adult offspring of Holocaust survivors: Relation to PTSD symptom severity in the parent and child. *Psychoneuroendocrinology*, 27(1–2), 171–180.

Yerkes, R.M. & Dodson, J.D. (1908). The relation of strength of stimulus to rapidity of habit-formation. *Punishment: Issues and Experiments*, 27–41.

Yumei, Z., Ning, Z., Zaizhu, H. et al. (2010). Magnetoencephalography of language: New approaches to understanding the cortical organization of Chinese processing. *Neurology Research*, 32(6), 625–628.

Zhang, Y., Zhang, N., Han, Z., Wang, Y., Wang, C., Chen, H., Wang, Y. & Zhang, X. (2010). Magnetoencephalography of language: New approaches to understanding the cortical organization of Chinese processing. *Neurological Research*, 32(6), 625–628.

Zubin, J. & Spring, B. (1977). Vulnerability: A new view of schizophrenia. *Journal of Abnormal Psychology*, 86, 103–126.

INDEX